the
conman

(What follows is based on a true story.)

by
Mike Murphey
with Keith Comstock

FROM THE TINY ACORN...
GROWS THE MIGHTY OAK

This is a work of fiction. References to real people, events, establishments, organizations, or locales are intended only to provide a sense of authenticity and are used fictitiously. All other characters, and all incidents and dialogue are drawn from the author's imagination and are not to be construed as real.

THE CONMAN. Copyright © 2019 Mike Murphey.
All rights reserved.
Printed in the United States of America. For information, address Acorn Publishing, LLC, 3943 Irvine Blvd. Ste. 218, Irvine, CA 92602

www.acornpublishingllc.com

Edited by Laura Taylor
Cover design by Damonza
Interior design by Debra Cranfield Kennedy

Anti-Piracy Warning: The unauthorized reproduction or distribution of a copyrighted work is illegal. Criminal copyright infringement, including infringement without monetary gain, is investigated by the FBI and is punishable by up to five years in federal prison and a fine of $250,000.

All rights reserved. No part of this book may be used or reproduced in any manner whatsoever, including Internet usage, without written permission from the author.

ISBN-13: 978-1-947392-65-6 (hardcover)
ISBN-13: 978-1-947392-64-9 (paperback)

◇ ◇ ◇

The Conman is dedicated to
the memory of Dave Henderson,
an extraordinary baseball player,
and even better human being.
Oh, man, Hendu,
do we ever miss that smile!

———

... there's a reason for living way down in the valley
that only the mountain knows.

—John Henry Bosworth
NOEL STOOKEY

one

Phoenix, Arizona
October 1992

FAILURE CAN BE AN ACUTE CONDITION, PERHAPS EVEN chronic, but quitting—quitting is fatal.

Conor Nash believed this to his marrow.

No stranger to failure, Conor had been released from professional baseball contracts ten times. He'd been released by major league teams. He'd been released by minor league affiliates. He'd been released in five countries encompassing three continents. He wasn't sure how to count Puerto Rico. And, technically, that release occurred in an aircraft somewhere over the Atlantic Ocean. He'd had a contract when the plane took off. When it landed, they told him, "Go home."

And Venezuela, well, they weren't satisfied with just releasing him. A pissed-off dictator banned him from the entire country.

Hope remained, though, and ultimately, he'd kept his vow. Conor Nash pitched in the major leagues. So, why did this champagne bottle clutched in his left hand cast a pall that felt like death?

Fat Brad Grady could have helped him sort through these confusing emotions. Brad loved debating the nuance of words, and he and Conor argued the semantics often enough. Where Conor saw a razor-sharp line distinguishing *fail* and *quit*, Brad found a middle ground he defined as *surrender to reality* or *honorable retreat*. Brad's intellect would help make sense of Conor's present struggle. Brad wasn't available, though, was he? Conor closed his eyes and took a deep breath, trying to slough off the guilty anger he still confronted when he thought of Brad.

Conor set the champagne atop a flat red rock beside one of those damned jumping cactus plants. He bent forward, hands on knees. Everything around him conveyed hostile intent. Towering saguaro, their spines like nails, prickly pears, sharp-edged Spanish Daggers. The cholla cacti were the worst, with needles that seemed to leap from the plant if you got too close.

Maybe he hadn't thought this through.

This was an occasion, and he would not visit a host of family, friends and adversaries dressed in sweatpants and a t-shirt. Cowboy boots, jeans and a knit polo were proving inappropriate, though, for scaling Camelback Mountain.

He squinted into the glare of afternoon sun and saw a pair of young women making their way down. They wore cargo shorts. Sweat-soaked tank tops seemed plastered to their skin. Their hiking boots bit into the steep slant of red rock and sand surface.

Conor shaded his eyes, stood straight and did his best to look ten years younger.

"Hi," he said.

They smiled politely and passed without comment.

Conor was not a womanizer. He'd put that behind him when he married Kate fifteen years ago. Still, if those women knew they'd been greeted by a genuine major league baseball player, they wouldn't just hurry on their way, would they?

Then, he amended his thought. *Ex-major league ballplayer.*

Other hikers—all the traffic seemed to be headed down—offered curious glances at his clothing and champagne bottle. A few wished him success on his climb. He thought it a happy coincidence they were leaving. After all, he sought solitude at the camel's hump.

Retrieving the bottle, he craned his neck toward the summit. *Damn.* He didn't remember the fucking mountain being this steep. A half dozen more steps and the slick soles of his cowboy boots betrayed him again. He caught himself with his free hand, protecting his champagne. Breaking the bottle after all these years would be catastrophic.

French. Moët-Chandon. Purchased for twenty-five dollars at an Idaho Falls liquor store during the summer of 1976. Conor hadn't a clue whether brand and vintage qualified as good, bad or indifferent. They'd been four minor league baseball players. Kids really. The *last man standing* pact was Conor's idea. The player remaining when the other three had officially retired from their playing careers got to drink the champagne. Sports Illustrated published a story about this pact when Kenny Shrom passed the bottle to Conor as the 1989 season ended.

The Idaho Falls Russets, a team named for a potato, represented the minor league ladder's lowest rung. And against all odds, three of the four pact members climbed from that first step to the majors. Mark Brouhard arrived first. He played a half-dozen seasons in Milwaukee, punctuated by a year with the Yakult Swallows, before Kenny took charge of the bottle. Kenny pitched for Minnesota and Cleveland until injury robbed him of 1988. His comeback the next season failed in El Paso.

Initially, the bottle sat on Conor's garage shelf, subjected to a quiet indignity of shared space with wrenches, bicycle tires and motor oil. Then Kate pointed out it should probably be refrigerated. So, he made room at the back of his garage ice box. It loomed like a grim reaper each time he opened the fridge to grab a beer. It also fed a sullen, brooding hostility that took seed following Conor's final shoulder surgery.

Since second grade, Conor Nash had lived with a single purpose: to be a big-league pitcher. Even through high school, adults and friends indulged him with smiles and chuckles and, "Yes, but what if you don't make the majors? What's your back-up plan?"

The only adult who might have swayed him from his path had been his father. Hugh Nash cast an enormous presence. A brawler, he literally fought his way into a leadership role with the Teamsters at the Port of Oakland.

"Conor, I know what I'm supposed to tell you," Hugh told his second-born son one grey fall Bay Area afternoon. Hugh had conceded he would not beat lung cancer, and that his five sons would make their way into the adult world without him. He called each boy individually into the living room of the two-story house on Melendy Drive in San Carlos, California, to address their futures.

"Even though you had a good year in Idaho, there's a long, tough road ahead," he told Conor. A deep, rasping cough forced a pause.

Conor made it a point not to wince or show concern, though he imagined what a painful fire the coughing built in his father's lungs. Hugh's failing body still held an iron will, and Conor refused to acknowledge the cancer. As his cough subsided, Hugh drank from a glass of water, gathering himself.

"No matter what the scouts said, only something like four or five percent of kids drafted ever make the majors," Hugh continued. "So, I'm supposed to say find something to fall back on, maybe school during the off-season, or see if I can hook you up driving a truck or working the docks."

Hugh shook his head.

"I'm supposed to say, don't put all your eggs in one basket. Conor, I've watched you try to change a tire. Son, you've only *got* one basket. That's it. If you have a fallback plan, that's just what you'll do—fall back. Since you were seven years old, you've aimed yourself like an arrow at one goal, and I've never seen anyone so focused, so single-minded. For the other boys, that would be a weakness. Not you. That's your strength."

And now, on an October afternoon sixteen years later, Conor climbed Camelback Mountain. Along with the bottle of champagne, he carried his father, his best friends—A.J., Basil, Brad—his brothers, his wife and children, a whole community of people who had celebrated his successes and commiserated over his shortcomings, teammates and coaches, both friend and foe. All who had shaped him for better or for worse.

He intended to sit atop a mountain overlooking Phoenix, drink his champagne, and reflect on people, places and events—try and understand what would become of Conor Nash now.

He honestly didn't know, though, whether he was attending a party or a funeral.

two

San Carlos, California
1961

CONOR FELL IN LOVE THE FIRST TIME HE STOOD ON A pitchers' mound. At age seven, the initial attraction had nothing to do with throwing the ball, or even the game itself. Pencil marks climbing his bedroom door frame placed him at four feet even. He weighed either forty or forty-one pounds, depending on what he ate for breakfast. The mound made him taller than everyone else.

The San Carlos Farm League, entry-level play with teams comprised of seven and eight-year-olds, served as his introduction to baseball. His older brother, Sam, coached the Braves. Sam brought all the experience and wisdom of a nine-year-old to the job.

"Conor, you're our pitcher," Sam announced the first day of practice.

"I wanna be the pitcher," said Stevie Bullock, the biggest kid there.

"No, you're our left fielder," Sam ordered.

"I don't wanna be left fielder. I wanna pitch."

"Don't you know anything?" Sam said with a note of menace. "Who's the best pitcher in the world?"

"Saaandy Koooufax!" shouted a unanimous chorus of tiny baseball fans seated cross-legged on the grass before Sam.

"Right," Sam said. "And Sandy Koufax isn't right-handed, is he? No, he's left-handed. So, the best pitchers are left-handed. What are you, Stevie?"

Stevie's defiance melted into downcast defeat. "Right-handed," he said, staring at the ground.

"And Conor's left-handed. He's our pitcher."

Besides making him taller, Conor liked pitching because no one could do anything until he threw the ball. They all waited for him. What really hooked him, though? When he threw it, most kids couldn't hit it.

Sam's Sandy Koufax reference inspired Conor to pay attention when Sandy's Dodgers came north to play his beloved Giants. While the seven-year-old enemy hurlers awkwardly did their best to guide the ball toward the vicinity of the strike zone with careful lobs, Conor did what Sandy did. He started with a high leg kick aimed at first base, dropped low and arched his back so his right knee nearly scraped the ground, then drove toward the plate, unleashing a thirty-four or thirty-five mile-an-hour fastball that either baffled or terrified most second graders.

The rules aided his effectiveness.

In Farm League baseball, adults wisely instilled an aggressive rather than passive approach to hitting. Many second graders figured out that standing and waiting for the inevitable four balls was the easiest way to get on base. So, league rules forbade walking. A batter either struck out, or he put the ball in play.

Thus, Conor reared back and threw for all he was worth, unpenalized while his opponents ducked and dodged for their very lives. Conor felt invincible, like one of the Old Testament characters nuns told him about in Sunday School, or maybe Superman, throwing lightning bolts at sinners who scrabbled below. Hitters quickly realized that, if they flailed at anything even approximately near the strike zone, they could retreat to the safety of the dugout.

Sam's nine-year-old concept of pitching instruction—remarkably similar to the approach of many professional pitching coaches, Conor later came to understand—was telling him to *throw strikes*.

"Hey, lame-o, throw strikes!" Sam yelled from the dugout.

Adult Farm League supervisors counseled Sam that he should not yell at his players or call them names.

"I don't yell at them except for my brother," Sam told them, "and I yell at him all the time, anyway. He's used to it."

The season's third game offered Conor an epiphany. He tugged at Sam's arm, breaking his characteristic silence. "Remember what you said t . . . t . . . to me last inning?"

"Yeah. I said 'Hey, ya little snotweasel, throw strikes!'"

"Why?"

"Why, what?" Sam asked.

"If I throw it where they can reach it, somebody might hit it."

"Because, lame-o, in real baseball you *have* to throw strikes. Or else you walk people. Sandy Koufax doesn't walk people."

Hmmmmm. Made sense.

Thus, at the age of seven, Conor began a life-long process of determined self-instruction.

He got a baseball, drew a box on a brick wall at his elementary school, and practiced throwing strikes. And, having added strikes to his repertoire, he led the Braves to the 1961 San Carlos Farm League pennant. He was hooked. His life's destiny might as well have been tattooed on his skinny seven-year-old bicep.

"Hey, Dad, know what I'm guh ... gonna be when I guh ... guh ... grow up?"

"Yeah. A gas station attendant. You told me last week."

"No. I'm guh ... gonna be a pitcher."

For the rest of his childhood, his answer remained the same. An adult would ask, "What are your plans?"

"I'm guh ... gonna be a major league pitcher."

An indulgent smile, maybe a chuckle, then, "Yeah, but really. What will you do for a living? If baseball doesn't work out?"

Conor only regarded them curiously and wondered to himself, *why wouldn't it work out?*

October 1992

CRADLING HIS BOTTLE OF CHAMPAGNE LIKE A NEWBORN, Conor found the natural bench at Camelback's summit just as he remembered. He sat, gently placing the bottle at his feet. Eyes closed, he leaned back and simply breathed while waiting for his heart to forgive him. He pulled the tail of his shirt from his jeans and dabbed at sweat dripping into his eyes. He faced west. A descending sun began to tint a covey of billowing, wandering clouds the colors of the desert. A breeze wound its way through the few cactus plants and grasses that somehow maintained footholds in the granite peak. Despite the heat, this breath of wind raised chill bumps along his arms as it brushed a sheen of perspiration.

He drank in the beauty below—rich greens of golf courses and baseball diamonds dotting the Phoenix cityscape, browns and reds and tans of the desert, sharply defined lines and curves of streets and freeways dissecting the urban palette.

Okay, now what?

Just as his choice of clothing proved ill-suited, so, perhaps, was his mental preparation. His plan to climb, drink, remember and reflect, which seemed perfectly sound at the mountain's base, now struck him as vague.

Recollection could be an exercise in chaos, his focus careening from place to place, event to event, like a marble bouncing in a pinball machine. Similarly, reflection required a disciplined order, or all his emotions might bleed together, allowing no individual incident of influence or support or betrayal its proper due.

And besides, he only had one bottle of champagne.

Raised in the Catholic Church, Conor easily related to concepts of saints and guilt and confession. At the age of five, he spilled a can of Drano into his eyes. Doctors feared he would be blinded. His eyes were ultimately saved, but he left the hospital with a persistent stutter that plagued him through adolescence. So, he considered divine intervention as a kind of heavenly quid pro quo in which miracle is balanced by affliction.

Conor listened to the desert—the voice of a mockingbird, the rustle of unseen creatures through weeds and bushes that clung to their arid existence—then explained himself to the mountain.

I've settled on a belief I was granted my life's baseball journey because of a wish I made in a tunnel. Which raised a question. Who could grant such a wish? Maybe a saint? My childhood priest, though, told me baseball has no patron saint. Father McCray called my attention to Saint Sebastian, the patron of athletes. But any theology assigning baseball and soccer to the same level of paradise made no sense to me.

A couple of years ago, I watched a baseball movie which,

through a convoluted blend of legend and circumstance, declared Saint Rita as baseball's patron. Rita's Google makes no mention of baseball. She is the official patron saint of abuse victims, sterility, loneliness, difficult marriages, infertility, sickness, widows, spousal abuse, forgotten causes, impossible causes and desperate causes.

Desperate causes.

Okay. Maybe Rita is my baseball angel, after all.

Conor liked the idea of saints. Confession rested among the most comfortable aspects of his Catholicism. Not only had confession gotten him off the hook on any number of occasions, he liked it because it demanded the spoken word. As a boy, Conor's wit and emotion were consigned to the silence of thought. His stutter left his brain racing ahead of his words, and his mind became a prison of those things that made him laugh and feel. As he defeated his stutter, he basked in gregariousness. Conor needed words the way most people needed oxygen.

He raised the bottle toward the blue Arizona sky and spoke to Rita, his angel, who, if she were real, had a lot to answer for.

Bless me, Rita, for right now things are pretty fucked up.

This will be part conversation, part confession. You damn well better listen. I climbed this rock to reflect and remember, so you will hear it all. Line by blessed line. You might have anointed my arm, but all that came after? All I can conclude is, a hell of a lot of the time, you just weren't paying attention.

Conor regarded his bottle. After sixteen years under God-knows-what conditions, suppose the champagne had gone flat? What an anticlimax that would be. He peeled its metallic wrapping, already more than a little tattered, released the wire bail, then carefully set to work with his thumbs, rocking its cork from one side to the other until it leapt away with a satisfying pop. Energized by the jostling climb, liquid erupted into white bubbles that flowed over his hand and wrist. He did his best to catch the overflow by holding the bottle high and swallowing the stream as it dripped off the base.

He waited for the eruption to subside, then drank deeply.

Here's to you, Dad. God, how I wish you could have been there.

three

Port of Oakland
1964

CONOR AND SAM WERE BEING PUNISHED. They'd accompanied their father to the Oakland trucking terminal he supervised where they'd been sentenced to wash semi-truck cabs. The day was hot and the work hard for a nine-year-old. Hugh periodically checked on his sons to shout dire threats when their work assignment deteriorated into water fights with the heavy hoses.

While he scrubbed, Conor took note of the sway his father held over this rugged kingdom of drivers and mechanics and loading dock workers. They made their respect for Hugh obvious. That he savored the crudeness and masculine camaraderie was equally apparent. Hugh did not require these workers to alter their comfortable profanity and blue-collar humor as an accommodation to his sons.

Early that afternoon, a truck pulled in, hissing its brakes and adding a loud blast of its horn. There followed a stream of livid epitaphs and accusations issued by the driver as he descended from his cab. Angry over the way his trailer had been loaded, the driver's curses spared no one. Until Hugh clasped a hand on the back of the trucker's thick neck, directing him toward an office one story up with windows overlooking the yard. Hostile, knowing eyes watched this little ceremony from all corners of the terminal.

Conor crept to the front of the truck he washed and watched as Hugh shoved the trucker inside. Conor rubbed an imaginary spot on the truck's front bumper as he checked the office windows.

Five minutes later, the trucker made his way downstairs, one eye swelling shut. He bled from his nose and from a cut on his forehead. Wearing a grim silence and ignoring grins of those he'd earlier berated, he climbed into his truck cab. The diesel shuddered to life.

Hugh reappeared several minutes later. As he descended the stairs unmarked, he caught Conor's wide-eyed stare. He walked directly to his son, squatted to Conor's eye-level, and said, "Nobody treats my people like that. Now get back to work."

Hugh grew up in East St. Louis among a family of Irish-Catholic brawlers. He loved boxing and country music, and none of his five sons feared a fight. Several of Conor's brothers were good at it. Conor wasn't, and Hugh didn't fault him for it.

But he wouldn't allow Conor to shrink from confrontation.

Conor remained smaller than most of his sixth-grade classmates when Gary Shaw picked him as a target. Conor came limping home one afternoon, displaying a bloody nose. Hugh placed a meaty hand under the boy's chin and issued an order. "If you don't stand up to him now, he'll never stop picking on you. Go wash your face. Tomorrow, after school, go to his house and fight him again."

Convinced his father knew something he did not, Conor accepted this assignment and hiked the two blocks down and one block over to Gary's house. Again, the bigger kid beat him up.

"Fight him again tomorrow afternoon," Hugh ordered.

Conor found himself uncertain of his father's strategy.

On the fourth day, Gary met Conor at his door. "Quit coming over here. My mom's getting mad!" He pounded Conor into submission once more.

Six days Conor trudged to his adversary's door. All six days, he lost the fight. The seventh day, Gary's mother answered.

"Gary," she called, "Conor's here."

Gary's voice carried from somewhere inside. "Tell him to go home. I don't wanna' fight. I'm tired of this!"

AS SAN CARLOS FARM LEAGUE CHAMPIONS, THE BRAVES' 1961 season culminated with a game against an all-star team comprised of the rest of the league's best players. Conor was mowing them down. Second grader after second grader trudged back to his bench under Conor's deft mixture of strikes and not strikes. The All Stars' frustration grew with each futile inning.

Conor's pitch count neared three hundred or so when the All Stars sent their last substitute to bat. The kid might have been the only boy small as Conor. He scowled his determination, pushing his glasses higher on his nose after each pitch, then sinking into an exaggerated squat that reduced his strike zone to the size of an index card.

With the count fifteen and two, both umpire and hitter became surly.

The batter squatted, pounded home plate twice, and screamed, "Throw strikes!"

Conor sneered and hurled a high, tight fastball, sending the batter diving for cover.

"Ball," sighed the umpire.

The thirteen-year-old base umpire called time-out and summoned the twelve-year-old plate umpire. They met halfway between home and the mound. Conor overheard their conversation.

"Score's twelve to three. We're gonna be here all night. How about expanding the strike zone a little? Like, anything close?"

The umpires returned to their respective posts. Conor kicked and fired a ball that skipped off the plate into the catcher's glove.

"Strike Three!"

The batter's mouth fell open in disbelief. He glared first at the plate ump, a boy roughly twice his size, then turned to the mound. Emitting a ninja scream he raised the bat high over his head, and charged, mayhem blazing in his eyes.

"Notfairnotfairnotfairnotfair . . . !"

Conor required a few seconds to process the intent of this miniature bat-wielding maniac.

"Notfairnotfairnotfairnotfair . . ."

My God, this kid's trying to kill me.

"Notfairnotfairnotfairnotfairnotfair . . ."

Conor ran, dodging and weaving with the kid on his heels. The other second graders watched in stunned silence until they got into the spirit of the chase. They began cheering each juke and jive as Conor fled his attacker. The umpires, who had not been instructed by their adult supervisors regarding felonious assault, hesitated to intervene. A chain-link fence separated the adults from any opportunity for direct involvement.

Finally, their journey took Conor and his pursuer onto the infield dirt where the kid tripped over second base. Conor's shortstop had the presence of mind to disarm him. He pounded the second base bag twice with his fists, and yelled, "Not! Fair!"

The umpires escorted him to the All Star's bench and left him in the custody of his teammates. Conor dispatched the game's final hitters.

The kid didn't participate during their end-of-game handshake ritual. Conor found him, disheartened and alone, in his dugout. He approached cautiously.

"Hey," he said.

The kid looked up and said nothing.

"Do you want t . . . t . . . to fight?" asked Conor.

"I dunno," the kid said, then squinted one eye and added, "Do you?"

Conor considered his options. "Not if you don't."

The kid said, "You talk funny."

"Yeah. I st . . . stutter. Sometimes." After another pause, he added, "I'm Conor. What's your name?"

"I'm A.J." He extended his hand. "A.J. Cohen. Good-tameetcha."

BY THE TIME THEY WERE FOURTH GRADERS, CONOR AND A.J. were inseparable.

A.J.—the second son of Myron Cohen, a well-to-do Jewish merchant—and his older brother shared an intended destiny in the carpet business.

Hugh came home from work one day to find Conor and another boy playing back-yard whiffle ball. The minute Hugh stepped onto his porch, the game halted as Conor's new friend marched toward Hugh with extended hand and determined stride.

"Howyadoin, Mr. Nash. A.J. Cohen, greattameetcha." He offered a firm and enthusiastic handshake. "Conor's told me all about ya. You gotta great kid here."

Hugh immediately liked A.J. As a sharp counterpoint to Conor, A.J. displayed an abundance of self-confidence and social ease. Hugh believed A.J. offered a good example for his son, who too often hid from his stutter.

Hugh understood that words flashed through Conor's brain while his tongue tripped like a scratched record over his g's and hard t's. At home, his brothers didn't call him by his name. They called him Guh… Guh. Hugh could have intervened. He didn't. The stutter presented another battle Conor must fight. Hugh knew, though, if any other kid made fun of Conor's stutter within their hearing, his brothers would pound the living daylights out of his tormentor. Conor bore the inevitable teasing with silence. Hugh and Nadine knew the tragedy of this self-imposed isolation, because at home, Conor fought past his stutter to constantly make his parents and brothers laugh. He displayed a rapier sense of humor, and all the makings of a first-class smart ass.

By sixth grade Hugh accorded A.J. the privileges and expectations of a Nash. A.J.'s parents were similarly welcoming of Conor, although Myron Cohen believed in more sharply defined lines between children and adults. Myron raised his sons within strict adherence of Jewish religious tradition. Though not a particularly religious man, according to his Catholic upbringing, Hugh herded his sons regularly to Mass. He granted Conor dispensation to occasionally attend A.J.'s Sunday School.

"Why do you want me t... to guh... go t... to Jewish Sunday school?" Conor asked A.J.

"Because Jews are lousy basketball players. Anyway, the ones who go to my temple are. And if you come to Sunday school, they'll let you play on our church team."

As they walked together to the synagogue, A.J. gave him a heads-up. "Some of the stuff's in Hebrew."

"I don't know Hebrew."

"That's okay. I'll get a cup of ice. When it comes your turn to read, fill your mouth with ice and stutter a little. It'll sound just the same."

Along with his outsized self-assurance, A.J. enjoyed a curiosity urging him beyond his father's religious and social boundaries. So, he welcomed the chance to accompany Conor and his family to Mass as the Cardinal presided over Conor's Confirmation. When their pew stood and filed toward the altar, twelve-year-old A.J. surpassed the line of people waiting to receive the sacrament and marched directly to the Cardinal with extended hand.

"A.J.," Hugh called with a harsh whisper. "A.J., get back in—"

"Howyadoin', Cardinal. I'm A.J. Cohen. I've never attended one of these things. I'm Jewish, so I didn't take one of the crackers, but I want to tell you how impressed I am with the way you handled yourself up there, how you said it."

"Um... well, thanks very much, A.J..."

"One question. I noticed a lot of these people are kissing your ring. What's that about?"

Hugh clamped a hand on A.J.'s shoulder. "I'm sorry, Your Holiness. A.J. is... well, he's... I apologize."

At about this same time, another boy, who would play a leading role in Conor's life story, fell under the paternal surrogacy of Hugh Nash—Basil Doan, a gangly, pimpled, buck-toothed kid who could hit a baseball out of sight.

Conor and Basil became friends as teammates during the summer of their thirteenth year when, eerily foreshadowing his professional career, Conor's mother negotiated his first release.

"You made the team," Nadine said, "but now you don't want to play?"

"Yeah, I want t... to play. But they've already guh... guh... got their pitchers," Conor explained. "I won't guh... get t... to pitch on this team. And I need t... to pitch. So I need t... to guh... go to the minors."

The summer program included both a major and minor league. Making the majors afforded more prestige than being one of the kids judged *not quite ready* for that level of competition.

"Don't you want to play in the best league?"

"No. I want t... to pitch."

His mother called Conor's coaches and arranged the transaction.

So, like A.J., Baze became a fixture at our house. And though he was quiet, the sincerity and determination with which he approached both baseball and life impressed my dad

The depth of my ineptitude always amazed my father. He saw Baze as my exact opposite. Baze could do anything, fix a car, build things. Hugh hoped some of that would rub off on me.

Our ultimate bond, though, has always been baseball.

As you get older, the game becomes less an exercise in varying degrees of ineptitude and acquires sophisticated nuances that make it so difficult. And Baze and A.J. were way ahead of me. While I remained trapped inside a hundred and thirty-pound body, they grew. A.J., a catcher, and Baze a third baseman, both displayed raw power at the plate.

On our high school freshman team, I was a slap-hitting center fielder and third-string pitcher with a mediocre fastball, which meant I hardly ever pitched. Adults considered me highly coachable, though, because when they told me to throw strikes, *I did.*

The fourth and least likely member of our crew showed up during that freshman year. Brad Grady, two years older than the rest of us, couldn't have been more different. While A.J., Baze and I approached academics with varying degrees of apathy, Brad focused on straight A's. In a few years, Brad looked old enough to buy us beer using a fake ID. When we caroused and drank on weekend evenings, though, Brad went home and studied. A.J. and Baze fought at the drop of an insult—either real or perceived— and because I accompanied them, I often got caught in the storm.

I don't remember Brad ever hitting anyone.

A.J could talk people into anything, including girls. Girls liked me, because I made them laugh. Despite his awkward looks, Baze met girls because he hung with us. Brad never had a bit of luck dating. Not ever.

Brad and I did share the gift of dogged focus. At about the same time I declared I'd be a major league pitcher, Brad decided he would attend Stanford Law School and become a judge. Granted, an odd ambition for a fourth grader, but it's true.

Despite Brad's utter lack of athletic ability, he loved baseball every bit as much as the rest of us. And he understood baseball on an intellectual level we didn't.

We met Brad at freshman baseball practice. He'd been cut from the varsity team where he tried to be a left-handed pitcher. The coaches felt bad because they liked Brad's enthusiasm. So, they gave him a uniform and made him assistant student coach of our freshman squad. And they gave him a scorebook. Brad kept the most detailed and accurate scorebook they'd ever seen.

Odd as this association among us three jocks and Brad might seem, his relationship with my dad appeared even more unlikely. Hugh, a blue-collar guy with hard fists and hard attitudes, believed his sons must be hard as well if they were to make a place for themselves in a demanding and unforgiving world. Yet, he accepted this soft, cerebral boy into the family circle just as he had A.J. and Baze, giving the same degree of attention to Brad's ambitions as he did to ours.

This is who we were—four friends, bound for eternity. Lots of high school buddies graduate and go their separate ways. Not us. To this day, we remain vital pieces of each other's lives. Somehow, my dad saw this future. I think he liked them so much, because he felt I'd surrounded myself with three guys who would always have my back. A.J, the brains and the dealmaker, Baze, the muscle, and Brad, the voice of reason.

four

Seattle Mariners
1991

WE EACH HAD OUR LITTLE BOY DREAMS OF PLAYING *professional baseball, Rita, but for some reason you picked me. And as their realities set in, they placed their hope and confidence in me. They kept faith during my failures. I included them in all my successes. My friends on all my teams were their friends, too. When I finally made it, I passed them off as relatives, so they had access to major league clubhouses.*

That only backfired once.

A member of the Mariners public relations staff, an enthusiastic woman in her twenties, found herself attracted to Baze. She asked around about him, and a clubbie told her he was my cousin.

She made it a point to chat Baze up the next time she saw him in a hallway outside the locker room. By then, Baze had acquired this mesmerizing power over women, and things took their normal course.

We left the next day on a road trip. When we got back, the

PR woman found me during pre-game workouts and said, "When's your cousin coming back?"

I didn't know about the liaison, so I drew a blank. The only cousin I could think of was cousin Pete who lived in Bellingham.

"You know my cousin?" I asked.

"Yeah. I met him last homestand. I think he's pretty hot."

My confusion multiplied. Why would Pete have come to a game without calling ahead to ask me for tickets? And I supposed, by some strange standards, Pete could be mistaken for someone, well, not hot, but lukewarm?

"Maybe so," I told her, "but he's married. He's got three kids."

She stared at me with disbelief, then simmered to a low boil. She turned and stomped away.

I remained puzzled until the next day when I heard a commotion outside the locker room.

"You asshole!" she screamed at Baze. "You didn't tell me you were married."

"I'm not married. Who said I'm married?"

I'd just stepped through the door. She pointed to me. "Your cousin!"

"But I'm not—"

I grabbed Baze's arm and gave him a warning look. The PR office handled players' requests for tickets and clubhouse passes for relatives. The major league has rules I didn't want to trifle with for the sake of Baze's libido.

Yeah. Major Leagues

Had it just been the minors, Rita, maybe this ending wouldn't be so hard. Maybe I wouldn't feel like I'd blown it, not only for me, but for my friends and family. Finally giving a hungry man a seat at the banquet and then snatching it all away borders on cruelty.

And believe me, the Major Leagues are a feast.

Or were you even present for that final insult? I guess I always took it for granted that an angel would be all-seeing. But maybe not. Maybe you're just some wandering spirit with a shitty sense of humor. Ducking in and out of my life every so often to set me up for the punchline.

July 1991

CONOR SAT IN A STERILE WAITING ROOM, THE ONE TO which a bubbly assistant guides you, then leaves you alone. He'd spent a claustrophobic hour listening to klinks and clanks from the magnetic resonance imager.

His doctor entered with a flourish, as if anxious to be somewhere else, slapped two images against the lighted wall panel, and spoke without preamble. "Both labrum and rotator cuff are torn. These injuries require major reconstructive surgery."

"What about, just, rehab—"

"Not if you ever want to throw a baseball again."

"And the chances of recovery? How long until I can pitch?"

The doctor sighed. "Odds are pretty long. Your damage is significant."

Conor heard the only part of that statement he wanted to hear. He'd been battling long odds all his life.

The first surgery took place a week later. With his arm constrained tightly to his chest by ace bandages and a sling, his doctor ordered him not to move the shoulder for six weeks. Beyond that, the only instruction given was *don't push it. Your shoulder will let you know when it's ready.* Conor kept waiting for his shoulder to let him know. Apparently, they didn't speak the same language.

"How's the shoulder?" a Mariners trainer asked during Conor's 1992 spring training physical.

"Good," Conor said. He'd been careful over the winter, finally beginning to throw in December. His arm felt okay, although he hadn't cut loose yet.

In only a few years, pitchers with reconstructed shoulders would be treated like newborns. Every step of rehabilitation carefully controlled and monitored for six months before they indulged in any throwing at all. These lessons were learned at the expense of guys like Conor Nash. He threw too hard, too soon. When the season began, the Mariners left him behind at extended spring training. Two weeks later, searing pain returned. An MRI showed new tears in both labrum and rotator cuff. Conor's second surgery occurred at the end of April.

A.J. had negotiated an excellent contract for 1992. The contract wasn't guaranteed, though. To collect, Conor had to be healthy. Because teams couldn't release players who are on the disabled list, Conor earned the major league minimum as he rehabbed through 1992.

The tedium of pain and rehabilitation dragged on. When he finally picked up a baseball again, nothing felt right. The pain returned, his arm unimproved. He became sullen. Depression and anger so foreign to his nature settled in. The Mariners executed their buyout clause at season end and cut him loose.

On the day following his release, he reached for a beer and saw the champagne at the back of his garage fridge. He slammed the door. He didn't even consider the possibility. Opening that bottle would be acceptance of the unacceptable.

He tried a different surgeon the third time around.

"We can do this again," the doctor said. "Honestly, though, I can't say you'll regain enough strength to pitch. So, what are your goals if we undertake this procedure?"

Conor shook his head, closed his eyes, and said, "All I want is my arm back. I'm thirty-seven years old. I just want to play catch without it hurting so bad."

"Well, if you're careful, we can do that."

In truth, he wanted some shred of hope he wasn't done. He needed hope. And as hope ebbed, and he saw that damned champagne bottle every time he opened his refrigerator, the distance between Kate and Conor grew a little more pronounced.

Camelback Mountain
October 1992

WHO IS CONOR NASH IF HE CAN'T PITCH?

He considered the bottle at arm's length. By shutting one eye, he hid the sun. Dark glass diffused light into soft ripples that seemed to skate through the liquid. He shook the bottle, and light glinted through each bubble as it swam a straight line from the depths to the surface, displaying a gentle persistence along their path.

Gentle persistence brought him to Kate.

She's pissed at me.

She's been here each step of the way, Rita, endured everything without complaint. For the first time, though, Kate doesn't understand.

Look, I know I've been a different person these past few months, brooding over this damned bottle. Given the circumstances, don't I get a pass? I mean, she watched me pitch at Candlestick

Park and Wrigley Field and Yankee Stadium. She heard the cheers. She claims she feels the same sizzle I feel when I'm taking that walk to the mound with a game on the line.

It all came to a head a few days ago. She was blunt. I'd been hard to be around for months. She said she understood to a point. "But when will you come back to us?"

She trotted out my ten-year rule.

See, whenever one of the kids—one of those with the physical talent who couldn't cope with pressure and disappointment and failure—said they'd decided to retire, I got all over them. You can't call it retiring until you've given at least ten years to the game—to the dream. Be honest and call it what it is. You're quitting.

"You've given it sixteen years," she told me. She said I didn't fail. "You climbed to the top. You showed everyone. You were good."

"I've been on this path three decades," I told her. "It's my body that won't let me do it. Not my mind or my heart. It still feels like quitting—like dying."

When we were young, I told her how scary the pressure felt, standing before thousands of people, half of them hoping I'd fail. But you know what? I love that pressure. Me and that guy holding a bat. Think you can beat me? Okay, let's go.

Pressure makes it all mean something.

Over all my years of professional baseball, I avoided the trap of alcohol and drugs because baseball was my drug. She doesn't understand how it feels when an addict realizes he'll never be that high again.

THE SOFA THEY USUALLY SHARED SAT EMPTY. THEY FACED each other in two chairs typically reserved for kids or guests. The television droned but neither heard it. The coffee table marked the distance between them.

Conor broke his brooding silence and tried to explain.

"By any standard other than professional sports," he said, "I'm a young man. But it's like my life is over. Once you've lived in that spotlight, you never forget it."

"Maybe it feels that way," Kate said. "In your heart, though, you must know it's not true. We have so much. Now you get to be a husband and a father."

Conor answered without thinking. "Yeah? Where's the spotlight in being a husband and father?"

He knew how wrong he was the moment those words left his mouth. He saw Kate fight back tears. He would never forget what she said next.

"I know how much you've dreaded this ending. But have you ever considered how much I've looked forward to it? I've lived through the failure, too. Every time they said you weren't good enough. I've seen you rise above every disappointment, and I'm proud to say I think I've helped. For fifteen years, though, I haven't been your wife. Since the moment we met, you've been married to baseball. I've been the mistress. And I've so looked forward to a day when it would finally be my turn."

He didn't trust himself to answer. She endured his silence for a long moment.

"Conor, it's up to you now. Your sense of self-worth, your success or failure, no longer bends to the whim of some manager or baseball executive or pitching coach. We have a whole lifetime ahead of us."

Right, he thought. *Yankee Stadium, Wrigley Field. Candlestick Park. Forget the sound of 40,000 people. Banish the memory of being better than anyone expected when I was a decade too old;*

the embrace and respect of teammates—that clubhouse family who knows exactly what life's about on this damned treadmill.

Still, he didn't speak. He sat smoldering inside, while she wore a look of helpless desperation. Again, it fell to Kate to break the silence. "I've never told you this. But there were times I wished you *would* have quit. When we were beyond broke. When I faced another moving van alone. When you felt so betrayed by the game, and I knew how badly you were hurting."

"Well, why didn't you say something?" he barked back to her.

"Because," she said softly, "if I had forced you to choose, I was never quite sure you'd choose us."

Conor's heart stopped. Not once had he doubted Kate. It hadn't occurred that she might have doubted him.

Her quiet statement drove him to mountain.

five

CONOR DRANK AND CONSIDERED HIS ANGEL.
 I will never cease to be amazed at how many things had to fall into place along this twisted path. And I've always wondered, Rita, if that's a matter of your design, or your neglect.
 When my brothers and I were little, Dad instilled the sacred rite of the tunnel. On the east side of the bay, the Caldecott Tunnel bores through the Berkeley Hills between Oakland and Orinda along California State Route 24. Dad told us if we closed our eyes, licked one finger, held our breath, and touched the roof while we passed through the tunnel, we could make a wish.
 My wish never varied. Please, let me pitch for the Giants. Until high school, when A.J. and Baze added power and strength and speed, while I didn't budge a scale past a hundred and thirty pounds. That's when I added: and please let me throw harder.
 A bridge was necessary, though, between the freshman third string pitcher and the professional prospect, something to get

hitters out while a mediocre fastball had time to develop an afterburner, something that earned me a starting spot during the last two years of high school.

Thank God, or maybe Rita, for Fat Brad Grady's knuckle curve.

In fairness, Fat Brad wasn't all that fat. Tall and slight, a minor paunch overhung his waistline. Picture a pregnant woman starting her second trimester—if she had hair on her stomach. As an adult, he cultivated his paunch into a serious beer gut. During high school, though, he earned the nickname because he suffered by comparison to me, A.J. and Basil. As a high school junior, Basil surpassed six feet with signs of impressive musculature. While A.J. would never be tall, he, too, packed on muscle. I raced A.J. toward the five-foot-five mark but remained slender as a fungo. I'd willingly have sold my youngest brother to Gypsies for real, honest-to-god biceps.

In my earlier description of Fat Brad, I may have erroneously created the image of an overly serious young man. Nothing could be further from the truth. Brad cracked us up all the time. We gave each other all kinds of crap and were brutal in attacking each other's vulnerabilities. I suffered barbs for my stuttering. We didn't give Basil a pass on his buck teeth and braces. As early as our senior year, A.J.'s hairline began to recede. "You don't have a forehead anymore," Brad told him. "You have a fivehead, or a sixhead." And with Brad, of course, we made all kinds of comments about his stomach.

He turned our barbs around, though, by making his growing pot belly a point of pride. He cultivated his stomach as one might cultivate a taste for fine wine. He became adept at pooching it out, exaggerating the effect. As he aged, his belly grew more prodigious and hairier.

He'd place golf bets with A.J., then walk the course with his stomach exposed, A.J. laughing so hard at other peoples' reactions he couldn't concentrate on his game.

Brad was dead serious about baseball, though.

He had one athletic gift—he could bend the flight of a ball. While mediocre hitters crushed any fastball, he managed to get over the plate, even accomplished batters flailed at his yakker.

As our freshman season moved along, we gradually accepted Brad into our company. Finally, he showed up in my backyard one Saturday afternoon.

BASIL READ SOMEWHERE THAT STAN MUSIAL HONED HIS batting eye by hitting bottle caps. So Conor sailed soft drink lids for him and A.J. They stopped their game when Brad appeared.

He got right to the point.

"Ya gotta learn to throw a curveball," he told Conor.

"I already throw a curveball."

"Yeah, but it sucks."

Conor looked to his compatriots for support. He faced an awkward silence until A.J. said, "It really does kind of suck."

Eager to hear any more salient instruction than *throw strikes*, Conor did not respond defensively.

"They call it a knuckle curve, because you put the tips of your first two fingers on the seam and push with those fingers when you throw it," Brad said.

"Hold it like this?"

"Yeah, then spin it by pushing it."

"Push it?"

Brad took the ball and offered a half-speed demonstration

of the pushing action, tossing it easily to Basil a few feet away.

A few minutes later, standing sixty feet apart, Brad wore Conor's baseball glove.

"Don't worry if it doesn't do much at first," Brad called. "Getting the feel of it takes a lot of practice."

"Okay. Sure you don't want a catcher's mask or something?"

"No, I can catch it."

"Should I throw it hard or soft?" Conor asked.

"Throw it hard. And remember, push it."

Conor wound up, paused at the peak of his balance point, kicked, drove, snapped and pushed. As the ball spun from his hand, he felt a tighter rotation than anything he'd thrown before.

Sixty feet away, Brad assumed a half squat, glove extended and ready. The pitch's velocity caught him by surprise, as did the ball's elevation out of Conor's hand. He raised the glove as compensation. At the last second, the ball darted down, missing the glove entirely and catching Brad square in the mouth.

Basil reached him first.

"Brad! Man, you're bleeding."

Brad got to his feet, displaying a rapidly swelling upper lip, and spit a series of red globs onto the ground.

He was ebullient, though, with praise.

"That wath the beth fuckin' curve ball I ever thaw, man!"

He spit again.

"You really puthed the thit outta' that one!"

Then, he realized he was bleeding.

He bent, hands on knees, and gasped as he saw blood pooling around two white objects gleaming under the afternoon sun.

"Thit! Thoth are my theeth!"

And he fainted.

six

THE SUN SETTLED LOWER AND CUMULUS TOWERS filling the western sky became washed with color. This was a fat, more friendly sun than the one hanging white and smoldering over the Phoenix landscape at mid-day. While these cloud bases remained pure white and contrasted sharply with a deepening blue of evening, their tops showed splashes of red and yellow.

I REMAINED CENTER FIELDER AND THIRD PITCHER IN A TWO-man rotation through our sophomore high school season. I kept working at the knuckle curve, though, throwing it at my square chalked onto the elementary school brick wall. The work paid off. During my junior season, I became San Carlos High's ace.

Though we still hung together on weekends, A.J. wasn't with us. His dad sent him to Mount Zion, a private high school for boys.

I grew to five-and-a-half feet, but our bathroom scale remained stuck at a hundred and thirty. The knuckle curve, though, converted my fastball from mediocre to sneaky, *the distinction being that a mediocre fastball gets pummeled, while a sneaky fastball—set up by an off-speed curve—gets people out.*

And, I could throw strikes.

I struck out so many, a scout from the Texas Rangers showed up. Brad and Hugh always sat together, watching me and Baze play. And on this day, I wondered about the guy sitting with them.

Ten opponents struck out that day, and when my dad introduced the man as a professional scout, I nearly peed my pants. Baze hit a ball twelve miles during the fifth inning, accounting for a 3-0 San Carlos victory. Maybe the scout would take Baze, too?

He said, "Nice job, Conor. I'll stop by and see how you're doing this summer."

Unfortunately, I didn't throw a single pitch that summer. I suffered a severe lapse of common sense, during which I certainly could have used the intervention of a guardian angel.

"Are you sure about this?" A.J. asked. "If Sam catches us, he'll kick our butts."

They huddled at the far end of the elementary school, looking at a trellis providing access to the one-story building's long, flat roof. Two weeks remained in the school year, and most seniors at San Carlos High, including Sam and his girlfriend, took much of that time off.

Sam and Carol Gibson had left Conor's house earlier, telling Hugh and Nadine they were going to a movie. Conor knew where they'd really be—the elementary school roof, a notorious make-out spot.

"He's been kicking my butt all my life," Conor said. "It's not that big a deal."

"Maybe not for you," Basil said, "but I like my teeth."

"He's never going t... to catch us," Conor said, shifting a bag of water balloons to his right hand, testing the trellis with his left. "His pants will probably be around his knees, and we'll be guh... gone before he can chase us."

They climbed the trellis, crouching low as they summited the roof. A half-moon diluted the darkness. Several couples occupied blankets spread along the building's length.

"Which ones are they?" A.J. whispered.

Conor suppressed a laugh. "Fourth blanket down. The one with the bare ass."

Into the spirit of things now, A.J. grinned.

They both looked at Basil.

"Okay, give me some balloons."

Thus armed, they tiptoed their approach.

Although occupants of some blankets glanced up as they crept by, Sam's dedication to his task rendered him oblivious. Conor nodded his chin once, twice, and on three, they gave a scream, sending Sam rolling sideways off Carol, who sat up with a scream of her own, pendulous breasts swaying in the moonlight.

The three attackers unloaded their munitions.

If Sam's pants *had* been around his knees, they might have escaped without incident. He was not, however, wearing pants. Thus unencumbered, he gave chase.

The assailants knew splitting up offered their best chance of survival. Basil headed for shadows cast by a tree growing alongside the structure. A.J. made for the trellis. Conor sprinted toward building's far end.

Sam chose Conor.

Laughing as he ran, Conor considered his alternatives. He could leap off the roof or surrender to his half-naked sibling.

One story. How far can it be? There's grass. I think.

Legs and arms flailing, he chose to jump. The grass didn't make much difference, though, as he felt fire bloom in his right ankle.

"THESE TWO I CAN UNDERSTAND," HUGH SAID WHEN A.J. and Basil hauled Conor home. "But you, Basil, you have more sense than to go running around on roofs."

Basil bowed his head and studied his feet.

"What were you doing up there, anyway?" Nadine asked them.

Conor started to mumble. He'd never been able to lie to his mother, though, so A.J. stepped in.

"Stupid thing, I know," he said. "We wanted to see it. Like Mount Everest. Because it's there."

"And how did you fall off?"

Again, A.J. handled the narrative.

"He tripped."

Hugh gave A.J. a half-disgusted, half-knowing look and rolled his eyes.

Nadine took Conor to a doctor the next morning.

"It's not a break. Be better if it was. It's a tendon. The good news is it will heal without surgery. The bad news," the doctor looked at Conor, "is it will always be weak, something you have to protect. You won't be able to pitch anymore."

Conor frowned and was about respond with an answer sure to land him in even more trouble.

His mother saved him. "Don't tell him that," she said. "You don't know my son."

I FACED A SUMMER WITHOUT BASEBALL. THE TEXAS SCOUT lost interest. I could only work to strengthen my arm with a five-pound fishing weight and concentrate on growing. I laid on my bedroom floor each evening and bench-pressed my bed. When lifting the rear legs up and down—banging the headboard against the wall—became too easy, I convinced my youngest brother and our cat to lie on the bed while I worked out.

As my ankle recovered enough that I could tolerate the pain, I headed back to the elementary school and threw an endless procession of baseballs against the brick wall.

The doctor was wrong. Everything accelerated during my senior year. I grew taller, even managed to gain another five pounds. The knuckle curve became deadly, and my fastball got less and less sneaky every day.

"You're throwing harder," Brad told me.

"Think so?"

"Absolutely. If I can find a state cop somewhere, I'll see if I can borrow a radar gun."

From his pre-law classes at Stanford, Brad drove home on game days. He continued keeping careful records of every aspect of my pitching and explaining his statistical theories. As a result, where most high school pitchers just took the mound and threw, I learned to create game plans and strategies.

Strikeouts mounted. Old guys with pork-pie hats, cigar stubs, stopwatches and notebooks became more and more common at the San Carlos High baseball diamond.

1974

A PERSON PLAYS THOUSANDS OF BASEBALL GAMES OVER THE course of his life, and they all sort of run together. You remember snippets here and there, but only a few retain their individuality. The day I faced A.J. with a high school record on the line is one I do remember.

"Hey, Connie, great game," Brad said as he and Hugh met Conor by the backstop. "I don't know if you realize it. You're only seven K's away from the San Carlos High School career strikeout record."

Conor accepted his father's handshake and offered Brad a quizzical look.

"Who even keeps t . . . track of stuff like that?"

"I did some research. A hundred and fifty-seven strikeouts is the record held by Dennis Dunlevy, and it took him three full seasons. You didn't pitch much your sophomore year. So, you've almost caught him in two seasons, with two games to go."

Conor smiled. "Next week we play A.J. Wouldn't it be something if . . . ?"

A.J. hit fifth for Mt. Zion, and his first time at bat, he caught a sneaky fastball that didn't sneak enough and drove it into the left-centerfield gap for a two-out double and RBI. Conor did his best to ignore A.J. standing atop second base, grinning, arms folded across his chest.

San Carlos led 2-1 as A.J. batted in the fourth, again with two down. Mt. Zion's leadoff hitter occupied second. He'd reached on a bunt Conor's third baseman threw into right field.

Foo Betts, the San Carlos catcher, hurried to the mound. "Ya gotta throw 'im the knuckle curve, Connie," Foo said. "He ain't seen nothin' like your knuckle curve."

"He's seen it about a million times in my backyard, Foo. He's looking for it. If we keep fastballs on his hands, he'll pop up."

Foo's shoulders slumped. He trotted to the plate, squatted, and extended one finger, though clearly, not an enthusiastic choice.

A.J. got under it just a bit. Conor held his breath until the center fielder settled below the towering fly a couple of feet shy of the fence. Conor had struck out six and allowed no more runs when A.J. hit again in the ninth. Basil had homered the previous inning, and San Carlos held a comfortable 5-1 lead.

A.J. pounded home plate with his bat and sneered his disdain. Conor scowled his derision. Foo put down two fingers.

Shit. I already told you. He shook his head.

Foo relented and asked for a fastball.

A.J. clobbered it, a few feet foul.

Foo put down two fingers. Conor shook his head. He nibbled—a pair of fastballs too far inside to tempt A.J.

Foo asked for a fastball and set his glove two inches off the outside corner.

Conor hit Foo's mitt and the umpire rewarded his effort by calling a strike. A.J. gasped, turned, snapped something to the ump, then looked again at Conor, redoubling his glare.

Now, Conor thought, using telepathy shared between pitcher and catcher.

Foo asked for the curve.

Conor dug his fingertips into the seam along the big part of the horseshoe, kicked, and pushed, imparting a wicked spin.

Seams grabbed at molecules of air, then bit hard. The ball, which left his hand on a line about a foot outside to right-handed A.J., took a quick dive and pounded down onto the plate's inside corner. Foo sank to his knees, blocking the ball off his chest protector.

Any other high school hitter facing a 2-2 count would commit to that ball before it dove out of sight. A.J.'s hands didn't move. Not even a twitch.

"Ball," the umpire said, almost as an aside.

A.J. adopted a half-grin, half-snarl, caught Conor's eye, and spit at his feet.

Foo put down two fingers. Conor shook his head. Foo put down two fingers, this time jabbing them for emphasis. He placed his glove a few inches from A.J.'s back leg, right below his knee.

Conor sighed. He'd never hear the end of it if he walked A.J.

He pushed the knuckle curve as he had that day when Brad's front teeth bit the dust. Foo didn't have to move his glove even a little.

"Strike Three!"

A.J. froze, offered the umpire a look of total disbelief, then turned again to Conor, his expression still protesting this injustice. For a moment, Conor remembered second grade. He steeled himself for A.J.'s charge. Instead, A.J. voiced one more criticism of the umpire's judgement and turned.

As they watched A.J. walk away following the game Brad pulled his dental plate from his mouth and grinned through the gap.

"Thit, man, that wath a good one."

Conor laughed. "Yep, that wath a *really* good one."

seven

---

*D*URING THE SUMMER SEASON FOLLOWING MY HIGH *school graduation, your angel powers worked overtime. The knuckle curve became irrelevant because a real fastball showed up. Nothing sneaky about it. Just a blazing comet with a sharp little tail no one believed could be generated by a five-ten kid so skinny he might blow away in a strong wind.*

Brad didn't borrow a radar detector from a state cop, because scouts brought their own. Lloyd Christopher represented the Angels. (Some irony there, don't you think, Rita, that the Angels were who wanted me?) Jack Night, baseball coach for the College of San Mateo, Northern California's most prestigious junior college baseball program, became another regular attendee.

We'd always played summer ball with our local San Carlos group. This year, though, A.J. convinced Baze and me to play for Walnut Tree, and Walnut Tree was loaded. We went 27-0 that summer and attracted attention all over the state. Now, we all faced a decision. Where would we go to school to take the next step along our baseball path?

"I GUESS I'M GOING TO COLLEGE OF SAN MATEO," CONOR told Basil and A.J. halfway through summer.

"Why?" A.J. asked.

"I thought you'd sign with CSM," Conor said.

"I know the girls going to CSM," A.J. said, "and believe me, Cañada will be more fun."

Cañada College, a JC a few miles south of San Carlos at Redwood City, had a long history of baseball mediocrity.

"The Cañada baseball program sucks. CSM is the best. I want to play with the best."

"Look around," A.J. said. "You're pretty much playing with the best right now."

"Well, yeah, but—"

"How much fun would it be for this group of guys to turn Cañada's program around? Steal a little of CSM's thunder?"

"Okay," Conor challenged, "who else is going to Cañada?"

"Trust me," A.J. said, "I'm working on it."

Conor shook his head. He didn't tell A.J. he'd already given CSM a verbal commitment.

"C'MON, CONNIE," A.J. SAID A COUPLE OF WEEKS BEFORE the semester started, "you've gotta come with us!"

Over the course of his life, Conor learned that A.J. Cohen hustled a deal like no one else. And, indeed, A.J. had been *working on it*. By his latest count, he'd sold a dozen Walnut

Tree stalwarts on the golden quest of turning Cañada into a baseball machine.

"I can't," Conor said. "I told CSM I'd go there."

"That doesn't matter. Tell 'em you changed your mind. Tell 'em all your friends are at Cañada, and you can't let your friends down. What can they do?"

Conor didn't answer. A.J. pressed ahead.

"How can you go over there when Baze and me will be at Cañada?"

Basil flushed, lowered his eyes to his shoes, and said, "Um . . . actually, A.J., I'm not."

"You said . . ."

"I know."

"Okay, A.J.," Conor said, "now you're the one who has to change. You can't go to Cañada when Baze and I are at CSM."

"Connie, I'm not going to CSM, either."

Conor regarded Basil with narrowed eyes. "So where—?"

"Alaska."

"Where's that?" A.J. asked.

Basil offered a puzzled look. "Alaska. It's way north, by Russia."

"Alaska, the state? I thought you were talking about a community college."

Conor couldn't believe Basil was serious. "Why Alaska? What's in Alaska?"

"Amanda. Her family's moving there."

During our sophomore year Baze had developed a relationship with Amanda Scollard, a tall, happy red-haired girl on the brink of becoming attractive. Like Baze, she suffered adolescent woes of braces and acne. They were ugly ducklings, leaning on each other and keeping faith that a metamorphosis was somewhere on their horizons. Amanda had metamorphosed more quickly than Baze.

"A girl?" A.J. said. "You're moving to Alaska for a girl?"

"Yeah. I'm kind of... in love. I think. And Alaska sounds like a pretty cool place."

"It's a fucking cold place!" A.J. said. "What about us?"

"What about baseball?" Conor added.

"Hey, I'll miss you guys. I'll come back and visit, though. And you can come see me. We've lived here our whole lives. Don't you want to see someplace else?"

"We'll see lots of places playing baseball," Conor said. "The scouts are after us."

"Scouts are after you, Connie," said Basil. "And I can play ball there. They've got those summer leagues where college guys go."

Conor and A.J. watched Basil head toward the cages for batting practice.

"Don't worry," A.J. told Conor. "He's not going to Alaska. I'll talk him out of it."

A week later, though, Basil left.

And a week after that, Conor entered the field house at College of San Mateo. He found his name above a locker in an expansive modern clubhouse featuring all the amenities. He greeted what few players he knew. Most of the guys were aware of Conor. Few of them went out of their way to be friendly, though, as they studied this rail thin kid with *the reputation*. Conor read their minds as skeptical glances found him. *What's so hot shit about you?*

Right now, fifteen of Conor's summer teammates were putting on Cañada uniforms at an antiquated, crowded, dank locker room reeking of mildew and frustration.

Conor wished desperately to be there.

He sat for a long time, staring at his name above the locker, hearing the clang of metal doors, a screech of spikes scraping concrete, sarcastic jibes and profanity characteristic of this game he so loved. He knew he couldn't stay.

CONOR TOOK A DEEP BREATH. "DAD, I KNOW I TOLD THEM I'd go to CSM, but I can't. All the guys I know are at Cañada. At the CSM clubhouse this afternoon, everything felt wrong."

Conor sat at the kitchen table, his father standing over him. He waited with trepidation. He knew how the sermon would go. *He'd made a commitment. Changing his mind now wasn't right. He should have thought about his friends from the start.*

Hugh sat. "So, what will you do?"

Conor looked at his father with surprise. *What happened to the lecture?*

"Well," he said, "I guess... I guess I'm gonna call and tell them I changed my mind."

"No," Hugh said. "Remember when you were thirteen, made the majors and then decided you'd rather play in the minors?"

Conor nodded.

"You had your mom call the coach and ask him to release you."

"Um... yeah."

"Believe me, if I'd known about it, it wouldn't have happened that way. This time, you'll do the right thing."

Conor's spirits sagged even further.

"Tomorrow," Hugh continued, "go to CSM, and be man enough to tell those coaches face-to-face you've changed your mind. No phone calls. No intermediaries."

"Yes, sir." Conor felt as if a weight had been lifted from his soul. He almost grinned, but somehow sensed the solemnity of the occasion.

As Hugh pushed back his chair and stood, Conor stammered, "I thought... I thought..."

"You thought what?"

"I thought you'd tell me to keep my word. I made a commitment so..."

Hugh settled in his chair and brought his hands together on the tabletop.

"Conor, commitments are important. But I watched those guys from CSM recruiting you all summer. I heard what they said. Those guys are pros. They're good at getting into the head of an eighteen-year-old kid and convincing him of all kinds of things. You've wanted to be a pro ballplayer your whole life, and I watched you work your ass off and make yourself successful despite your limitations. Then, something happened over the past summer and now, you really do have a shot at a pro contract. This game will become your job. And believe me, if you don't do your job, you'll get fired. Loyalty and promises won't save you. That's the real world."

Hugh stared hard into Conor's eyes.

"The thing about talent... you'll find all kinds of people who only care about your talent and don't care about you. Any number of people will want a piece of your ability. And the most important thing you can do is develop a trust and belief about yourself—about things you feel. This is your life we're talking about. If you feel Cañada is the right place, then go and don't look back. It's up to you now. Not me or anyone else."

"Mr. Knight?"

Jack Knight, CSM's head coach, glanced from his desk and offered a smile.

"Conor, it's good to—"

"I'm sorry, sir," Conor said. "I appreciate that you want me to play here... but I'm not comfortable with my decision. I know you've got a great program and... I know... I'm sorry. I can't be here. I just can't."

Knight stared at Conor for several seconds, then asked, "Where will you play ball?"

"Cañada. I know everyone there and—"

"Conor, you've got talent. You've got a real future ahead of you. You should make the most of your opportunities. The best opportunity for scouts to find you is here. Cañada isn't—"

"I'm sorry, Mr. Knight. If I'm good enough, they'll find me wherever I am."

That evening, Conor again sat at his kitchen table.

The phone rang. His mother answered.

"Hugh, phone's for you."

His father strode into the kitchen.

"Yes... yes, and I appreciate that you offered him an opportunity... Yes, it might be a mistake. Everybody knows how good CSM has been... Okay, okay, look. Here's the difference between you guys and Cañada. If Conor was still the average pitcher he was in high school, he could've walked on at Cañada, and gotten an opportunity to compete for a job. Without a ninety-mile-an-hour fastball, though, you folks wouldn't have given him the time of day... No. It's his decision, not mine."

eight

*I*UNDERSTAND THAT A PERSON NEEDS AN EGO TO SUCCEED *in a competitive situation. And as a nineteen-year-old phenom, Rita, I had plenty of that. I was lucky, though. I understood I owned no real claim to my talent. The ability to throw a baseball at warp speed, or hit it four hundred feet, is a gift bestowed by genetics and happenstance—or some stupid angel.*

I've seen so many young men enter pro ball wearing a sense of entitlement. At their high schools and their summer leagues, they'd always been the best. Their gift set them a notch above, earned them admiration and deference. Eventually, of course, they learned, at the professional level, their gift wasn't as unique as they believed. And it's a hard, hard lesson as they get weeded out. They never understood that ascending to the next level requires grueling, grinding work with which lesser mortals had been cursed all along.

Cliff Holland, a left-hander, held every pitching record at Cañada. He'd been drafted, and by the time I got there, served at some minor league outpost. I'd held him as my role model since junior high school. During my first week at Cañada, head baseball coach Lyman Ashley asked me about my goals. I told him I wanted to break all Cliff Holland's records.

From that moment, Ashley held the lever he needed.

Behind the campus, beyond the athletic fields, stands a hill—a long, rising grassy slope—the jocks call Mount Vial, named for a past Cañada football coach who hammered his players into shape by running them to the top and back.

Ashley offered pitchers that example as an extracurricular activity.

"Remember, boys," he said, "you pitch with your legs."

I accepted the challenge.

"How many did you run today?" Ashley asked me as I sat sweating and panting at my locker.

"Five times."

"That's good. But remember, son, a baseball game has nine innings."

Soon, I was making that round trip nine times.

Until Ashley asked, "What if we go extra innings?"

I added a tenth. And I swore that was it. Then Ashley said, "I've seen Cliff Holland do twelve."

I finally met Cliff when I was inducted into Cañada's Hall of Fame in 2013. By then, of course, he knew I was the guy who'd surpassed him in Cañada's record books. I thanked him for the motivation. I told him chasing his records helped me improve—that and running Mount Vial.

"Mount Vial?" He didn't seem to understand my reference.

"Yeah, when Coach Ashley told me how many times you ran the mountain, I knew I had to do it, too."

Holland laughed and shook his head. "I hate to tell you this, Conor. I never ran the damn mountain. Not even once."

1975

During their first season at Cañada, things occurred pretty much the way A.J. predicted. Conor and the Walnut Tree guys did, indeed, take the program to new heights. The College of San Mateo no longer stood as the only JC program big city newspapers wrote about. More significantly, Lyman Ashley found the current crop of high school seniors, including several kids he previously had little hope of recruiting, were expressing interest in playing baseball at Cañada.

CSM and the community of San Mateo, which abutted San Carlos, owned this territory. These were *their* recruits, *their* kids who were being spirited away. Conor became a focus of irritation among locals who felt he'd forsaken home-town loyalties just as his skills blossomed.

None of that mattered to Lloyd Christopher.

Conor intrigued Christopher, a veteran California Angels scout, when he watched Conor throw the knuckle curve as a high schooler. Not that a knuckle curve impressed Christopher. Professional hitters would demolish that pitch.

He saw an undersized kid who, despite his limitations, found and mastered a vehicle that kept him alive—for the time being. This kid manufactured a way not only to survive, but to thrive with mediocre stuff. The knuckle curve worked because he also teased his below-average fastball at the edges of the strike zone.

And the thing about skinny kids who kept their heads above water with knuckle curves and mediocre fastballs? They learned *how to pitch*. Christopher counted plenty of professionals who threw the piss out of the ball but never learned *how to pitch*. Competing at the professional level is all about adjustment.

Hitters improve. Fastballs fade. Pitchers who endure are the creative ones, those who learn early to find that next something, securing a few more games, a few more months, a few more seasons of survival.

The other thing about skinny kids, Christopher knew, is they didn't stay skinny forever. And every once in a long while, you combined a kid who learned *how to pitch*, with a body that finally flowered to bear the fruit of a genuine fastball, and you discovered you'd struck gold.

And, oh yeah, the kid's left-handed.

So, during Conor's first season Lloyd became a regular at Cañada baseball games, sitting alongside Hugh and Brad, watching the fastball mature. Lloyd didn't concern himself about competition from other scouts and other teams. He knew how their report on Conor would read.

While his fastball is impressive, his breaking ball needs work— the knuckle curve didn't factor into that equation, because now that Conor threw hard, his velocity simply overpowered the two-fingered push. Scouts were inherently skeptical of little guys who threw hard, because small bodies were prone to breaking down under long-term stress. *And,* the other scouts would point out, *he is racking up numbers against a bunch of junior college hitters who've already reached the pinnacle of their careers.*

The other scouts would look at bigger guys first.

So, Lloyd often had the ballpark to himself as he watched Conor go eight and one while Cañada won twenty-five games and reached the Northern California regional finals.

"CONNIE, WANNA HEAR SOMETHING FUNNY?" A.J. ASKED. "Go listen to Lloyd Christopher trying to cultivate your dad.

That's kind of like trying to cultivate a brick wall."

Hugh and Lloyd sat on metal bleachers, absently watching mini-camp workouts for the Palo Alto Oaks, the summer team for which both Conor and A.J. had agreed to play following their second season at Cañada. Lloyd, though, wanted to ensure Conor would not be available.

The Angels selected Conor Nash in the fifth round of Major League Baseball's January supplemental draft. Negotiations between Hugh and Lloyd became more intense with each game Conor pitched during his sophomore season. Conor produced a spectacular 10-0 record. He K'd at least fifteen hitters every start. And when he'd set a school record by striking out twenty-two a few weeks ago, Hugh smiled at Lloyd and said, "I believe the price just went up."

The two men shared an animated exchange of point, counter-point. As Conor, A.J., and other players finished raking the infield and tarping the mound and plate areas, Conor drifted toward the discussion.

"The money's not what's important, right now," Lloyd said. "You *have* to understand that, Hugh. The important thing is getting him on his way. The money will be there. Major League salaries will only get bigger."

"The money's not important?" Hugh said. "Not important to who? The guy who owns the team? I'll tell you, for damn sure, it's important to us. Conor's got options. He doesn't have to sign with anyone. He's got plenty of bids from major colleges. And a lot of them are offering more than you are."

"Colleges can't—"

"Oh, come on, Lloyd. This is the real world. You and I both know they can, and they do."

True enough.

Lyman Ashley told Conor he'd gotten inquiries about Conor from all over the country. "We're getting more calls about you than I've ever gotten about anyone. You can get a full ride practically anywhere."

A full ride, and all the little extras it included, sounded good to Conor.

For Hugh, though, university offers represented bargaining chips.

"Maybe getting an education would be a good thing—" Conor suggested.

"For a lot of people, yes," Hugh told him. "Not for you. I find it difficult to believe you'll take getting an education seriously at a place where they'll do everything for you, as long as you're pitching well. College programs aren't about developing players. They're about preserving coaches' jobs. It's just a two-year delay getting your professional career started."

Of course, Hugh would never admit that to Lloyd Christopher.

Hugh initially set the price of Conor's signature on an Angels' contract at $50,000.

"Hugh, that's crazy," said Christopher. "We gave our supplemental first-round pick a $25,000 signing bonus. And Conor is a fifth-rounder."

"He's only a fifth-rounder because you guys didn't have second or third-round picks. So, he's actually on a par with a third-round choice," Hugh argued.

Christopher offered $8,000, and throughout Conor's sophomore season, the scout didn't budge.

During the last week of May, Conor prepared himself to pitch the Palo Alto Oaks' season-opener the coming Sunday, when Lloyd called. Conor heard Hugh's half of the conversation.

"Lloyd, I'm tired of this. We're getting nowhere. Don't insult us with an $8,000 offer again. If you call one more time and there's not more money—and I mean a lot more money—on the table, Conor will *never* sign a contract with the Angels. He'll go play college ball, or we'll wait a year, and other teams will get their shot."

On May 30, 1976, Lloyd made a new offer. Hugh, Lloyd and Conor sat at the kitchen table as Conor scribbled his name to a contract paying him a $30,000 signing bonus. He would report to the Idaho Falls Russets—the Angels Class A representative in the Pioneer league.

While they shared congratulations, Conor smiled broadly as he told his dad, "The great thing about this? I can still pitch against San Mateo Sunday."

Lloyd shook his head. "No, Conor. We've given you a lot of money. We don't want you to get hurt playing amateur baseball a week before you report."

Conor's face fell as he turned and offered a silent plea to his father.

On Sunday, Conor and the Palo Alto Oaks would face the College of San Mateo's summer league team. For two years, as Conor and his friends dominated the Camino Norte Conference, CSM had done the same in the California Central Coast Conference.

For two years, Conor and Hugh read newspaper accounts of the California Coast Conference's superiority. Hugh suffered jibes from friends and neighbors who, still smarting from Conor's defection to Cañada, suggested Conor might not be doing so well if he'd chosen a more competitive conference. Conor hadn't faced CSM during the two years of his JC career. Sunday's game was his chance to erase the skepticism.

Hugh told Lloyd, "The boy wants to pitch Sunday. He *needs* to pitch this game."

"Hugh, we can't do it. It's out of your hands. He's signed a contract. We can't jeopardize—"

"The contract is still sitting on my kitchen table. I can tear it up as easily as I can let you leave here with it."

"Oh, come on. It's one game. He's got a whole career ahead of him."

"You're right," Hugh countered. "It's one game. Let him pitch it."

Lloyd closed his eyes. "Hugh, find your son an agent. Because next time I negotiate his contract, it won't be with you."

He turned to Conor and added, "You just be damn sure you don't break your arm, or anything else. And, Hugh, I hope you enjoy your game."

My dad, though, didn't see me pitch that Sunday. My dad would never see me pitch again.

CONOR DRANK. HE FELT A CHILL OF REGRET SWEEP through him. If he could have done one thing different, he wouldn't have bought that damned car.

Thirty thousand dollars! How could anyone even begin to spend thirty thousand dollars? One splurge. That's all I wanted. Just one splurge. The only car I'd ever had was a fifty-dollar beater my dad provided for high school. The thing used nearly as much oil as it did gas, and all I knew about cars was if you pushed the gas pedal they went, and the harder you pushed, the more exciting they became. That car lasted only a few months. Billowing smoke and making sounds like a whale song, I managed to get it home, but it never ran again.

"I got you a car," Hugh said, *"and now I gotta pay someone to come and tow it away. Last car I get for you."*

Now I had Thirty Thousand Dollars! I suppose angels can't relate to such blatant materialism, but my dream was a Starsky and Hutch car. David Starsky, played by Paul Michael Glaser on a weekly television series, drove a bright red two-door Ford Torino with a wide, white vector stripe along both sides. The closest thing I found was an orange Chevy Monte Carlo featuring an off-center brown stripe running along the hood, continuing onto the roof and trunk. I bought it used for $3,500 from a Redwood City kid, who needed money to pay speeding tickets.

I sold it the following November for pretty much the same reason.

"WHAT THE HELL IS THAT?" HUGH DEMANDED.

"My car," Conor said.

"Are you crazy? You need a car like you need the measles. You parked the damn thing right in front of the Johnson's house. You know how pissed he gets—"

"He doesn't own the street."

Hugh stared at his second-oldest son and shook his head with disgust. "How long do you think your bonus money will last if you spend it like this?"

"Hey, I got a good deal." Conor folded his arms across his chest and gazed out the window at his beautiful machine.

"Anything you paid is too much. You don't need a car. Next week you'll be in Idaho. It'll sit here and be an eyesore in my driveway all summer."

Conor dismissed his father with a sarcastic wave before stomping away.

"And get the damn thing out of the street!" Hugh yelled after him.

The feud still simmered a day later when Conor drove the Monte Carlo to Menlo Park on a perfect Sunday afternoon for the showdown against CSM. A.J. and Brad were still at Conor's house, pleading with Hugh.

"This is crazy," A.J. said. "I know Conor's acting like an ass, but it's his last amateur game. Both of you've been looking forward to it for months. And you're not going?"

"You're not really gonna make me go watch the game by myself, are you?" Brad pleaded.

Hugh sat at the table, his big arms folded across his chest. "I'm sorry, A.J. I'll miss watching you play today. I'll be there the rest of the summer. He's wrong, though. And he's got to wake up, or he'll blow this chance. I can't validate his actions by going and watching like nothing's happened."

"YOU'RE A FUCKING IDIOT," A.J. TOLD CONOR. "YOUR DAD should be here."

A.J. stood at the dugout steps, bat on his shoulder. Conor, who had retired the first three Menlo hitters, two of them via strikeout, leaned against the railing next to him.

Despite adrenaline coursing through him, Conor felt empty. He knew A.J. was right. He should have made peace with Hugh. His dad should be seated with Brad, savoring his son's crowning home-town performance.

A.J., the Oaks' number three hitter, stepped to the plate with two gone. CSM's best pitcher tried throwing a fastball by him. A.J. drove the pitch a good ten feet over the centerfield wall.

Several CSM players were guys from rival high school

teams, and they remembered Conor as the corner painter and knuckle curve guy. They discovered a different pitcher living in Conor's skin. This guy had little use for finesse. He simply blazed three fast balls right past them.

As Conor warmed up, he felt his feet slip in his new spikes. The shoes didn't fit exactly right. He threw a few pitches, then tapped each toe behind the pitching rubber to adjust the fit.

When he struck out the game's first hitter, he tapped his toes. He repeated the gesture after his second strikeout, and a howl arose from CSM's dugout. They perceived the gesture as a hot-dog move—showing them up. They vowed revenge.

Conor made it a point to tap his toes each time he dismissed a CSM hitter via strikeout. He tapped fifteen times that afternoon. The day unfolded as one of those dreams in which everything fell into place. He threw nine innings, using a hundred and seven pitches. Eighty of them, according to Brad, strikes. He allowed one hit.

A.J. punctuated the game with a second home run in the eighth as the Oaks won 3-0.

Brad and Conor drove home together. Brad walked straight to the kitchen carrying his scorebook, where he reconstructed the game almost pitch-by-pitch for Hugh.

After he'd showered and changed, Conor found them still seated at the table.

"Good job," Hugh said.

"Thanks. I'm sorry about the car. I'll be more careful with my money. I promise."

"I SHOULD DO SOMETHING FOR THEM," CONOR TOLD A.J.

and Brad. "My dad won't be happy if I spend more money, but I need to do something. A trip, maybe?"

The three lounged in Conor's yard, site of a thousand whiffle ball games, the home field of their childhood, sharing a final afternoon before Conor left for Idaho.

"Well," Brad said, "you know how your dad feels about Hawaii."

"Hawaii? I've never heard him talk about Hawaii."

"Really?" Brad said. "He's told me all about it. Some of his buddies were there during the war, and they talked about how nice it was. He's told me several times he wanted to take your mom there."

"Hawaii? Okay. How can we put something together?"

"You're leaving," A.J. said. "Brad and I will make the arrangements."

Hugh and Nadine departed that July for a two-week dream vacation. The first day at the beach Nadine noticed a lump on Hugh's back. By the end of the second week, the lump had grown larger.

nine

Idaho Falls Russets
Rookie Baseball
1976

A YOUNG MAN GREETED CONOR WITH EXTENDED hand and a face so black it reflected the glow of the 40-watt motel desk lamp. His broad smile revealed pearl-like jewels set in an ebony frame.

"Hey," drawled a high-pitched voice from the back roads of Mississippi, "I'm Goodrum Martin, and I guess we're roommates. I gotta warn ya' though, I ain't never lived with no white boy."

"Um ... hi. I'm Conor ... Nash. And ... I'm not sure I got your first name?"

"Goodrum." His smile glowed again. "I'm from a little place where po-leese used to come lookin' whenever somethin' happened. So, my Daddy named me Goodrum, 'cause good rum is hard to find."

Conor laughed.

"I play infield, second base mostly." Goodrum made a show of looking Conor up and down. "You're too skinny to be anything other than a second-baseman or a pitcher."

"Pitcher. You've got second base to yourself."

Goodrum sat on one of two single beds. It sagged under his weight. "Conor, huh? What your folks call you?"

"Well, *they* call me Conor. A lot of friends call me Connie. Which always pisses off my dad. He says if he wanted to give me a girl's name, he'd have named me Sue."

Goodrum threw back his head and offered a laugh from deep in his chest. "Yeah, like the song. Well, I can't go tellin' folks my roommate's a Connie. We call you... let's see... we call you the Conman. That's your baseball name."

Minor leaguers roomed at the Bonneville Hotel, a former Idaho Falls gem now gone to seed. It offered a variety of rooming plans, ranging from one hour to monthly. Conor and Goodrum shared a room featuring war-surplus twin beds, a bathroom with curling linoleum tile, and two bed-side lamps. The single bit of décor was a framed photo of Spiro Agnew.

When Conor peeled back heavy drapes, the sunlight worked its way through a set of bars fixed to the exterior window frame, protecting a view of an alley.

I'll tell you, Rita, Idaho Falls, Idaho, a land of flat prairie, distant mountains, Sunday blue laws and Mormon churches, represented quite an adjustment for a twenty-year-old raised in a San Francisco suburb.

Hugh bailed from the big city early during the sixties when the culture changed all around him. San Francisco, with its ever more brazen gay population, the rise of the Black Power movement and rampant liberalism, was no place he wanted to raise five sons. So, he moved his family south to San Carlos, a mostly white enclave where civil rights movements and Caesar Chavez were a decade distant. Nobody preached white separatism to us. Race and diversity were simply subjects that didn't come up.

By the time I got to Idaho, though, I knew racism and baseball no longer mixed. Baseball endured its integration trauma years ahead of the rest of the country. If judging a person on merit rather than skin color is the social ideal, baseball proved to be a garden where that philosophy flourished. Not that minority players had gained a completely level playing field. Blacks and Hispanics could not afford to be average. Those jobs still belonged mostly to white kids. Generally, though, on a baseball diamond ability tended to speak loudest of all. If you were a good player, you were a good player. If you were an asshole, you were not a white asshole or a black asshole. You were just an asshole.

GOODRUM MADE THE INTRODUCTIONS. HE POINTED TO A big outfielder. "Conman, this is Mark Brouhard."

"Yeah," Brouhard said. "I saw your bullpen. For a little guy, you can really bring it."

Conor grinned.

"Hey, give me a minute," Brouhard said. "I gotta say hi to a friend."

As the Lethbridge Expos filed into their dugout, Brouhard called a name and crossed the infield. An Expo met him halfway, and they shook hands. After a few moments of conversation, broken up by a Lethbridge coach, Brouhard returned.

"Richey Cobb," said Brouhard. "He's a good guy."

As it turned out, Miguel Montoya, the Russets' starting pitcher, didn't share Brouhard's opinion of Richey Cobb.

Cobb hit second for the Expos. Montoya buried his best fastball between Cobb's shoulder blades with his first pitch.

Cobb's batting helmet bounded toward the backstop as he fell to all fours and gathered himself. The Expo trainer trotted toward him when Cobb sprang to his feet and charged, fury glowing like embers in his eyes. Montoya closed the distance by leaping from the mound, meeting Cobb's challenge.

Conor led the Russets' bullpen charge to join the battle. He quickly learned if you arrive first to the fray, you find yourself at the bottom of the pile. Being the smallest among three of his four brothers, Conor was no stranger to the bottom of a pile. The pilers to which he was accustomed, though, weren't chewing tobacco or wearing baseball cleats.

He laid a good three layers deep as he struggled for breath. He could feel his arms and legs and wiggle his toes. He held a clear view of Goodrum flying ninja-like, spikes first, into the melee, and a gush of blood leaping from whoever's whatever he'd landed on.

Next, he saw Brouhard materialize above him as Mark's right fist smashed into Richey Cobb's jaw. Cobb's face went all smushed and flat before he staggered beyond Conor's view.

Soon, the fight degenerated to a scrum, everyone holding onto everyone else. Then, like a windup toy slowly running down, the whole thing lost its energy.

Brouhard helped Conor to his feet.

"I thought," Conor gasped, "you said Richey Cobb was your friend."

Brouhard appeared puzzled for a moment. "Well," he said, "I guess not right now, and not right here."

I'll never forget what Carlos Estrada said after watching me throw.

"Son, I don't know how somebody who weighs a hundred and fifty pounds can generate a fastball like yours, but let me tell you, the Good Lord fucked up a helluva' truck driver when He gave you that arm."

Carlos was the Angels roving pitching instructor. Major League organizations did not yet supply individual pitching coaches to minor league affiliates. Larry Hopp managed the Idaho Falls team. A trainer assisted him, while a third guy served as more of a gofer than anything else. The roving pitching instructor traveled among the affiliates.

Carlos saw me throw a bullpen, grinned a tobacco-stained grin, and fell in love.

"Conman," he said, "you need to read my book. I wrote it for guys exactly like you."

His book consisted of a hundred or so type-written pages bound in a three-ring binder saying, *fifty different ways,* Throw the Shit Out of the Ball. A loving ode to cheese, this journal didn't reference curve balls or changeups. Throw hard, it preached, and when your back is to the wall, throw harder. Blow the bastards away. Dedicate yourself to the heater. And if anyone gives you crap, hit 'em in the neck. With a fastball.

ONLY ABOUT TEN PAGES INTO ESTRADA'S SOLILOQUY TO dead red, Conor made his professional debut two games into the season, but he'd gotten the gist.

He was called to protect a 3-1 lead with one gone during the eighth.

Conor did not yet know enough about competing at a professional level to be particularly nervous. He felt a few things crawling around his stomach as he warmed up. When he stepped onto the mound, runners at first and second, and took a sign from his catcher, though, he saw the hitter as just another kid like him, and he'd been getting kids like him out his whole life. The last two years had endowed him with supreme confidence and a cockiness bolstering his belief.

He retired all five batters he faced, throwing only fastballs.

Trotting off the field, Conor saw Estrada turn to Hopp and say, "Larry, I think we got ourselves a prospect."

ten

LOWER NOW THE SUN BEGAN PAINTING CLOUDS IN earnest. Conor raised his champagne bottle toward the western sky.

I don't know if this was you or not, Rita. One thing I've always treasured, though, is a gift of appreciation, not only of the spectacular, but the ordinary, everyday beauty of things like sunsets. I know. Most people appreciate sunsets. How many stop to study nuances of color, though, or compare differences between this one and another? Not that I do it every day. I do it, though. And taking time to notice those kinds of things set me apart from most ball players. Leant me an air of eccentricity that helped build the legend of the Conman.

I remember talking with Ken Griffey Junior when we were at Fenway Park. It's Saturday, I told him. This is the day I smell the grass and eat a hot dog. Why don't you come with me? He looked at me like he was being set up for some kind of joke.

Bus rides have become a cliché for the hardships of the minors.

And the Pioneer League is more spread out than most. Our bus took us to far-flung destinations like Great Falls, Lethbridge, Billings, and Helena. The bench seats seemed dedicated to lower back pain. We had no bathroom. Guys peed into Gatorade bottles and emptied them out the rear door as we rolled along those two-lane highways at fifty miles an hour.

I enjoyed those rides, though. Unless it was too cold, I kept the window next to my seat open. Nothing in San Carlos smelled like the prairie after a rain, or a forest of pines. I'd never seen anything like a full moon hanging above a distant, snow-capped mountain range, or the endless sharp blue of a Montana sky. At Lethbridge, located on a poverty-stricken Indian reservation, I was shocked by lumpy forms of the homeless who camped along the streets. If San Carlos had homeless people, they were well hidden.

I didn't talk about any of those things with the other guys, though, because you don't talk about stuff like that when you're twenty years old and throw a baseball ninety miles an hour. You mostly talk about getting laid, or beer, or rock-n-roll. You don't express your fears. You simply hide them behind the bravado of outrageous behavior and profanity.

Take the F-bomb, for example. Throughout high school and college, the F-word served as an exceptionally utilitarian baseball declarative, sprinkled almost unconsciously into our language. I assumed I'd heard it exercised in all its forms. I'd personally used it as adjective, verb and noun within a single, concise and alliterative sentence. That fucking fucker is fucked!

In amateur baseball, though, we seldom heard the F-bomb used as an offensive weapon calculated to stun or maim. Or dropped with profusion amounting to carpet bombing. And among high school and college ranks, no one survived an F-bomb lobbed at an umpire.

My manager, Larry Hopp, did it all the time.

The rules permit F-bombing of an umpire all you want, and they can F-bomb you right back, as long as neither of you uses the word as an adjective to describe the other. This is hard-bound baseball tradition, and if nothing else, Larry was a traditionalist.

The most infuriated I ever saw Larry, in fact, was when he F-bombed a home plate ump who refused to respond in kind.

ON THE DIAMOND IN LETHBRIDGE, AND AFTER A particularly scathing string of expletives, the umpire stared into the visitor's dugout and said, "Quit yelling at me, Larry."

Larry's jaw dropped so far his chaw fell to the ground. He stormed onto the field. "What the fuck did you say?"

"I said quit yelling at me, Larry."

Even from the dugout, Conor saw his manager glow a beet red.

"Fuck!" Larry screamed. "We are not gonna stand here and talk to each other like a couple of fucking old ladies having a fucking cup of tea!"

The umpire removed his mask. "Larry, go back to your bench and calm down."

Larry stood for a long moment. The carotid arteries on both sides of his neck throbbed visibly. He'd been struck speechless. With a dumbfounded expression, he plodded away.

By half-inning's end, though, he'd gathered himself. He told the Russet's catcher, "Take your time getting your gear on. I'll warm him up."

Larry squatted at the plate and nodded for his pitcher to go ahead. His intent, though, was the renewal of his assault at closer range. His F-bombs fell without mercy, to the extent that Larry became distracted by his purpose. He anticipated a curve ball as the pitcher's final warm-up delivery, glanced at the ump to punctuate his dissertation with one more blast, and a fastball nailed him squarely in the sternum.

Larry gasped, wheezed, croaked, and slowly rolled into a fetal position. Trainers from both teams sprinted to his aid. The umpire arrived at a more leisurely pace. As he bent to ascertain the fallen manager's condition, Larry managed only a pitiful, final squeak. "Fuuuuuuuuuuuuck."

"Not that it matters at this point, Larry," the umpire said as Larry was loaded onto a stretcher bound for the clubhouse, "but you have been officially tossed from this fucking game. Enjoy the rest of your evening."

THE CONMAN WAS ON A ROLL, AND HE GREW IN CARLOS Estrada's esteem with every outing. As a closer, Conor approached the season's half-way point with fifteen appearances, a 3.50 ERA and forty strikeouts. When Estrada's travels returned him to Idaho Falls, he quizzed Conor about his approach to various hitters.

"Okay, Conman, you face this guy in the ninth, how will you handle him?"

"Throw the shit out of the ball."

Estrada slapped Conor's back and said to Hopp, "Smartest kid I ever coached."

When Estrada left for another Angels' affiliate, Hopp called Conor into his office.

"Yeah, Skip?"

"The organization wants me to give you some starts," Hopp said. "You're doing great closing games, but all you need for that is your fastball. Doesn't give you a chance to develop other pitches."

Conor grinned. He loved starting.

"I want you to work on your curve in the pen this week. You get the ball next Monday. If you can find a breaking ball, you'll be moving along pretty quick. You're tearing up rookie ball. You could close for Quad Cities right now, maybe get to Salinas if they make the playoffs."

Conor practically floated from Hopp' office. The timing couldn't be better. A.J., Basil and Brad intended to fly into Idaho Falls the following week to watch a couple of games. His parents planned a visit during the next homestand.

Nothing could stop him now.

BASIL DOAN WAS ON A ROLL OF HIS OWN. ALTHOUGH Amanda no longer played a part, Alaska suited him. Amanda left for college in the lower forty-eight at summer's end. Basil managed to weather the blow, though, because he was making more money than he'd ever imagined.

Amanda's father had moved to Palmer, Alaska, for work on the pipeline, and he convinced his employer to give Basil a shot as an apprentice welder. The company discovered Basil was an artist with a welding torch. He soon earned nineteen dollars an hour in a part of the world offering few opportunities to squander it.

He bought a small piece of land, a house trailer, and a brand-new Harley Davidson Electra Glide. The braces came off. His pimples dried up. He enjoyed his work, and his body responded by packing on more muscle.

He experienced an epiphany one late summer night when, with the Alaska sun still shining, he rode his Harley to the only bar in Palmer and walked into the restroom to comb his hair. His long blond locks were blown straight back, exposing his ears and forehead with a James Dean kind of muss. He took the comb from his pocket, then reconsidered.

He walked directly to a pay phone and called the Russets' clubhouse.

"I just looked in a mirror . . ." Basil told Conor.

"Baze? I'm supposed to be getting ready—"

". . . and you know what?"

"Okay, what?"

"I'm a damn good-looking man."

HIS FIRST START WENT WELL.

Conor threw five innings adding five K's to his strikeout total. Although his ERA climbed a little because of the curve ball, everyone was happy with his performance.

"Lethbridge? Where the fuck is Lethbridge?" A.J. asked.

"You should have looked at the schedule," Conor said.

"We did," Basil said. "But we figured we'd see you pitch here. We didn't know we'd have to go to Lethbridge."

"You were a reliever when we booked our tickets," Brad added.

"Now I'm a starter. Next start is Saturday in Lethbridge. I can see if they'll let you ride the bus."

"How long is the drive to Lethbridge?"

"About twelve hours . . ."

"On that thing?" A.J. protested. "No way. Basil's got bucks. He can rent us a car. Something hot. I understand Montana highways don't have speed limits."

CONOR THREW TWO FASTBALLS BY LETHBRIDGE'S LEADOFF hitter, then missed with a curve. The hitter's only choice was to gear up for another heater. He took a weak, lunging swing and tapped the bender toward third base. Conor smiled. *Maybe this breaking ball thing will work out.*

The second hitter, who stood no chance against Conor's smoke, took a half-swing at a shoulder-high fastball, falling behind 0-1. Another opportunity for a curve. The Lethbridge hitter might not have expected this gift, but he took full advantage of it. As Conor's curve ball hung—huge, like a big, yellow, full moon rising—belt high and mid-plate, the hitter crushed it right back at Conor. The ball caught him flush on the ankle he'd injured three years earlier.

"Take a couple of throws," Hopp advised him as he, trainer and umpire gathered at the mound. Conor climbed gingerly onto the pitching rubber. When he landed to finish his pitch, a jolt of pain shot up his leg.

"We'll get you to a hospital for X-rays," the trainer said as Conor limped beside him.

Basil, A.J. and Brad waited as he emerged from the emergency room, wearing a foot-to-knee plaster cast.

"Broken," Conor told them, downcast. "Hairline fracture. I'm done for the season."

Team rules prevented Conor from returning to Idaho Falls with his buddies. He suffered the ordeal with an itchy cast and a throbbing foot while A.J. and Basil flew home in a rented Pontiac Firebird.

"COME ON, CONOR, YOU'VE GOT TO SEE THIS," A.J. SAID. "You won't believe it."

"My leg hurts, and I look like a dork with this cast," Conor told him. "I don't feel like bar-hopping tonight."

"Well, we sure won't be hopping, because near as I can tell, there's only one bar," A.J. said.

More than one bar existed in Idaho Falls, but baseball players hung out at the Snake River Bar. Located near the ballpark, the Snake River catered to ball players, girls who wanted to meet themselves a real-live baseball player, and cowboys or farmers' sons making sure their girlfriends didn't get hustled by baseball players.

Conor, A.J. and Basil walked into semi-crowded darkness. Brad, who'd enrolled in Stanford's summer session, remained at the motel to study. As they entered, a couple of girls recognized Conor. Noticing his cast, they hurried over to see if he needed comforting. They chatted for a moment, leaving the door open to later possibilities.

"Okay, what did we come to see?" Conor asked. "Where's Baze?"

A.J. pointed across the room, where Basil sat on the tallest stool, situated directly beneath a ceiling can casting a soft circle of light.

Although Conor and Basil spoke often enough by telephone, Conor had not seen his friend in the flesh for almost two years. And, Conor conceded, the transformation was significant. Without question, this Basil vastly improved on the high school version. Until this moment, though, with dramatic lighting—as if Basil was on some center-stage—and holding his glass of scotch, Conor had not witnessed the full effect.

"What's he doing?"

"Just watch," A.J. said.

"He's trying to attract girls? He was always so shy he couldn't bear speaking to girls."

"Oh, he still doesn't speak much. Like I said, watch."

His leg throbbing, Conor found a high top nearby, climbed onto the stool and sat. When he glanced again, a girl had engaged Basil in conversation, although she seemed to be doing most of the talking. Basil's side of the discussion consisted mostly of smiles and nods and shrugs. And not *just* a girl. The best-looking girl in the place. And then another one. And another. And another.

Conor thought of sparrows flocking to a feeder.

Now girls were laughing, touching Basil's shoulder or arm with painfully intimate gestures. Basil mostly smiled and sipped his scotch. As soon as ice cubes showed above the lapping brown liquid, a full glass appeared. The bartender pointed to yet another girl, this one seated farther down the bar. Basil grinned, raising his glass in her direction.

"I told you," said A.J., joining Conor at the high top.

"You've gotta be kidding me."

Halfway into his second scotch, Basil entered the conversation, apparently speaking actual sentences. Girls laughed, as if engaging the smoothest and most witty operator they'd ever encountered. And now gentle touches and nudges and even a little squeeze here and there accompanied Basil's comments. He and the original girl locked lips. Conor heard dark, mumbled threats somewhere behind him along with the sound of stools being shoved and boots scraping the floor.

Just to fill you in, Rita, my older brother Sam is still known as the toughest guy around San Carlos, and I sometimes felt the weight of his reputation. But he warned me off. On those occasions when I suggested I might confront so-and-so because of some perceived insult or matter of disrespect, Sam counseled otherwise.

"Nah, you don't want to do that."

"Why not?"

"Because the guy will kill you. Trust me, you aren't much of a fighter. I'll give you this, you can take a punch. But, see, fighting is kind of about not taking punches, okay?"

Basil, though, could fight. He was slow to provocation, unlike A.J., who would take on anyone at the drop of an insult.

REACHING FROM THE SHADOWS, A MAN WEARING A cowboy hat pulled at Basil's shoulder and A.J. was off like a shot.

"A.J., no!" Conor called. "A.J., we can't..."

Conor clumped after A.J. as quickly as his cast allowed.

He heard a pop. Basil stood. A cowboy hat rested upside down on the bar. The covey of girls separated enough for Conor to see a pair of cowboy boots, toes pointed up, their occupant swallowed by shadow. Other cowboy hats converged.

"A.J., don't..." Conor tried again.

A.J. spun one of the hats by the shoulder, yanking him away from Basil, and pummeled the man with lefts and rights.

Conor clumped onward.

A third hat engaged Basil, faring no better than the first. Basil turned slowly, looking for another adversary, when Conor yelled, "Baze! Stop!"

A tall man next to Conor shoved him. "You're with these guys?" He blasted Conor on the jaw.

"IT'S NOT MY FAULT."

They'd retreated to the parking lot, Conor massaging his face, hoping the lump he felt there would disappear by morning.

He opened his mouth, gingerly wiggled his jaw, and checked a couple of molars with his tongue.

"What do you mean, it's not your fault?"

"It's not my fault. I go into a place. I sit. Girls show up. I don't invite them. I don't ask them to buy me drinks. They just do. It's not my fault."

"Yeah? Who was the guy who started copping little feels for all the local boys to see?"

"Oh, him," Basil said. "That's Touchy Teddy. Touchy Teddy shows up during my second scotch."

"Guys?" A soft voice wafted from the darkness.

Conor turned and saw two women, including the original contact, approaching through a background glow of neon.

"We wanted to make sure you guys were okay," first girl said.

Conor stood with a half-lean against the Firebird, his casted leg propped along the hood, his jaw puffed and throbbing. A knot had sprouted on A.J.'s forehead, against which he held a cloth napkin full of ice cubes.

The girls headed straight to Basil.

"Did you hurt your hand?" second girl asked.

"Did I tell you I'm from Alaska?"

First girl leaned forward, kissed his cheek, and whispered something.

Basil grinned.

The girls walked toward a pickup parked a few spaces away.

"Um … guys," Basil said, "I think I'm going to have to … you know … go?"

"Baze!" Conor called.

"It's not my fault," Basil answered over his shoulder.

The pickup's engine growled. Tires spun gravel as it skidded onto the street.

"I told you," A.J. said, "that you wouldn't believe it."
"Well, crap," Conor said. "*I'm* the baseball player."

eleven

"I ALREADY KNOW WHAT CONOR LOOKS LIKE IN A baseball uniform," Hugh Nash told his wife. "I'm not going all the way to Idaho for that."

"You haven't seen him wearing a professional uniform," Nadine said.

"He can send us a picture. The only reason I'd go is to see him pitch. He's injured. Besides, I've got that doctor's appointment."

So, Rita, they canceled their airline tickets. Which turned out just as well, because ten days into the second half of our season, the Angels sent me to Los Angeles to see the team doctor. He fitted me with a walking boot and told me to go home.

Neither the doctor nor the organization offered rehabilitation instructions. They said get well—a medical equivalent of throw strikes. I wore the boot for six weeks, then returned to the elementary school where I threw baseballs at a brick wall. The mindless repetition was as much grief therapy as exercise for my arm. My dad's doctor's appointment produced devastating news. The lump was a manifestation of lung cancer. The cancer moved fast. With chemotherapy still in the experimental stage, doctors prescribed radiation. And following each treatment, a little bit more of my dad seemed to be missing.

Ever the realist, Hugh accepted before the rest of us that he would not survive. He did not, though, become a victim of melancholy. As his body suffered devastation from radiation, he mentally and emotionally strove to remain the same man who set strict standards for his sons and himself.

During this ordeal of our father's failing health, Sam, now twenty-two, grew angrier each day. The biggest and smartest of the Nash boys, Sam always seemed balanced on a knife edge between brilliance and destruction. He fought more than ever and became notorious among local law enforcement. He hung on the fringe of a biker gang. He drank too much.

At seventeen, Mike directed anger related to his grief at his oldest brother. In Mike's eyes, Sam's behavior only made things worse, and they initiated a feud destined to flare for years to come. Fourteen-year-old Brandan approached Dad's situation with a stoicism that worried our mom the most. His somber silence might have been denial. No one knew for sure. Dylan, the youngest at eleven, just seemed overwhelmed.

None of us could accept that the brusk, burly, self-assured man, who established values for us, forced us to church on Sundays, stood as an emblem of doing the right thing and demanded our competence, would be taken from us by an enemy we couldn't see, much less bare our knuckles and fight against.

When I called Baze, he cried and said he'd come home right away. I told him to stay where he was. I promised to keep him *informed. Baze called Hugh several times a week. Brad spent hours at Hugh's bedside. A.J. suffered the most devastation of the three, though he hid his grief the best. He seemed determined to keep things as normal as possible around Dad.*

"Howyadoin', Mr. Nash?"

Hugh, weak and emaciated, stretched on his recliner and regarded A.J. with a look of incredulity. "Not particularly well, A.J. I'm dying here, if you haven't heard."

"I mean other than that."

Hugh's laughter degenerated into a coughing spasm. "Put it that way, I guess I can't complain."

"I've got something I need to ask you about. Get some advice, I mean."

"Okay."

"It's the carpet store," A.J. said. "My dad told me it's time for me to start learning the business."

"That business holds a good future, A.J. Your father's built something significant. You'll have security."

"Yeah, that's the thing. I think security is the last thing I want, you know? I want to build something of my own."

"So, what are your plans?"

"Well, I want to take some business courses at UCLA. Maybe start a restaurant."

"Food service is a tough business."

"I'm a tough guy."

"Yes," Hugh said. "You are."

"Well, what can I do?"

"A person has to be who he is, not who someone else wants him to be," Hugh said.

"Even if the someone is his father?"
"Yes, A.J. Maybe especially if the someone is his father."

WHEN THINGS LOOKED WORST, WE FOUND A SLIVER OF HOPE. Early that November, Hugh felt better. His appetite returned. He regained weight. "Maybe," the doctor said, "the radiation is working. We'll just have to see." Hugh wasn't fooled by the respite. As this brief period of optimism played itself out, he called his sons to his side, one-by-one. That's when he gave me his one-basket speech.

Hugh finished the meeting with one more assignment.

"Dylan will need some help. You and the other boys have been around me long enough that you understand me, and why I've raised you the way I—"

I interrupted him. "Dad, you're getting better."

Hugh offered a rueful smile. "No, Conor, I'm not. And as I was saying, I'm not sure Dylan has known me long enough. Sam will take this the hardest. He'll be lost for a while. Meantime, I need you to be someone Dylan can see as an example. I need you to kick his ass when it needs kicking, show him the right way."

At that moment, I accepted that my father would die.

"A.J. PUT ME ON HOLD AGAIN." HUGH OFFERED THE telephone receiver to Conor. "Tell him he shouldn't put me on hold. I don't want to die on hold."

Conor took the phone and waited.

"Okay, I'm back."

"A.J., it's me. Dad's pissed cause you put him on hold. You shouldn't—"

"Connie, good. Tell your dad I'm sorry, but I've got a deal going here."

"A deal?"

"Yeah. Land. Phoenix. You need to give me five thousand dollars. You'll be an investor."

"I'm not going to give you five thousand dollars. I promised my dad I'd be more careful with my bonus money. And what do you know about land?"

"We'll get to that. Right now, let me talk to your dad."

He died two days later. December 17, 1976. Basil flew home for the funeral. We put Hugh Nash to rest December 22nd, one day before my twenty-first birthday.

I look back on my dad and the difficult standards he set for us, and I often wonder how he would have raised a girl child. Whether a daughter might have softened him around the edges? Most certainly, he would have expected his five sons to be her protector. God save the hapless teenage boy who brought her home late from a date or bragged about his conquest of the Nash sister. We four younger boys could only hope Sam didn't get to him first, because there wouldn't be much left for the rest of us.

I wonder if our father would have been less strident and more indulgent of a daughter, or if his protective instincts would have doomed her to the life of a cloistered nun? Of course, she'd be a Nash. In the latter case, her rebellion might have been spectacular.

I can only guess, though.

Our sister Valarie—Hugh and Nadine's first-born child—died of leukemia at the age of eight months. Although none of us boys ever met her, we all know her. Our parents saw to that. We always noted her birthday. We knew about her happy spirit, despite the pain of her brief life. We know our parents mourned her death to the day they each left this earth.

And I know one other thing, Rita. She would have loved baseball.

ALTHOUGH NADINE NASH STOOD FIVE FEET AND ONE INCH tall, her sons never underestimated her. Conor and his brothers didn't remember a single occasion when she said, "Wait until your father gets home." She handled the discipline herself. She broke up their fights with a whiffle ball bat or a broom handle.

She felt fulfilled as wife and mother. She'd never held a job outside her home or driven a car. The day after she buried her husband, though, she found a job as a secretarial assistant, and passed her driving test.

That evening, she gathered her sons around the kitchen table.

"Facing your father's death may be the hardest thing you'll ever do," she told them, "but we can do it. It's what he'd expect of us. And no matter what else comes along, whatever you face, you'll know you've already handled the most difficult thing you can imagine."

Mike mumbled something under his breath.

"What was that?" Nadine asked.

"Why did God take him away? Why did he make us go to church to worship a God who doesn't care about—"

"Don't you think that," Nadine said sharply. "Not for one minute. You were able to know your dad, to understand what he wanted for you. Remember, there's another member of this family. Now, it's Valerie's turn to have her father."

SUNSET WASHED THE ENTIRE WESTERN HORIZON. Freeways crawled with commuters heading home, each car a dot of light along an undulating chain.

Mom was right. Nothing anyone threw at me compared to facing life without my dad. Dealing with his death, though, let me find a toughness I didn't know I possessed. Toughness I'd need to face everyone who would doubt me. Mental toughness to rise above disappointment. Physical toughness to push me through injuries.

Of course, I cheated a little there, didn't I?

Being an angel and all, with more important angel things to do, you probably couldn't be bothered to keep count. I sought the refuge of cortisone one hundred and sixty-eight times over the course of sixteen years. One hundred and sixty-eight!

So, here's a toast to cortisone, my blessing and my curse. These injections kept me going long enough to get there, but only until they finally drained the magic you zapped into my left arm before I'd been there anywhere near long enough.

"YOU STARTED THROWING TOO SOON AFTER THEY INJURY," Dr. Jacobs told Conor.

"I broke my ankle. Why does my shoulder hurt?"

Conor's shoulder pain increased steadily during the month before his reporting date for 1977's Spring Training. Trainers watched him struggle through his first bullpen session and took him aside.

"What's wrong?"

"Nothing. I'm fine."

"You don't look fine. You look like you've got a sore shoulder."

"My shoulder's tight. I'll work it out."

The next bullpen session showed no improvement. Trainers said a cortisone shot might help.

"I don't want to get shot up," said Conor. He'd heard stories about pills and injections—training room witchcraft that polluted body and soul—and he swore he would not choose that path.

The organization sent him to Los Angeles and Dr. Jacobs.

"You're experiencing soreness because you compensated for your ankle and foot tenderness by adjusting your throwing motion," Jacobs told him. "The ankle's fine now, so you should be okay."

"My shoulder still hurts."

"Cortisone will help."

"I'd rather just work through it."

Jacobs peered at Conor over his glasses and shook his head. "Take off your shirt and sit here."

The doctor stood behind him and probed Conor's shoulder.

"Hurts here?" he asked jabbing a finger into tender flesh.

"Yes," grunted Conor.

"Here?"

"Uh huh."

Next came a sharp jab, then a tiny, focused flow of heat.

"Ow! What was that?"

"A cortisone injection," Jacobs said. "You'll feel better soon."

When Conor began an angry protest, Jacobs cut him off.

"You're a professional, son," he said. "Your employers aren't paying you to work through it. They're paying you to perform."

I left the doctor's office feeling betrayed. Not for long, though, because that shot produced a miracle. My shoulder pain disappeared. The ball jumped from my hand. On that same day, though, someone or something visited us with The Curse.

twelve

Quad Cities Angels
Low A Baseball
1977

"**D**ID YOU SEE JIMMY'S BULLPEN TODAY?" Conor asked Ken Shrom, carefully looking over his shoulder to be sure Jimmy Dial wasn't anywhere nearby.

"Yeah. He couldn't find the damn plate."

The Angels' minor leaguers finished their final day of spring workouts and packed for their various assignments. The high drama occurred the day before when minor league rosters were posted. Those who hadn't made a list packed to go home. Among those unfortunates was Goodrum Martin.

Conor felt bad for Goodrum. He didn't dwell on it, though. He found himself disengaging quickly from those who slipped by the wayside. Conor would not consider the possibility of his own failure. Not for one minute. Not even when his shoulder ached, and his ankle throbbed. He was, after all, chosen.

And sure enough, a solution presented itself at the sharp end of a syringe.

When they entered into their last-man-standing agreement,

the fourth pact member, Jimmy Dial, had also been among the chosen. A high-round draft pick, featuring a solid fastball and a big, heavy curve, Jimmy had been Idaho Fall's most reliable starter the previous year.

Three of the four were bound for Davenport, Iowa and the Quad Cities Angels of the Low A Midwest League. Mark Brouhard, who hit .314, pounding seven homers and driving in fifty-four runs at Idaho Falls, jumped one rung higher to High A Salinas, but Conor, Ken Shrom and Jimmy Dial remained together. Like Conor and Ken, Jimmy wore the label *Prospect*. Meaning, he figured prominently in the organization's plans.

The Quad Cities consisted of Davenport—the ballpark location—East Moline, Rockford and Bettendorf. Among the first rituals of any minor league campaign is locating a place to live and roommates to share rent. Outfielder Dave Holland found a house in Bettendorf that fit minor league budgets and invited Jimmy and Conor to join him.

"We'll each have our own bedroom," Dave told them. "No one has to share."

While the house sported an abundance of bedrooms, it did not come with furniture.

"What do we do for beds?" Conor asked.

"What, you've never been camping?"

Dave and Conor found an Army surplus store and bought sleeping bags.

Jimmy splurged and purchased a bed.

"Ooooh, Yimmy."

A soft moan drifted through the closed door of Jimmy Dial's bedroom.

Conor and Dave, watching television in the living room, glanced at each other with raised eyebrows.

"Oooohhh, Yiiimmy."

Louder this time.

"Ooooooooooohhhhhh Yimmy, Yimmy, Yimmy!"

The volume continued to increase. The next quick series of *Yimmies* approximated a sort of breathless scream.

"We should get a tape recorder," Conor said.

Dave turned up the television. Walter Cronkite, though, could not compete with the pretty Hispanic girl Jimmy hosted that evening. And Jimmy hung in there for a good half hour before her *Yimmies* played themselves out and the bedroom door finally opened.

Conor held his tongue as Jimmy and his date left.

"Way to go, Yimmy," he said as soon as the front door closed behind them.

IF YOU ARE A PARTICULARLY PRUDISH ANGEL—AND I HAVE to say Rita sounds like a pretty strait-laced kind of name—I apologize in advance, but sooner or later, we have to broach the subject of sex. Long before pro ball, I knew girls found jocks attractive. Between my stutter and my pitching success, I'd plowed that field several times back home. Visitors to the Nash household saw a wall of photos chronicling the five Nash boys' relationships. My brothers chose steady connections, and photo after photo over their high school years pictured the same young women. My pictures featured a dozen different companions.

I liked girls, and girls liked me. Although I still tripped sometimes over my t's and g's, I was far less self-conscious. And, while I wasn't the greatest looking kid in the world, I had a gift for making them laugh. And a lot of girls didn't mind my stutter at all.

"What is it with you and girls?" asked Basil, who remained painfully shy.

"I think they like the stutter. They kind of feel sorry for me. They want t . . . to see if they can fix me."

Many of these relationships were platonic, but enough of them were not.

One sexual encounter stood paramount in Conor Nash lore and became legendary among my friends. This event occurred during our senior year of high school when I attended a party hosted by A.J.'s father.

A.J. lived in a huge house, complete with a swimming pool, making him the envy of his friends, and Myron Cohen entertained often. A high school girl I'd lusted after for some time attended this party and agreed to her role as lustee. I snuck her into an upstairs bedroom while the festivities proceeded below.

Things had reached a critical stage when the bedroom door opened. Myron Cohen, momentarily taken aback, gathered himself, chuckled, and said, "Conor, m'boy, I'll give you twenty dollars for a motel room, but not under my roof."

By the time I reached Quad Cities, I'd conquered my stutter, partly because I no longer needed it. A professional baseball uniform is an even more powerful aphrodisiac than a minor speech defect. Many of my teammates, young and at their peak of horniness, sought variety. A few, like Dave Holland, looked for love and spent their season with just one girl.

Though not as much of a hound as some of the others, I wanted to get laid like anyone else. My aversion to throwing up, though, meant I didn't drink as much my friends did. And being sober, for the most part, meant I saw women through more discerning eyes at closing time than did my more well-lubricated associates.

We quickly discovered Davenport featured a nursing school, and the nurses frequented a favorite bar. That's where I met Karate Girl, an aspiring nurse and part-time karate instructor, tall with a solid build, and clearly not a slave to femininity. I feared she could hurt me if she wanted to. She chose a direct approach. She had early morning classes. If we were going to sleep together, she said, we must do it now.

"Um... well, I'm here with my friends," Conor said. "I don't have a car..."

"I've got a car."

Conor balanced the degree of injury she might inflict upon him in bed, against what she might do if he refused her offer. They drove to Bettendorf and Karate Girl began to disrobe as soon as they crossed the threshold. She removed her bra as they entered Conor's room.

"Where's your bed?" Karate Girl demanded.

"Well... um... I don't actually have one..."

"I am not gonna fuck anyone on a sleeping bag." She dressed and left. Conor felt he'd dodged a bullet. Until late the next evening when Conor, Jimmy and Dave arrived home from the ballpark.

"Who is that?" Jimmy asked, as our headlights played over a person sitting on the front steps of their porch.

"Oh, my God," said Conor. "It's Karate Girl."

"What's that against the wall?" Dave asked.

Jimmy said, "I think it's a bed."

Jimmy and Dave stayed in the car as Conor approached the porch.

"I'm back," said Karate Girl.

"Yes, you are."

"Get the frame, I'll get the mattress."

Effortlessly, she hoisted the twin mattress and tucked it under one arm.

Jimmy and Dave waited in the living room, wondering at an ominous series of bangs and bumps. Karate Girl exited twenty minutes later. She did not speak. They cautiously peered into Conor's chamber, where they found him breathing heavily and awash in a sheen of perspiration.

"Are you okay?" Dave asked.

"That was weird," Jimmy said.

"Yeah, well, at least I've got a bed now."

TWO NIGHTS LATER, RAIN HALTED PROCEEDINGS DURING the third inning. Jimmy, who hadn't pitched for days, pleaded for Conor to accompany him to the bar.

"I don't want to start drinking alone," Jimmy told him. "I'm afraid I might end up killing myself."

Passed over for his last two starts, Jimmy worried and fretted over the desertion of his ability to locate a baseball.

"I met a nurse, and she wants to go to the house," Jimmy told Conor a few moments after they entered the bar.

"Okay, let's go."

"It's not that simple. She has a friend."

"Oh, come on . . ."

"Her friend says you're cute."

Conor tried a subtle lean around Jimmy to check the women Jimmy indicated.

"I don't know, Jimmy, I . . ."

Jimmy offered a plea. "Come on, Conman, I really need this."

Conor and his nurse shared the rear seat as Jimmy drove home. As they pulled into the driveway, Jimmy said, "Uh, oh."

Karate girl sat on the stoop in the glare of headlights. "Crap," said Conor.

"Is there something wrong?" asked back-seat nurse.

Karate Girl walked toward them. She saw Conor and glared, making a motion for him to roll his window down. "What the fuck is this?" she demanded.

"Um . . . well, I didn't expect you to—"

"Is she with you?" Karate Girl demanded, pointing at Conor's nurse.

"Well, sort of, I guess—"

"Give me your keys."

"What?"

"Your house keys. Give them to me. Now!"

Conor handed over his keys.

"What should we do?" Jimmy asked as they watched Karate girl disappear into their house.

"We should probably wait here, where it's safe."

A moment later, Karate girl re-emerged, a mattress under one arm, a bedframe under the other.

"She's taking your bed," Jimmy said. "Shouldn't we stop her?"

"I don't think so," said Conor.

"You don't have a bed?" asked back seat nurse.

JIMMY COULDN'T THROW A STRIKE.

His decline began innocently enough. At the start of spring workouts, he didn't hit his spots with any consistency. A fastball intended for the plate's inside corner drifted to the outside corner, instead. He'd miss high, compensate for the next delivery, and miss low.

"Oh, Yimmy," Kenny said as he and Conor watched their friend struggle.

Coaches attributed the problem to off-season rust, and sure enough, Jimmy's control made a brief reappearance. When his location abandoned him again shortly before they broke camp, though, the variation seemed more dramatic. Now, his fastball produced lunging dives and leaps by his catcher.

Trainers probed and questioned Jimmy, suspecting soreness or an injury being hidden from them.

"I actually wish I had an injury," Jimmy confessed. "Then I'd at least know what was going on."

By the time he threw his first Quad Cities bullpen, the issue became less whether he could throw a strike than whether his catcher would even reach the ball. No one wanted to warm up with Jimmy. His teammates began treating him as if he suffered some airborne contagion they might contract if they got too close.

Conor volunteer to catch him.

"Let's start short, like five feet, and work our way back," he suggested.

They tossed back and forth without incident until they reached sixty feet, six inches. Conor spent the rest of their workout sprinting into the outfield after the ball.

"Okay, let's try starting far apart and working our way in."

They set up a hundred feet apart and Jimmy hit his target. Until Conor again reached the distance from home plate to pitching rubber.

Jimmy bordered on hysteria.

"I've got no idea what to do. I feel like I'm doing everything like I used to, but the ball goes wherever it wants. It's like, once it leaves my hand, it's got a mind of its own."

"Well, have you tried . . ." Ken Shrom asked.

"Yes! Yes! I've tried everything. Some fan who watched me hollered that I should throw with my eyes closed. He said I needed to eliminate any distractions and let my body flow. So, I tried it."

"Did it help?"

"The guy was standing, like, five rows back and I hit him. Right in the chest. I think he's gonna sue me."

A month into the season, the Angels handed Jimmy his release. A guy who'd been a solid starter the previous year had a 1977 season lasting a total of three innings. He allowed three hits, struck out one, and walked twelve. He packed his stuff early in the morning and caught a Greyhound for somewhere in Indiana.

"I didn't want to say anything while he was still here," Ken said, "because it's not something you want to jinx a guy with by saying it out loud." He motioned Conor closer. "He got," he paused, looked both directions, and whispered, "the yips."

"The yips?"

"Shhhhhh. Don't just *say* it like that. Yeah."

"How do you get the . . . those?" Conor asked.

"Nobody knows. It just happens. Happens to more people than you'd think. And there's no cure."

We grieved over Jimmy Dial the rest of that day, then let it go. There would be no champagne for Jimmy. Like Goodrum Martin, he represented a kind of death, something we dared not contemplate. We hadn't committed whatever egregious sin prompted Jimmy's baseball angel to scorn him.

We were golden. We would survive anything.

thirteen

*B*ECAUSE I CONTINUED TO EXPERIENCE SOME SHOULDER soreness, my manager at Quad Cities used me sparingly. I made a late-inning appearance only every fourth or fifth day. On each occasion, though, Chuck Cottier saw more evidence of the fastball everyone had told him about.

"How are you feeling?" Cottier asked about a month into the season.

"Good," I told him. "I could use more work."

Cottier smiled. "Well, I talked with the operations people yesterday. I told them I wanted to give you a couple of starts."

My face lit up.

"Don't get too excited. They're worried about you getting hurt again. They said they like you out of the pen. They see you as a closer. So, you'll be getting more work, anyway."

I caught fire. Over my next eighteen appearances, I K'd thirty-nine, with very little finesse. Mostly, I just threw the shit out of the ball.

"Thank God," said Dave Holland. "I thought we'd never get any rain."

As a kid, Conor regarded even a drop of game-day rain as tragedy. He remembered sitting on his porch, wearing a uniform, watching puddles deepen, and praying it wasn't raining this hard three blocks away at the ballpark.

On this morning, though, he, Dave and Kenny were roused from their beds by a peal of thunder. They stepped out the front doors of their adjoining Waterloo, Iowa, motel rooms into a downpour. Cottier made the rounds before noon, informing his minions the night's game had been canceled. Conor watched Cottier only a few minutes later, twirling a set of car keys, walking across the parking lot, a little skip to his step.

The Quad Cities Angels neared the end of their longest road trip. They'd played twenty-one days straight, and everyone needed a break. They walked a few blocks to a movie theatre, napped, splurged for a nice meal at a restaurant across the highway from the hotel and got a couple of six packs.

"Guys, this is crazy," Kenny said. "We need to find some girls."

"Okay, where?"

They'd already stopped by a neighborhood-looking pub within walking distance. They found a bunch of old guys playing darts. The youngest woman there might have been somebody's grandmother.

"I know a great pickup bar," said Gary Tebetts, who'd played in Quad Cities the previous year and knew the exotic backwaters of Iowa. "Only it's in Cedar Falls."

"What good does that do us?"

"We could pool our money, get a cab."

"If I spend money for a cab, I won't have anything left for beer. We don't get paid again until next week."

A general groan of agreement made its way around the motel room.

Until Conor said, "I can drive a bus."

The Quad Cities Angels owned a 1950's-era GMC Silversides, several incarnations removed from its proud service in the Greyhound fleet. Immediately prior to its acquisition by Quad Cities, it apparently lived south of the border, as instructional signs were in Spanish, and empty tequila bottles sometimes rattled from way under a random seat when the brakes were applied with too much enthusiasm.

The Silversides featured its original diesel engine, unencumbered by emission control devices, eight forward gears, and a reverse the ballplayers considered only a rumor. Doc Hartman, who doubled as both team trainer and bus driver, hailed from the same era as the bus and they apparently understood each other.

Conor enjoyed watching Doc drive during their endless journeys, cajoling and threatening as he ground through the gears, his cigarette smoke sucked outside by means of a tiny wing window.

"Where did you learn to drive a bus?"

"One of my summer jobs," Conor said. "I drove an airport shuttle."

He did not mention that the Silversides dwarfed his airport shuttle, or that he'd been fired for kissing one too many bumpers in the departures lane. He figured a bus is a bus is a bus.

"How do we get the keys?"

Conor checked his watch.

"It's after nine," he said. "Doc's asleep. Someone has to sneak into his room."

"Are you crazy?"

"No. He's half deaf. He's seventy-two, for Chrissake."

"Okay, how are you gonna get into his room?"

CONOR AND KEN SHROM RANG THE NIGHT DESK BELL. A bleary-eyed teen-aged boy yawned as he opened the door behind the counter.

"Yeah?"

Conor turned up the collar of his jacket, pulled his baseball cap low over his forehead and puffed on a cigarette.

"I'm Doc Hartman. I need a key to my room."

The desk boy squinted and rubbed one eye with the back of his wrist. He thumbed through a set of index cards representing the day's registrations.

"We got a problem," he said, glancing from a card to Conor.

Kenny edged toward the door.

"And what's that?" Conor asked without flinching.

"You gotta pay five dollars for a duplicate key."

"Okay . . . can I just charge it to the room?"

"I don't see why not."

Kenny stood guard as Conor eased inside. Long, wheezing snores drifted into the night. The snoring stuttered as Conor lifted a set of keys from the dresser. He froze and held his breath. Doc rolled onto his side and resumed his snore. Conor emerged holding a ring of at least forty-seven keys.

By then, eight ballplayers had signed up for the trip. They waited while Conor sorted through the ring, finding a key that unlocked the bus door on his thirty-fifth attempt.

"We can't start it here," Conor advised his crew. "It'll make too much noise. Let's push it down the street."

He tried each key again, found one that brought the bus's electrical system to life, fumbled with a heavy, floor-mounted gear shift and—according to the pattern printed on the knob—discovered neutral. The baseball players rocked the bus a couple of times and shoved it onto a slight decline that rolled it a block away.

Conor saw gauges jump to life as he turned the key. He searched for a starter button, finding it mounted on the floor to left of the clutch. The diesel clattered to life.

The shift knob showed him positions for eight gears. The transmission gave a shriek as he searched for the clutch's correct friction point. And, eventually, they were off along a dark two-lane roadway headed toward Cedar Falls.

With much clanking and grinding, Conor found the first five gears. The bus, though, refused him access to the other three. Still, they managed a reasonable forty miles an hour as the tachometer needle hovered near the red line.

THE EIGHT-BALL SAT AT THE LIP OF A CORNER POCKET, the six blocking Conor's shot. He picked his spot on a far rail. He needed to kiss the eight ball slightly off center, so the cue ball wouldn't follow it into the pocket. He hit it exactly right.

"You want to go again," he grinned as he pocketed a stack of bills resting on the rail. The morose farm boy leaning on his cue grunted and shook his head no.

"Hey, you might make a living with that stick," Ken said. "You never told me you were a pool shark."

"I'm not. My brother Sam taught me some things, but he's

the real shark. I'm good enough to make some money in a place like this. My brother and his friends would eat me alive, though."

"They aren't here, are they?"

"Nope," Conor said, "and tonight I made two hundred and thirty-five bucks shooting against the locals. I'll buy dinner."

Brady's Pub & Grub featured beer, pool, and rural Midwest cuisine. Brady's main room consisted of a bar and a bunch of high tops scattered around three pool tables. A pair of French doors opened onto a second room lighted by dim wall sconces where customers wanting some separation from the more raucous bar crowd occupied shadowed booths lining the walls.

As the official bus driver, Conor nursed a single beer all evening. His teammates seemed determined to compensate for Conor's sobriety. And Gary hadn't exaggerated his promise of girls. A noisy gaggle of young women, in various stages of impairment, clustered around the ball players. The juke box roared. The party rocked.

"This is the Conman," Dave slurred as he introduced a young woman displaying spectacular cleavage.

"We want to ride your bus," she said.

"Okay." Conor grinned. "Where to?"

"Back to the motel," Dave said in a theatrical whisper.

"Yeah. There."

BEING SEVENTY-TWO YEARS OLD, DOC HARTMAN RARELY slept through the night. He usually had to pee at least twice, and as long as he had to get up, he used the occasion to enjoy a smoke. He stepped onto the sidewalk, embracing the cool of the evening. He inhaled deeply and studied his view of the parking lot when some little something picked at the corners of his brain. He frowned. He inhaled. He squinted.

Where did I park the bus?

He leaned over the second story railing to see a dirt strip way down alongside the building. No. He parked the bus in the parking lot. He was almost sure. *Maybe I put it around back...* Doc liked a nip of bourbon each evening. This wouldn't be the first time he'd misplaced his bus.

He'd get the keys and go check around... His keys were gone! His bus was gone!

"Somebody stole my goddam bus!"

CONOR PEEKED AT THE RAUCOUS CELEBRATION AS HE drove. His rearview mirror reflected that not everyone remained entirely clothed. He felt proud. He'd performed a humanitarian service for his teammates. He'd told them he'd drive the bus, and he did. All they needed to do now was get it to the parking lot and return Doc's keys.

Conor signaled for a left turn into the lot. He slowed, found second gear, and began muscling the Silversides though the turn. He misjudged the bus's length only a little. Big rear wheels bounced over a curb. Which would have been okay, except for the fire hydrant.

The bus lurched, and the engine died. Conor heard a bang and a sort of rushing noise he didn't immediately identify. Behind him, his passengers observed a moment of silence. Rain began to fall. Conor flipped on the windshield wipers.

At the back, though, where some windows were open, a fat torrent of water spewed skyward in a majestic arc.

"Abandon ship!" someone yelled, and a stampede of humanity

left Conor alone as he tried to restart the engine. He didn't notice the blue and red lights. The roaring sound of the flood initially masked a wet policeman's voice shouting, "Hands on your head, and get out of the bus!"

"I'M SORRY ABOUT THE PUDDLE."

The policeman gave Conor a puzzled look. With his hands cuffed behind him, Conor could only nod at his head toward the police car.

"I dripped on your seat."

He'd tried explaining he hadn't stolen the bus. This bus, after all, belonged to the baseball team. He worked for the team. He'd only borrowed it.

"They reported a stolen bus," the cop told him, "so you're under arrest."

Conor wasn't particularly worried. He'd been arrested before, back home, for siphoning gas. A.J. and Basil had dared him to do it. And, like this time, his buddies had escaped, leaving Conor holding the evidence. Then, he'd been scared. Then, he'd had to face his father.

Now, though, he figured he'd be okay. The cop fingerprinting him became angry because Conor kept dripping on the print card, but Conor knew he'd pass a breathalyzer and he didn't think the team would press charges against their closer.

He decided to savor the experience.

"Quit smiling!" the next cop yelled as Conor stood for his booking photo. "This isn't your senior prom."

"Yeah, well, I still want to look nice." Conor configured his face into the expected convict scowl. Carefully, he timed his grin for the moment the camera flashed.

"Shit," said the cop.

For his profile shot, he timed it right again, this time striking a *Walk Like an Egyptian* pose. He decided asking for a couple of eight-by-tens would be pushing his luck.

Conor spent the night in a holding cell with a couple of drunken baseball fans. His manager retrieved him the next morning.

"No charges filed," said the officer, who opened Conor's cell door. "Don't show up here again."

Cottier dropped Conor at the motel. "Come see me as soon as I get to the ballyard."

"YOU STOLE A DAMN BUS," COTTIER SAID.

Wearing his uniform pants and an undershirt, Conor did his best to appear contrite. "I—"

"Hey, I don't want to hear it. You can't do shit like that. I'm gonna fine you."

Conor gulped. He'd completely overlooked this aspect of professional baseball.

Cottier stared at him for a long moment. "You shoot a pretty good game of pool," he said finally.

"I . . . what?"

"I said you shoot a pretty good game of pool." He paused, letting his observation register, and added, "A bit of advice. If you go out to drink and chase a little tail, just be sure you don't choose the same bar your manager does. It's an unwritten rule."

"You were—"

"Yeah. Darkest corner, behind the pool table. At the time, though, I didn't know you'd stolen the goddam bus."

Conor waited through another awkward silence.

"Normally, I'd fine you a hundred bucks," Cottier finally said. "In this case, the fine's two hundred and thirty-five dollars. I happen to know you can afford it."

fourteen

"IF WE DO THIS," KATE TOLD HIM, "I WILL NOT BE ONE of those baseball wives who smiles and looks the other way. I will not accept that boys-will-be-boys. I don't want to marry a boy. I want to marry a man. I want to marry your father's son."

Kate Dunnigan had been on Conor's radar since his freshman year at Cañada. They met at the San Carlos High School Nude Relays—although both were fully clothed. A sort of formalized version of the streaking craze, this event was, surprisingly, embraced by the community.

"You guys running in the nude relays?" Hugh asked Conor and Basil.

"Um . . . yes?"

"Good," Hugh said. "I don't want any son of mine wimping out when it comes to tradition."

Technically, the competition was limited to San Carlos High School seniors. But Conor snuck A.J. and Brad into the mix. They wore Lone Ranger masks.

"This mask won't do any good," A.J. said. "It's not covering the part of me girls will recognize."

"Yeah, you wish," said Basil.

The team of Nash, Cohen, Leary and Doan finished first, thus drawing the responsibility to organize the following year's Nude Relays. A.J. worked hard at recruiting the first-ever female entrants. He'd obtained a solid commitment, but they bailed at the last minute.

Kate, a year younger than Conor, attended a different high school. The Nude Relays, though, enjoyed a wide following. She met Conor when she sought him out to inquire about the semi-secret location of this year's course. Soon, she took her place among a pantheon of Conor's female friends. They dated occasionally. They had fun.

Kate felt a certain amount of apprehension. People didn't live around San Carlos without knowing of the Nash family. "The boys were either famous or notorious, depending on whether or not Sam had beaten up someone you knew," she explained.

She only had to know Hugh, though, to understand that, in Conor's company, she was safe.

When Conor and Kate walked into Conor's living room together the first time, Hugh turned to his wife and said, "Uh, oh."

Nadine told Conor, "Pay more attention to her. She's good for you."

They dated more seriously during his second year at Cañada, although their relationship proved occasionally contentious. While Kate accepted Conor's garrulous nature, even where other girls were concerned, Conor did not extend her the same courtesy. He declared their relationship over after seeing her chatting with a former boyfriend. Kate's persistence won out, though, and the more time they spent together, the more he appreciated his father's assessment. Both pretty and funny, he found an inner strength about her he hadn't seen in others.

Uh, oh, indeed.

One aspect of being my father's son, though, was practicality. Having already experienced the reality of minor league baseball, I headed off for Quad Cities with no desire to make a long-distance commitment I doubted I would be able to keep.

"You wanted to see me, Skip?"

"Yeah," Cottier said. "Shut the door."

Conor warily stepped into his manager's office. He'd thought the whole bus thing had blown over. No one had said anything about it the past week. In the meantime, he'd closed two games without allowing a base runner. This thing about shutting the door, though, gave him pause. A closed door translated into bad news for a couple of guys who'd recently been sent home.

Conor suffered an awkward silence as Cottier scribbled something on some kind of form.

"Pack your bags . . ." he said.

Conor felt the floor almost collapse beneath his feet. Until Cottier completed the sentence.

"You've been called up. They want you in Salinas tomorrow. Here's your plane ticket."

Salinas Angels
High A Baseball
1977

I WAS PRACTICALLY HOME.

Salinas, California, located eighty-four miles south of San Carlos along Highway 101, hosted the Angels' High A affiliate. Mark Brouhard started his season there, so I had a friend to introduce me around and help me adjust to the challenges of a higher level of play.

Gary Tebetts moved up, too, and he broadcast news of our bus adventure throughout the clubhouse. I became the go-to guy for comic relief. My teammates learned that, on a dare, I'd do practically anything—perform a sliding act across an infield tarp during a rainstorm, break a sprinkler to flood an opposing ballpark when we needed a day off, hide the mascot's costume.

Moose Stubing—nobody called him Lawrence—whose size and relative grace reflected his nickname, managed Salinas. He watched me throw a bullpen. "Lefty, you're my closer. Try and gain some weight."

The best thing about Salinas? My family and friends could drive a little more than an hour to see me play. And more and more often, Kate accompanied my mom.

The worst thing about Salinas? My family and friends could drive a little more than an hour and see me play. A month after I arrived, owners of the Blue Boar Bar banned me.

"You can't come in," the bouncer said.

"Why not? What did I do?"

"You didn't do anything, but last week your brothers were here. We're afraid if we let you in, they might come back."

PROXIMITY COMPLICATED THE KATE ISSUE. PARTICULARLY *when A.J. or Baze were around.*

"I've got us a sure thing," A.J. told Conor. He pointed at two women seated about a dozen rows behind the home dugout. He waved. They waved back.

A.J. stood at the first row of seats.

"What do you mean a sure thing?"

"They'll meet us after the game."

Conor made eye contact with these women. They wore low-cut tank tops and short shorts. And they were hot—in a dangerous sort of way. Conor had not seen tattooed women before. They waved again. Conor tentatively lifted his hand. They smiled.

"So, what's the catch?" he asked.

"Come on, Connie, I talked to them and they like me. They like that you're one of the players."

Conor stared at A.J. "And what else? Why are they *a sure thing*?"

"They're here to visit their boyfriends."

"To visit . . . what?"

"Their boyfriends are in prison. They'll be horny as hell."

Twin pillars of the Salinas economy were agriculture and a few nearby penal institutions. Local motels and bars did a thriving business, serving friends and family members as they visited their beloved felons.

"A.J., I am not going to sleep with someone's gun moll," Conor said, unable to resist one more glance. The women waved again.

"Come on," A.J. said. "Think about it. They're not looking

for a relationship. They already have one or will in two-to-five years. They're like us. They're just looking to get laid."

"Baze will be here tomorrow," Conor said. "He'll probably be happy to help out. I'm not going."

"I already made the date," A.J. protested. "We're meeting them at—"

"I'm not going."

A.J. pouted all night.

Basil arrived the next day. His Alaska fortunes continued to thrive. Brad met him at the San Francisco airport, and they drove to Salinas.

"They're sending me to underwater welding school this fall," Basil told them.

"Are you sure that's a good idea?" Brad asked.

"They pay me twenty dollars an hour welding on the pipeline. I get my underwater certificate and it'll be twenty-seven."

"Yeah, but when you're welding on the pipeline, at least you can't drown."

"And I'm selling my trailer. I'm buying ten acres of land and a house."

"Land?" A.J.'s ears perked up. "Can you buy twenty acres?"

"I could buy a hundred acres if I wanted to. Alaska has plenty of land."

"And this is close to the pipeline? Conor, you've still got your bonus money. We should—"

"I already told you, A.J., I'm not giving you any of my bonus money."

"If you guys buy something," Brad said, "don't sign a contract until I've seen it."

Conor protected a one-run lead with a popup and two strikeouts.

They chose the Blue Boar to celebrate. They were granted entry only after Conor assured the bouncer that none of his brothers were within eighty miles.

"Okay, where'd Baze go?" Conor asked, returning from the bathroom. A.J. grinned and pointed. Baze sat high on a stool, holding a glass of scotch, a gaggle of women surrounding him.

"And look who it is," A.J. added.

"Oh, no. The prison girls."

The women from the previous evening were hanging all over Basil, accompanied by three other tattooed ladies. Conor watched with trepidation as one of them handed Basil a second glass of scotch.

"Brad," Conor said urgently, "go tell Baze we need to leave. He'll listen to you."

His admonition came too late. One of the prison girls tucked herself into Basil's left arm. The other leaned into a long kiss.

"Thank God, they aren't local." Conor scanned the room for angry cowboys as a scowling woman grabbed the kissee by her hair and threw a punch to her jaw. A five-woman melee erupted. Basil stood calm at the epicenter, his scotch raised high, safe above the storm.

"Come on, A.J." Conor said. "We've gotta get him out of there."

He rushed forward. From his left, he heard someone say, "Hey, here's one of the assholes who stood us up last night."

She hit Conor with a chair.

"COME ON, CONNIE, IT'S NOT MY FAULT," BASIL SAID. "Nobody told me they were prison girls."

Once again, they stood in the parking lot seeing to Conor's wounds.

"I talked with the owner," Brad said. "If you pay for the chair you broke, they won't bring any charges."

"I didn't break the damn chair," Conor said. "It was... uh oh."

The prison girls approached.

Brad stepped toward them, raising his hands as an offering of peace. The prison girls apologized. "You didn't tell us you were with Basil," said prison girl A. "Yeah, we never met anyone from Alaska," added prison girl B.

"Okay," Basil said. "Are we good?"

Everyone seemed to agree, except Conor, whose back hurt.

"So..." Basil added, "If you guys don't need me for anything else, I said I'd have one more drink..."

Each of the prison girls took one of his arms and guided him toward a car at the far end of the lot.

"Whose gonna pay for the damn chair?" Conor called after them.

A voice wafted from parking lot shadows.

"It's not my fault."

I ENJOYED A SPECTACULAR SECOND HALF. WITH THE HELP OF a solid defense over my twenty-three appearances, I recorded forty-one strikeouts and didn't blow a single save opportunity. I was named to the All-Star teams for both the California and Midwest Leagues.

Stubing shared his end-of-season evaluation report.

"Conman, you don't have anything left to prove here. You should be closing at triple-A next year. Anyway, that's my recommendation."

Triple A! One short step from the Majors.

I spent my off season considering a life pocked with Karate Girls and Prison Girls and bar fights, or a life with Kate. I proposed in December. We married after the 1978 season, about the time my baseball career began to fall apart.

fifteen

Spring, 1978

"WHY AM I GOING BACK TO SALINAS?"

Conor might not seek physical confrontation the same way his brothers or A.J. did, but he'd learned his father's lessons. He wouldn't just smile and take it. He owned a sharply honed sense of basic fairness. So, when Mitchell Preston arrived at his office at the California Angels Palm Springs spring training facility, Conor waited at his door.

"You're Conor Nash, right?" Preston asked as he directed Conor inside.

Preston, a tall man with a long face and a high forehead, was the newly minted Director of Angels' Minor League Operations. Mark Brouhard and a couple of other guys advised Conor against approaching Preston. They suggested he relay his questions through one of the few remaining coaches they knew, like Moose Stubing or Chuck Cottier. That's not how Conor's dad would have done it, though. During the winter of 1977-78, Conor deeply felt his father's absence, particularly in situations when he needed paternal advice.

"Moose showed me his evaluation report last September," Conor said. "He recommended that I jump to triple-A."

"Moose doesn't run the Angels farm system," Preston said. "I do. I'll come to my own conclusions. Here's the thing. You don't fit our prototype. Little guys who throw hard break down too often. I wouldn't have drafted you. You're here, though, and we've got an investment. So, do well at Salinas, and you'll move up. Now, if you'll excuse me..."

In January the Angels had announced a sweeping reorganization of their minor league operations and coaching staff. The administration that drafted Conor was gone, the scouting system restructured. Many coaches who were Conman advocates, including Carlos Estrada, had been fired.

Conor knew his father would want him to stick up for himself. While trying to harness his anger at being summarily dismissed from Preston's office, he heard his father's reminder that baseball wasn't a game anymore. *You are a professional. Baseball is a business. And an expectation of fairness is naive.*

Salinas Angels
1978

"I DON'T KNOW WHY YOU'RE STILL HERE, CONMAN. As long you are, though, you're one of my starters." Chuck Cottier had also made the jump to Salinas. "Improve your curve ball and develop a change-up. We'll see if Spaldy can help."

Along with a starting opportunity, the prospect of learning at the feet of the great Wilbur Spalding mitigated Conor's disappointment. The Hall-of-Famer replaced Estrada as roving pitching instructor under the new administration. Every left-handed child of the 1960s worshipped two idols: Sandy Koufax and Wilbur Spalding, left-handed legends of the game. Spalding pitched until age forty-four. He retired in 1965, followed by election to the National Baseball Hall of Fame in 1973. Like Conor, he'd been a rail-thin southpaw when he broke into professional ball. Surely Wilbur Spalding would hold a special affinity for a fellow skinny lefty who threw smoke.

Conor's happy anticipation of being mentored by Spalding, though, was tempered by his second confrontation with Mitchell Preston.

"WHY IS MY CHECK ONLY FIVE HUNDRED DOLLARS?" Conor asked his manager. "Did I get some kind of pay cut I don't know about?"

During Conor's rookie Idaho Falls season, he'd made a grand total of three thousand dollars for six months work. His monthly salary jumped to five hundred twenty-five dollars his second year, and now, his third year, he should be making five seventy-five.

Cottier examined the stub. "I don't know. Check with the front office."

"We were directed by Mr. Preston to withdraw seventy-five dollars a month due to an unpaid debt," the front office lady told him.

"What unpaid debt?"

"You'd have to ask Mr. Preston."

"We were contacted by a dentist," Preston told him. "He said you refuse to pay your bill. I won't tolerate deadbeat employees. Seventy-five dollars will be held from each paycheck until this debt is settled."

Conor came unglued.

"I didn't pay the fucking bill," he screamed into the phone, "because he pulled the wrong fucking tooth!"

Last January, Conor had suffered a toothache. He tried to see his family dentist, who was in Acapulco. His tooth got worse. He found another dentist. Who pulled the wrong tooth. The dentist apologized. He said he'd be happy to try again. Conor did not want a dentist who pulled the wrong tooth anywhere near his mouth a second time.

The dentist sent him a bill for six hundred dollars. The next month, the dentist sent him a second bill, with interest due and a threat to sue.

"Don't pay the bill," Brad advised him. "He won't sue. He doesn't want everybody to know he pulled the wrong tooth."

Brad removed his two false teeth. "If he doth thue, we'll counter-thue and embarrath the thit out of him."

"Well," said Preston without a hint of apology, "I don't know anything about that. All I know is there's a bad debt and..."

"What the fuck gives you the right to pay my bills?" Conor yelled. "You aren't my father. You don't get to teach me any goddam lessons. Maybe you can bury me in Salinas, but you damn sure better keep your hands off my bank account!"

WILBUR SPALDING ARRIVED THREE WEEKS INTO THE season.

"I've been told how much all you kid pitchers liked Carlos Estrada," Spalding said with his Oklahoma drawl. "Well, forget everything Estrada said. I don't know what *his* record was. I won 363 games in the Major Leagues, I struck out 2,583 batters and I could still strike out half the hitters on this team."

Spalding glared as the Salinas pitching staff gathered in. A frown creased his face. His ears were long and his forehead high. Smack in the center of this elongated oval, a bulbous nose lay a little to one side and hooked at the end. A long stem of a neck connected Spalding's head and shoulders. The word *gangly* might have been invented just for him. A sportswriter once described him as *goose-necked and stork-legged.*

Of course, Conor didn't care how Spalding looked. Spalding's implied denigration of Carlos Estrada did not sit well. *But, hey, the guy's Wilbur Spalding, right?*

His estimation of Spalding fell further a couple of days later as Conor warmed for his fourth start. His first three outings had been solid. His fastball jumped and tailed—he'd already recorded nineteen strikeouts. His curve ball was coming along, the change-up a work-in-progress.

"Your delivery's not deceptive enough," Spalding said.

Conor had seen Spalding's approach. He'd interrupt pitchers mid-workout and advise some sort of significant change of motion, harkening back to days of herky-jerky deliveries with lots of moving parts.

"What I want you to do," Spalding told Conor, "is extend your right hand, stick your glove right out in front. Yeah, like that. Then, put your left hand by your side, now swing it up to the glove, and then go. And change the number of times you swing your arm. Sometimes do it twice before you pitch, maybe even three times. Okay, let's see it."

And right then, Conor realized the unthinkable: he didn't like Wilbur Spalding. Not because Spalding asked Conor to do something awkward and stupid at a point when Conor should be building focus for his start. Spalding, though, was just... unlikable. Which bothered Conor.

How can someone not like Wilbur Spalding? Spaldy the legend. Spaldy the Hall-of-Famer. Spaldy the war hero.

Under Spalding's penetrating glare, Conor attempted half a dozen pitches using the awkward motion. The first five sent his catcher leaping and diving. The sixth found a corner of the plate.

"There you go," Spalding said, and headed toward the outfield.

"What were you doing over there," Brouhard asked Conor as he toweled off his warm-up sweat. "You looked like a swinging door."

Conor rolled his eyes. "You wouldn't believe me if I told you."

Conor walked two hitters before he recovered the comfort zone of his familiar compact delivery. He pitched into the seventh for the win, though, striking out six.

Spalding found Conor at his locker.

"I didn't see any attempt to vary your delivery tonight."

"No," Conor said. "What you had me doing was awkward. It's not something I—"

"Son," Spalding said, "a kid who won't listen is what we call *uncoachable*. You don't want to be that."

He walked away.

Despite the growing animosity he and Spalding shared, Conor enjoyed a solid season as a starter. He won six and lost four with a 2.85 ERA. He made twenty-seven appearances, striking out seventy-one.

Mark Brouhard, Conor's closest friend on the team, flourished. He had a monster year elevating him to the Major's two seasons later. He hit .310, belting twenty-one home runs and ninety-one RBI.

Each time Spalding's rounds brought him to Salinas, my recovery—my ability to rediscover the mechanical groove that afforded me success and confidence—took a little longer. And my shoulder hurt.

My growing frustrations with Spalding were set aside, though, when Kate and I married that September. Our wedding took place in the same Catholic Church where I'd been confirmed a dozen years before. A.J., Basil and Brad were co-best men. My brothers were groomsmen, so the line-up standing on my side of the church extended almost to the wall.

As we prepared to walk down the aisle, I turned to A.J.

"Don't go making any explanations to the priest about being Jewish. And don't interrupt him to tell him what a good job he's doing."

"Don't worry," A.J. said, *"I already slipped him a twenty. I told him there'd be twenty more if he doesn't screw it up."*

I SHOULD HAVE GIVEN A.J. THE MONEY. REMEMBER THAT five thousand he wanted from my signing bonus for his Arizona land deal? A decade later, A.J. sold the land for almost a million bucks.

How was I to guess he actually might know what he was talking about? I mean, A.J. always had some kind of scheme going. When we were kids, he charged girls from my high school a fee for arranging dates with guys from his high school. He printed business cards that read A.J.'s Pimp Service. I didn't invest in that business, either.

I still don't know how the deals keep coming. He's always buying shopping centers or partnering in real estate developments. He's got a gift of schmooze—he calls it his rap, and no one raps like

A.J. I've asked him how he does it. I mean, what does A.J. Cohen know about shopping centers? "I don't need to know anything about shopping centers," he said. "I speak the universal language—the language of money."

The other thing I should have done is let him be my agent a lot sooner.

Same problem. How could I know?

You're not an accountant or a lawyer, I told him when he suggested it. What do you know about being an agent?

Nothing, maybe, he told me. "But I can make deals."

A.J. is a multimillionaire. Who knows, maybe he has an investment angel who was *paying attention the day A.J. nearly got roped into the carpet business.*

MY DAD DIED RIGHT BEFORE MY TWENTY-FIRST BIRTHDAY. SO, *a year later—December of 1977, the guys hijacked me to Tahoe to celebrate the birthday I'd missed. I was halfway to Sacramento before they told me where we were going. I told them Kate would be worried. They said I could call her from the casino. Which I did.*

She was a little irritated.

"Conor, you're engaged now. You can just go off with your buddies without telling anyone. Let me talk to A.J."

She reamed A.J. pretty good. "One of these days," she told him, "you have to grow up. Conor needs to be an adult now, and I'm not sure he ever will be, as long as you're not."

I stayed only because Don Rickles was playing at Harrah's, and because we agreed Baze would not pick up any women, A.J. wouldn't get sucked into the blackjack tables, and Brad would be sure we followed the rules.

Ha!

Lake Tahoe

"The day we get back, I have to go with my father and brother to a carpet factory, so I can meet our suppliers, start learning everything about carpet." A. J. had finally succumbed to his father's pressure to embrace the family business. He displayed an utter lack of enthusiasm for his commitment, moping with the fatalism of a man on death row.

"Well," Brad said, "maybe it'll be interesting."

A.J. sighed. "Believe me, that's the worst possible outcome."

They'd been at the casino only a few hours, though, when A.J. brightened.

"Here, Connie, hold onto this." He shoved a wad of bills into Conor's shirt pocket.

"Holy, shit, there's almost a thousand dollars here."

Conor, Basil and Brad sat at a table in a lounge situated adjacent to Harrah's casino floor. When Basil initially headed alone toward the bar, Conor intervened. "You agreed to the rules. You're not doing your voodoo girl mesmerizing trick. Just stay here and enjoy the company of your friends."

A.J., though, had departed under the pretense of a restroom break.

"I won it, playing blackjack," A.J. said. "Yeah, I know I wasn't supposed to. But it's crazy, man. It's like I can't lose."

"Why are you giving it to me?"

"I'm covering our expenses. As of now, everything's on me. I've kept a couple of hundred bucks to play with. If I blow the two hundred and ask you for more, don't let me have it."

"Why don't we let Brad hold the money?"

"No, because he'd just give it to me. Wouldn't you, Brad?"

"Well, probably."

Conor pocketed the money. Five minutes later, A.J. returned.

"I need two hundred dollars."

"No," Conor said.

"Come on. It's my money."

"No. You told me not to give it to you."

"That's when I didn't think I'd need it. Now, I need it."

"Five minutes ago, you *had* two hundred dollars."

"Right. And now I don't. So, give me two hundred of *my* dollars."

The whirr and ding of slot machines drifted through the darkness of the lounge. Cigarette smoke lingered everywhere.

"Fine," said Conor, shifting in his chair and withdrawing the wad of cash from his jeans. "Here's your money."

"Not all of it. Two hundred dollars. Then don't—"

"Hey, I'm not holding your money anymore." He shoved the bills across the table. "Give it to Brad."

"All right," A.J. said. "Brad, I'm counting on you. Don't give me any more."

The interval this time lasted ten minutes.

"Brad, I need the money."

"Okay, here."

As A.J. disappeared into the casino a cocktail waitress, wearing a non-existent sort of costume displaying her bulging breasts as if they were being offered on a platter, placed a glass of scotch over ice before Basil.

"Here ya' go, honey," she said, adding a wink. "This is from me and the girls."

"No," said Conor. "No. Take it away. He's allergic. Baze, you agreed . . ."

Basil raised the glass as tribute and returned her wink. "Hey, it's not my fault."

A flurry of activity followed by shouts cut his response short. They saw A.J. flash past the lounge entry at a dead run.

"What's going on?" Basil stood and took a few tentative steps.

"Stop that guy!" someone yelled. A pair of burly security guards raced past.

"They're after A.J.!" Basil sprinted in pursuit.

"Oh, shit," Conor said. "Basil's going after the security guys. We've gotta stop him." He flung a few bills on the table. He and Brad turned the corner just as Basil was swallowed by darkness outside the Harrah's entrance.

Conor envisioned a scrum with Basil and A.J. beaten bloody by an entire company of security guards. Instead, they found Basil under a streetlight kissing the cocktail waitress. Although she wore a trench coat to protect her against the cold, she still managed to display two thirds of her boobs.

"Where'd A.J. go?" Conor demanded.

Basil disengaged himself.

"I lost him."

"And you found her?"

"She told me *Happy New Year*."

"So, you had to stop and kiss her?"

"Well, yeah . . ."

"Okay, say good night, because we've got to find A.J."

The waitress offered Basil an alluring smile and got into a car.

"Where do we even begin—" Brad said.

"There!" shouted Basil.

He pointed to the Harvey's Casino entrance on the other side of the street.

A.J. ran into the distance, followed by a different set of security guards.

They searched for three hours, looking through casinos and bars and scanning shrubbery at the edges of parking lots.

"All we can do," Brad said finally, "is wait until morning and see if he's been arrested."

"We've got an early-morning flight," Conor said. "A.J. has to be on it, or he'll miss his carpet meeting."

They made the rounds again. Finally, their only alternative was returning to their rooms and packing.

"I'll meet you at the airport," Basil told them. "I've got an appointment."

Conor unlocked his door, opened his suitcase and threw it onto the bed. The bed sneezed.

"A.J.?"

"Are you alone?"

"Why are you under my bed?"

"I assumed sooner or later they'd figure out who I am and search my room. The safest thing is hiding here."

He wiggled into view and brushed dust bunnies from his shirt and hair.

"Why were security guards chasing you?"

"A misunderstanding at a blackjack table. Well, okay, two blackjack tables."

A.J. shook his head and confessed. He'd lost the rest of his thousand dollars over the course of a few minutes at Harrah's. He went into his wallet for the emergency hundred-dollar bill he stashed there.

"Money plays."

The dealer showed a ten. A.J. held two kings. The dealer turned over a six. A.J. prepared to receive his payout. Until the dealer hit with a five.

"I don't know what happened," A.J. said. "The guy's been pulling cards out of his ass for a dozen straight hands. I grabbed my hundred dollars before *he* could, and I ran."

"Jesus, A.J., you can't—"

Someone tapped at the door. A.J. dove back under the bed.

Brad entered carrying a small bag.

"Come out, A.J. It's only Brad."

A.J. repeated his story to the point of Brad's interruption.

"I outran the security guards, hid behind some cars, and then I joined a bunch of Chinese people who were getting off a bus and snuck into Harvey's."

"Yes, we saw you running *from* Harvey's being chased by *their* security guards," Brad said.

"Yeah, well, all the Chinese people were going to the blackjack pit. I figured I'd blend in. After all, I still had my hundred bucks."

"Money plays."

Again, his heart soared as he found himself holding a ten and a queen against a dealer's jack. The dealer flipped over an ace.

"So, I grabbed my money again. I don't think they got a good look at me there."

"How did you get away from two different sets of security guards?"

"Casinos should hire security guards who don't weigh so much. Those guys are really slow."

They shared a moment of silence.

"So," A.J. asked Brad, "how much trouble am I in?"

"A lot, if they catch you. Nevada's laws are pretty harsh when it comes to casino theft and cheating."

"And then there's the Mob," said Conor. "Doesn't the Mob run casinos?"

Color drained from A.J.'s face.

"Look," Conor said, "let's just leave. Get packed and—"

"No. Forget my stuff. I can't go to my room. They might be waiting."

Conor bought a Lake Tahoe baseball hat at a gift shop. A.J. pulled it low, right above his eyes. They left the elevator and lingered among slot machines until they spotted a throng of retirees heading toward a tour bus.

"What about Baze?" A.J. asked. "Where's he?"

"Out with some of the cocktail waitresses," Conor said.

"Shit, we can't wait. I can't miss this flight. I can't be late to my carpet meeting."

"Basil's a resourceful guy. He can get to the airport by himself."

They dropped their rental car at the Reno airport and sprinted through the terminal, each clock they passed ticking toward A.J.'s doom.

"We're not gonna make it," Conor called to A.J.

"Yes, we will. We're almost . . ."

They skidded around the corner to find the gate entry closed, the aircraft slowly backing away. A.J. ran straight to a woman standing behind the desk guarding the gate. He spoke using broad, imploring gestures, and urgent whispers.

She shook her head no.

"What do you suppose he's telling her?" Conor asked Brad.

The woman's expression softened, then evolved to a look of concern. She lifted a phone. The plane began a slow turn toward the runway. A man wearing an official-looking blazer strode purposefully toward the woman. A.J. repeated his imploring gestures and urgent whispers. The man shook his head no. The woman offered imploring gestures and urgent whispers of her own. The man took the phone. The airplane stopped, reversed its turn, and crept back toward the terminal.

A.J., Conor and Brad boarded, confronting a host of angry glares from other passengers. As they buckled their seatbelts, one more commotion occurred at the forward cabin.

Basil walked down the aisle, being led by a smiling stewardess.

"Boy, it's lucky your departure was late," Basil told them, "or I'd have missed the flight."

As Basil fastened his seatbelt, the stewardess returned.

"Sir," she said, "we'd be happy to offer a vacant seat in our first-class section."

As the plane repeated its slow backing turn, A.J. glanced frantically at his watch.

"Damn, I'll have to go straight to the carpet factory."

"You need to change clothes and shower," Conor said. "You look like you've been hiding under a bed all night. And you don't smell very good, either."

A.J. ran his hand over a stubble of beard.

"Let me borrow your razor. I'll shave on the plane."

Conor reached under the seat ahead of him and unzipped his bag. "Here, I don't have any shaving cream."

As soon as the seat belt sign flashed off, A.J. rose and made his way to the aft lavatory.

Conor settled himself for a brief and bumpy ride over the Sierras into San Francisco.

A.J. emerged from the lavatory ten minutes later. He'd gotten his hair under control. His face, though, was covered with dots of toilet paper stained by tiny red blotches.

"Never shave during turbulence," he said.

A.J. didn't make his meeting on time. When he finally did appear, he was disheveled, wrinkled, lacerated, and generally unpresentable.

I saw A.J. that night.

"My dad fired me. He said he finally realized my heart would never be in the family business. He gave me a hug and told me to go find myself."

sixteen

El Paso Diablos
Double A Baseball
1979

"**M**OOSE, I NEED A FAVOR."

Conor only reluctantly asked his manager's indulgence, because, for the first time in his professional career, he was struggling. He counted Stubing among his strongest advocates. Conor had been the ace of Stubing's Salinas pitching staff the year before and they'd been promoted together to El Paso.

Stubing sat behind a steel war-surplus desk in a sweltering cubbyhole of an office cooled only by the rhythmic sweep of an undersized electric fan.

The Diablos played at Dudley Field, circa 1924. Located adjacent to the El Paso Zoo, Dudley Field stood a few miles south of the Texas border with New Mexico, and a few miles north of Juarez. Metal bleachers faced unrelenting sun along the first and third baselines, flanking a covered grandstand crafted of adobe bricks. Cramped and stifling locker room facilities smelled like fifty years of sweat, tobacco, pine tar and Flex-All.

Infield and outfield grass baked under the Texas sun, and offered the only relief from the brown tones of the desert.

"What do you need, Conman?"

"My friend A.J. is here this week. He and I've played baseball together since we were seven years old. He's like a brother..." Stubing's eyebrows arched. He'd met Conor's brothers in Salinas. "... and I wondered if you might let him participate in pre-game workouts while he's here. He's a good player. He'd love to get on the field."

Stubing aimed a stream of tobacco at a metal wastebasket and regarded Conor with a furrowed brow.

"Okay," he said finally. "He can play some catch before the games. As long as it doesn't disrupt anyone's workout routines."

For A.J., slipping into the baseball culture was like putting on a comfortable old suit. He borrowed a pair of Conor's pants and a t-shirt, played catch and bantered with the players before batting practice, then showered and sat with Kate and Mark's wife behind home plate.

The Brouhards and Nashes shared the same apartment complex located at the edge of Biggs Airfield and the Fort Bliss Army base, a rough neighborhood at best.

A.J. slept on Conor's couch, and during the mornings before he and Conor left for the ballpark, talked about his plan to buy a sandwich shop on an attractive downtown San Francisco corner.

"You've gotta start somewhere," he said proudly, "and this will be my start. I've got my financing put together. We close right after I get back."

A.J.'s personality beamed full force during his week among the Diablos. Everyone liked him. Moose liked him so much that the day before they departed for a road trip, he invited A.J. to take a few cuts at batting practice.

Players teased A.J. as he stepped to the plate.

"Hey, don't hurt yourself." and "Try and get at least one into the outfield."

A.J. lunged at the first pitch, dribbling the ball along the third base line. The second pitch, though, he drove toward the left-centerfield gap.

Stubing snapped his head around at the sound of the ball off A.J.'s bat. A.J. blasted the next pitch into the desert beyond centerfield. Moose and a couple of players sharing A.J.'s hitting group gathered behind the turtle to watch.

"Your friend has a good swing," Stubing told Conor, who joined the others. "He's got some power."

At the close of BP, Conor headed toward the bullpen and A.J. retreated to the clubhouse to shower. Conor saw Kate find her seat and expected A.J. to join her. A.J. remained absent, though, until he appeared behind the dugout wearing a huge grin. He beckoned to Conor.

"You won't believe this," A.J. said.

"What did you do now?" Conor asked.

"He offered me a contract."

"Who offered . . . what kind of contract?"

"Moose. He offered me a contract to play baseball. He said I might have to go to Salinas for a while, but he thinks I can hit at this level."

He pumped his fist. "Wouldn't that be something, Connie? Playing ball together again. It's what we've talked about since the second grade!"

"Yeah," Conor said, forcing a smile. "Yeah. That would be something."

Conor brooded through the game. Every time he looked at Kate and A.J., he saw his friend talking with excited animation.

And each time, an empty place at the pit of his stomach felt a little emptier.

Had Conor not been struggling so mightily, had he not been staring his own baseball mortality in the face, he might have been more willing to celebrate his best friend's happiness.

A.J.'s excitement continued during their drive to the apartment. Brouhard offered his congratulations. Conor rode in silence. As they walked into Conor's living room, A.J. asked, "Okay, Connie, what's wrong?"

Conor studied his shoes and took a moment to gather himself.

"A.J., it's great that Moose made the offer. Now, I'm asking you to turn it down." A.J.'s expression of puzzled injury tore at him. "You know I love you like a brother," Conor said. "That's why I have be honest."

"What, you don't believe I'm good enough?"

"Yeah, you're good enough. For here. I've also heard you talking for weeks about your sandwich shop, that it's your starting point. You'd have to give it up."

"Yeah..."

"I've been around these guys for three years. I can tell who the good ones are. Mark, Kenny Shrom, Brian Hunter, they've got a real chance. Here's what will happen if *you* sign. You'll go to Salinas and do well. Come here a year later and do okay. Then you'll start bumping your head against the next level. They sign guys who are good enough for A or Double A, because they've gotta have teammates and opponents for the real prospects to test their talent.

"Another three years or five years, and those guys will be in the majors. And you'll be three or five years older and get released. Now, compare that to what you'll accomplish with your sandwich shop. Think about what the next step will be, and the one after that. That's where you belong. We both know it."

A.J. said nothing, only stared at Conor for long, long minutes.

"I'm sorry," Conor said. "I hate to—"

A.J. forced a smile. He hugged Conor, then stepped back. "Don't be sorry. Don't ever be sorry for telling me the truth."

"Hey, go be a millionaire," Conor said. "I'll play baseball for both of us."

El Paso
1979

MY COLLAPSE STARTED WITH A SINGLE ERRANT PITCH.

Following my year at Salinas, my shoulder soreness persisted so I didn't play winter ball at Golden Gate Park. I didn't pick up a ball again until Spring Training. When I did, my shoulder felt okay, but something was still off. The simple act of playing catch felt awkward. I attributed the problem to inactivity.

Wilbur Spaulding remained minor league pitching coordinator for the 1979 season. He messed with all the lefthanders' mechanics throughout spring training. Regardless of their past effectiveness, Spalding insisted on tweaking some nuance of their delivery. He offered no explanation. He just said do it and remained stoic and unapproachable.

I stepped onto the mound to throw my first bullpen under Spalding's critical eye. He watched my medium speed warm-up pitches with an air of impatience.

"Okay, okay, let's go."

Conor's catcher had to lunge for the first fastball.

"Throw the ball over the plate," Spalding said, shaking his head as a show of disgust.

Conor's next pitch came a foot outside.

"I said, throw the ball over the plate," Spalding demanded.

Conor buried his next offering by five feet.

"Are you shitting me?"

Despite the warmth of the Arizona sun, Conor felt a chill. Fleeting images of Jimmy Dial darkened his memory.

The yips.

"Get the fuck off my mound," Spalding said. "Come back when you're gonna take this seriously."

Things deteriorated from there.

Conor came to Spring Training determined to forge a better relationship with Spalding and, at least, try to execute the instructions he received. Each encounter, though, nagged at his confidence. That touch of arrogance, so critical to competing against hitters who preyed on uncertainty like a wounded animal, leaked away.

When he received his double A El Paso assignment, he felt uneasy because he knew, for the first time since he'd worn a baseball uniform, he hadn't earned his place on the team.

"You were my best pitcher last year," Stubing told him. "I'm gonna bring you to El Paso, and we'll get this thing whipped."

Though unspectacular, his first two starts resulted in wins. Then Spalding returned. The hall-of-famer looked on as Conor warmed for his third start. Spalding offered his confidence-crushing critique, and Conor did his best to suppress the anger boiling inside him.

His catcher signaled a first-pitch fastball. Conor missed home plate by eight feet. An immediate roar of derisive laughter issued from the opposite dugout. Conor barely heard it, though, over Spalding's apoplectic screaming from his own dugout.

"What are you doing out there? Goddammit, throw strikes!"

His next pitch skipped off home plate. The umpire gifted Conor with a strike a couple of inches off the outside corner. His catcher, though, had set up inside. He threw a second strike with a curveball. The catcher leaped for a fastball, and the hitter walked on the next pitch.

Spalding sauntered to the mound at the pace of a three-toed sloth. He waved for the infielders to join him. Arms folded across his chest, he said, "Throw. Strikes."

Conor tamped down his anger and said nothing. He'd allowed nine runs when Stubing pulled him with one gone in the second. As Conor slammed his glove onto the dugout bench, Spalding called from the water cooler, "Boy, Conman, they sure gave *you* the right name. I don't see how you've convinced anyone that you can pitch."

Spalding left and Conor found himself on a downward spiral he could not control.

Stubing tried letting him work as a reliever. They tried extra bullpens. They tried extended rest. Conor became so erratic none of his teammates would catch him. Except Mark, whose break-out season would make him 1979's Texas League Player of the Year.

"Come on, Connie. Let's go to the bullpen."

"No, Mark. You just finished nine innings."

"No man. We need to figure this out."

Their bullpen workouts extended until the grounds crew shut off the lights.

Conor's patience collapsed the next time Spalding visited El Paso.

During an off-day pitchers' meeting, Monte Mossburn—a

kiss-ass lefty—asked Spalding why didn't he write a book.

"If I wrote a book," Spalding said, "everybody would know my secrets. And no one would have to pay me to teach you mutts about pitching."

"Okay," Conor said. "Okay, Spaldy. What *are* your secrets? How do you win three hundred and sixty-three games, and get two-thousand and five hundred strikeouts? I think that's something we'd all love to know."

Spalding offered a condescending smirk. "Two thousand five hundred and *thirty-eight*. And if I told you, they wouldn't be secrets anymore, would they?"

At that moment, I realized Spalding knew nothing about the mechanics of pitching. I saw that the ability to perform a complex task and the ability to dissect that task and teach it are unrelated. People of extraordinary talent simply do it, absent analysis or thought. Sometimes, they are also blessed with a capacity to break down the nuances of their success, and—just as important—with patience to convey that understanding to lesser mortals.

This particular hall-of-famer, though, didn't have a clue.

CONOR FEARED EACH DAY WOULD BE HIS LAST. SURVIVAL to the Fourth of July All-Star break became his goal. He'd go home for a few days. Settle his mind. Search for the pitcher he'd once been.

When Spalding's tour returned him to El Paso the first of July, Conor determined he would simply ignore the man. He wouldn't rise to insults—be seen and not heard.

"Somebody needs to show you fellows how to take a real batting practice," Spalding said two days later as the Diablos began their pre-game hitting routine.

Afternoon heat sent waves shimmering off the infield dirt. Occasionally rising columns of air formed vortexes called dust devils that swept across the baseball field. These miniature tornadoes captured napkins, hotdog wrappers and loose sand, sending the mixture spiraling high above the grandstand. Players closed their eyes and tucked their chins to their chests when these whirlwinds crossed their paths.

A batting turtle surrounded the plate on three sides. An L-screed sat halfway between the plate and mound. Behind the screen, Stubing's mechanical throws—medium speed offerings down the middle, inside corner, outside corner—allowed hitters to focus on the nuances of their swings. This exercise is designed to groove a batting stroke, build confidence and allow subtle adjustments.

As groups of four or five took their cuts, pitchers shagged fly balls. Infielders engaged in a ballet old as baseball itself. Stubing delivered a ball. As soon as the hitter made contact, players holding fungo bats behind the first and third baselines slapped grounders to infielders. As Stubing reached for another baseball, infielders tossed balls along a graceful arc back to the fungo hitters, hitting a precise spot along the dirt base path, allowing a true one-bounce hop the fungo man caught without bending or reaching.

This fluid chiclé, a mindless sequence repeated over and over, lent itself to happy chatter, gentle jibes, and the luxury of nonchalance.

Normally, Conor would be with the pitchers, each trying to convince the others of their athletic prowess tracking fly balls. Today, though, fate handed him a fungo bat.

"Hey, Conman, could you pick me up? I've gotta..."

"Sure, no sweat."

So Conor stood just outside the third baseline, within easy hearing distance, as Spalding started needling the hitters.

What kind of swing is that? . . . Sure, you can hit it out of the park when Moose grooves it . . . I can still get every one of you by cutting the ball on your hands . . .

"Okay, next group," Stubing called.

"I'll take these guys, Moose," Spalding said. "They need somebody who's not just throwing cookies at 'em."

Big John Harrold, a power-hitting outfielder, stepped into the turtle. He flailed at Spalding's dips and darts during his initial round. Conor heard Harrold complain to Stubing. "You want to tell me what the fuck I'm getting out of this? He's just trying to make us look bad."

"Hey, Spaldy, can you at least tell 'em what's coming—?"

"They won't know what's coming in a game!"

Stubing turned to Harrold and the other four members of the hitting group. "Do your best. Let him have his fun. Okay?"

Brouhard stepped in next and offered a good-natured smile.

"Okay, Spaldy, don't worry about me. I know you can get me out. I'd like fastballs down and away. Help me get my eye—"

"Oh, no, man," Spalding said with a cackle. "I'm breakin' your bat today, stud. Don't use your gamer."

Conor squeezed the fungo and stewed. Minor league players bought their own bats and Louisville Sluggers didn't come cheap.

Brouhard offered a token laugh. "Don't do that, Spaldy. I don't have any BP bats. All I've got are two gamers."

Just leave it alone. Conor bit the inside of his cheek.

Spalding served Brouhard a fastball, and it left the park like a rocket. Conor smiled to himself. Brouhard waited, expressionless.

"All right," Spalding said. "I've got something for you."

He threw again. This ball became a desert companion to the first.

The sound of a baseball resonating off the sweet spot—the heart of the barrel where wood is like granite and launches a ball as if fueled by afterburners—rang through the empty stadium time and again. Conor heard the hiss of air over the seams as Brouhard drove one within inches of the L-screen. Instinctively, Spalding ducked.

Mark stepped from the turtle and offered Conor a surreptitious wink.

Conor could almost see the steam coming from Spalding's ears. He served the rest of the group a series of diving and cutting throws, leaving them shaking their heads in disgust. Brouhard began his second round, and Spalding's first offering was a fastball aimed at his head. Mark escaped by falling straight backwards into the turtle's mesh netting. Conor looked first to Brouhard, then Stubing. Neither offered a protest.

Just leave it alone.

Mark found his bat and resumed his stance.

Spalding followed with two deliveries boring onto Brouhard's hands, the kind that sting and buzz.

Keep your mouth shut!

Throughout the round, Spalding chirped. *Told you so . . . Oh, that looked like it hurt . . . What's the matter, can't you hit it?*

Brouhard stepped into the turtle for his third set of swings. Spalding threw a cutter and Conor heard a crack, like a dry branch in a campfire. Brouhard offered a look of disgust as he examined a split running from the bat handle toward its barrel.

Spalding did a little dance. "Got 'im! Oh, yeah. Got 'im, Moose. Told ya'll I'd get 'im!"

And like the bat, Conor snapped.

"What did you get?" he shouted at Spalding. "Just what exactly did you prove? You're pitching thirty feet away, and you're proud of breaking someone's game bat?"

"Connie, don't," Brouhard said.

"Yeah, when was the last time *you* broke someone's bat?" Spalding yelled.

"Oh, right. I know. But this isn't about my problems. What are you accomplishing? These guys need to get ready for a game and all you—"

"Conor," Brouhard said more forcefully, "don't do this."

"Hey, if you'd pop off less and pay more attention, you might actually learn something!" Now Spalding stood behind the L-screen, arms folded across his chest.

"The only thing any of us have learned from you," Conor said, "is that you won three hundred and sixty-three games and had twenty-five hundred strikeouts..."

"Twenty-five hundred and thirty-eight!" said Spalding.

"... you've screwed up more people on this pitching staff than you've helped, and now you're messing with our best hitter!"

Spalding threw his glove and balled his fists. Conor flipped the fungo aside. Spalding stepped around the L-screen.

"Conor! No!"

Spalding sneered. "You ain't got the nerve..."

Oh, yes, I do.

Conor charged the bigger man. Spalding's swing was awkward and wild. Conor side-stepped. Spalding's big round melon was wide open. One punch would put him away. Even in the heat of anger, Conor knew better. Instead, he clamped Spalding in a headlock and flipped him over his hip to the ground.

"Goddmf mffuerre, spfittle itll pssant..." Spalding sputtered through the headlock. He bounced and struggled, flailing at Conor with weak, powerless shots, but Conor kept him pinned.

Conor began to consider an exit strategy when he felt himself flying. Stubing, who stood six-six and weighed two hundred and eighty pounds, plucked Conor like a daisy and tossed him aside.

"What were you thinking?" Brouhard demanded. They remained on the dugout bench following the game. All afternoon and evening, players and coaches from both teams viewed Conor with a mixture of awe and disbelief.

Conor shrugged at Brouhard's question.

"You beat up Wilbur Spalding," Brouhard said with exasperation.

"Well, I wouldn't say I beat him up. We just rolled around a little bit..."

"No, you had him in a headlock and were giving him, like, atomic nooggies or something. Wilbur Spalding is, like, beloved."

"Not by me."

Brouhard stood, placed a hand on Conor's shoulder, started to say something more, then shook his head and walked toward the clubhouse.

Through the long afternoon and into the evening game, in which he did not participate, Conor brooded over the inevitability of his release. He felt an odd sort of relief. He dreaded going home, facing friends and brothers under an indictment of failure. He could, though, find some dignity in being released because he refused to be bullied by a Hall-of-Famer.

Stubing spilled the wind from that sail the following day.

"I'm sorry, Conman. I tried. I argued and argued we should send you to Salinas, or even Idaho, and let you work out of it. Mitchell Preston refused. He said he wants to cut ties."

"How much of this is because of the thing yesterday?"

"Nothing," Stubing said. "I didn't even report it."

Stubing rubbed a meaty hand across his eyes. "You can pitch. You can help a lot of clubs. Sometimes, though, Conman, you are your own worst enemy. You got on Preston's bad side right off the bat, and I don't think he's the type who ever forgets stuff like that."

Conor turned, then looked back. "Thanks for giving me a chance, Moose." He reached across the desk and offered his hand. "You've always been fair."

"Find a way to get this thing ironed out," Stubing said.

Conor nodded and went to pack his stuff.

Several teammates met him with tears. Because of his control issues, they weren't surprised at the release. They did not, however, want to contemplate the loss of his clubhouse presence. Through all his struggles, Conor never lost his sense of humor. He made the other guys laugh. How many teammates would steal a bus if they needed him to? After emotional goodbyes, after best wishes and reassurances, Conor sat alone at his locker while the others left for work. He lay among the dead. For the others, life continued.

He wanted to believe Stubing, but he'd seen many teammates released over the past three years. As far as he knew, they remained buried. He lacked faith to believe in even the possibility of resurrection.

HERE'S THE THING, RITA. HEROES FALL HARD WHEN THEY *tumble off their pedestals.*

I genuinely wanted to like Wilbur Spalding. I made the mistake, though, of requiring him to be more than a great pitcher. I wanted him to be the man we hope our heroes will be.

Koufax stood as the left-handed idol of my generation. Every kid who knew anything about baseball, though, knew of the legendary Spalding. I respected his accomplishments. I wanted to please the master. I became confused when I realized I didn't like the master, and then royally pissed off when the fallible man *couldn't command my respect.*

And even though, up until that last day, I didn't say the words out loud, I understand now I communicated my lack of respect in a dozen subtle ways.

Our paths crossed one more time—1981. I was a starter for Oakland's Double-A West Haven affiliate, and Spalding remained the Angel's roving pitching instructor. We played the Holyoak Angels. I still wasn't the pitcher I'd been before the yips. I'd made progress, though, and seeing Spalding in their dugout ... well, the effect was like gas finding a flame. In that moment I rediscovered my competitive arrogance and ego his hostile indifference had all but extinguished.

I stuck it up their ass, and he had to stand there and watch.

So, while he didn't teach me much about pitching, Spalding did teach me a lot about myself. He made me a better pitcher—a better man—in the process

I dressed quickly after the game and hurried to the Holyoak clubhouse. A clubby told me Spalding had already left. "He didn't wait around tonight. Probably a good thing. He was pretty pissed off."

I asked, "What about?"

"You. He was all over our hitters. Said you were the biggest cocksucker he'd ever come across."

I laughed. "Well, there's probably a lot of truth to that."

I never saw Spaldy again.

Conor raised his champagne bottle to the emerging stars.

Spaldy, I'm sorry. I should have handled it better. I salute your three hundred and sixty-three wins. I salute two thousand five hundred and thirty-eight *strikeouts, your twelve All Star appearances. You were a helluva pitcher.*

I just wish you'd waited around long enough that night, so I could've apologized in person.

AFTER A SLEEPLESS NIGHT, CONOR SWALLOWED HIS PRIDE and called Mitch Preston to offer an apology, and—although it grated on every sensibility he had—appeal for another chance. He owed it to Kate, A.J., Brad and Basil, all the people who believed in him. Although Moose told him he hadn't reported the fight, Conor couldn't imagine the front office didn't know.

"Mr. Preston, this is Conor Nash. I wanted—"

"Wanted to what?" Preston demanded. "Beg for your job back? Not so cocksure of yourself now, are you?"

"Look, I just felt like I owed it—"

"Save it, *Con-Man*." He dragged out the name, emphasizing his sarcasm. "I knew the first time I saw you that you didn't have the mental makeup to handle the pressure. I knew you'd never pitch in the Major Leagues. And after those stunts you've pulled, that's exactly what I'll tell anyone who asks."

Conor heard the flat buzz of a disconnection.

He and Kate mournfully packed their car and began the

long drive home. Their route followed Interstate 10 from El Paso through Arizona, where they would hang a right when they got to California. Reading the map, Conor saw that their path included Tucson. He knew the manager of Tucson's Triple A team, Jake Burroughs, who'd managed in the Angels' system before the purge. They stopped at a pay phone and Conor told Burroughs about his release. Burroughs invited him to stop by the ballpark so he could see Conor throw.

Kate and Conor waited at empty Hi Corbett Stadium for Burroughs and a catcher. When they arrived, Conor put on his spikes and threw with velocity. His fastball tailed. His curve ball bit hard. And while he might have located better, he was around the plate. "That's the way," the catcher reassured him, pitch after pitch. "Hey, that one had some smoke."

Kate grinned as he climbed over the rail.

"You threw strikes," she said.

"Well, closer to strikes than I have been," he answered, baffled at the mystery of it all.

"I'll make some calls," Burroughs said. "I don't know why they let you go. I can think of a half-dozen Double-A clubs you can help."

Winter bled into spring. Conor's phone remained silent.

seventeen

CONOR'S FAILURE CONFRONTED HIM AT EVERY TURN. The tires were so bad Conor borrowed money for replacements just to drive home. He and Kate moved into his mother's house. He needed a job.

When Conor and Kate arrived at San Carlos, his youngest brother, who did not yet know of Conor's release, shared big news.

"I made the fifteen-year-old All-Star team," Dylan said proudly.

Nobody made the fifteens team when they were thirteen. Conor saw his brother's sheer joy and mourned that he might never feel such enthusiasm again. He shook Dylan's hand and grinned. "Good job, kid. Good job."

As his brother dashed upstairs, Conor told his mother, "Well, at least there's still a chance one of Dad's sons will play in the Majors."

"Yeah," she said. "And it'll be you. Dylan might have the ability, but he doesn't have your heart."

Conor hugged his mother and smiled at what he considered her naiveté. She didn't understand—

The phone rang.

"You got your ass released? You said you were gonna play for both of us. If you're going to play for me, you need to play a helluva lot better."

"Hi, A.J. How... um... how did you know?"

"Fat Brad told me. He has an El Paso newspaper subscription so he can follow the team. You all right?"

"I... I guess so. I'm just... embarrassed. I feel like I let everyone down. I feel like—"

"Yeah, well, don't do anything drastic. Brad and I will be over this evening. Meanwhile, tell Kate to keep you away from sharp objects."

With her accounting degree, Kate soon found work at a contracting company. As my dad predicted, the poverty wages paid minor league ballplayers always forced me to work over the off-season. The past three winters I'd taken part-time jobs with the parks department, organizing youth sports and coaching girls' basketball. Now, I needed something full-time.

"My dad knows a guy at the Filoli Estate," Brad said. "He can probably get you on there."

The Filoli Estate, set against a backdrop of the Santa Cruz Mountains in Woodside, California, had been purchased by the National Trust for Historic Preservation about the time Conor signed his first Angels contract.

The estate included a 36,000 square-foot Georgian mansion dating back to 1915, a sixteen-acre English Renaissance Garden, a seven-acre Gentlemen's Heritage Orchard, and an elaborate system of hiking and biking trails. Conor loved the gardens' beauty. He enjoyed working with plants, mowing the vast expanses of grass, competing in riding-mower races against other gardeners, tending to swimming pools and ponds.

They gave him a gun—a .22 caliber pistol he holstered low on his hip, like Marshall Dillon—to protect himself from boars, snakes and other varmints stalking the grounds.

"They have no idea who they've armed," Conor told A.J. and Brad. "I shoot at anything that moves."

"Don't forget how much we need this job!" hollered Kate from the next room.

"I spent an hour today practicing my quick draw in the woods."

"Shoot someone, and they'll fire you," Kate called again.

"You guys should come by," Conor continued. "They're filming a new television show about some rich family, using the big house and gardens."

"So, you like it there?" A.J. asked.

"Yeah, I do. The grass reminds me of baseball diamonds. Today I thought about enrolling in school somewhere so I can learn more about grass and soil. I might get back into baseball as a groundskeeper somewhere."

"You'll get back into baseball as a pitcher," Brad told him.

"Yeah... I don't know. When they release you, I think you're pretty much done. I haven't heard of many people who—"

"Wait a minute." A.J. cut him off. "Baseball didn't release you. The Angels did. Last I heard there's twenty-five other Major League teams. And they need pitchers, too."

Yeah, but not pitchers with the yips.

"Guess what?"

Conor greeted Kate as he walked into his mother's kitchen.

"What?"

"I saw Nancy Drew naked today."

"You did not! I read the Nancy Drew books when I was a kid. Nancy Drew was never naked in her whole life."

"No, really."

Conor, assigned to clean the main house's swimming pool after the *Dynasty* crew wrapped for the day, organized his chemicals and skimmers and poles. The woman who had played Nancy Drew in a television series walked from the huge house wrapped in a beach towel. She shook her long, dark hair, dropped her towel, gave a luxuriant, feline stretch, and glided into the water. Conor found himself suffering a momentary paralysis as she swam gracefully to his end of the pool, floated on her back for a moment as water cleared from her eyes, then gave a start.

"Oh," she said, standing at the shallow end. "I didn't see you there."

A variety of responses tumbled through Conor's mind. All he could manage was, "Well, okay."

"I'm not trespassing or anything. I'm with the TV show. I play Fallon Carrington. Dumb name, I know. Am I in your way? I can always—"

Conor found his voice. "Oh... no. No. Take your time. I've got other stuff I can do."

She smiled and back stroked in the opposite direction. Conor rearranged his skimmers and chemicals and poles. On her return lap, two additional gardeners trimming the edges of the lawn ambled over.

They spoke to Conor, their eyes glued to the nude Nancy Drew. "Hey, Connie, we thought you might need some help with . . . you know, the thing. The one that's . . ."

"Um, sure. Here, hang out a couple of minutes while I . . ."

"Yeah. Yeah, we'll wait."

One more gardener stopped and sought a consultation with Conor about pruning when a shrill voice jolted them from their semi-hypnotic state.

"What is going on here?" Mrs. Barton, an assistant estate administrator, demanded.

Nancy Drew interrupted her laps. Again, she stood at the shallow end and brushed water from her eyes.

"Miss Martin!" Ms. Barton said. "Miss Martin! You can't . . . we're having tour groups . . . there might be children."

"Oh. I'm sorry." Nancy Drew smiled and pointed to Conor. "This nice man told me I wasn't in anyone's way. Well, all right. Thank you."

She offered Conor a wave as she retrieved her towel. Conor considered returning the wave. Mrs. Barton's glare made him think better of it.

Kate shook her head and rolled her eyes as he finished his story. "Why would she do such a thing?"

"I don't know. I didn't question her motive."

"So, are you in trouble?"

"I'm not sure. It's not like I tore off her towel and threw her in the pool."

"But you didn't tell her to stop."

"Well, no. No. I'm not sure I could live with myself if I'd done that."

"I'LL CATCH YOU," BRAD TOLD ME.

"No, it's okay. You need all the teeth you've got left."

A.J., who was better equipped to handle the movement and velocity of my fastball than Fat Brad, also volunteered. I rejected A.J.'s offer, as well. "I need a break. Give my shoulder some rest. I'll let you know when I'm ready."

My shoulder felt fine. I just didn't want my friends to know the true extent of my disability. I hadn't told any of them about the yips. A.J. knew I hadn't been getting much playing time, but he didn't know the whole truth.

As I watched Jim Dial's career fall apart, I tried being sympathetic. I attributed Jimmy's failure, though, to some character flaw. For whatever reason, he lacked the mental strength to cope with the pressure.

Throwing strikes is a physical process, a combination of a dozen different muscular commands fitting together like pieces of a jigsaw puzzle. Success is born of endless and precise repetition that muscles remember. And it works best when your brain just sort of stays out of the way.

You don't reason with yourself. You don't say okay, now I'm going to put this ball three inches to the left and two inches higher than where I put it last time. No, your eyes select a target, your body reacts, and some big ugly guy dragging a club sits down.

The brain complicates everything. Doubt, analysis, anger, fear are rooted in that lump of gunk sitting on your neck. And a strong person, by sheer force of will, should find the discipline to exorcise whatever demons were fucking with my fastball.

I faced a hard truth.

I wasn't the person my father believed me to be. I'd been fooling myself all along. My self-loathing became merciless. I wouldn't admit to friends and family that I didn't possess the mental strength to defeat this thing. I wouldn't play catch with anyone else, lest they discover how screwed up I really was. If my affliction could be beaten—if I could find the person I used to be—I would do it alone.

So, I took the bucket of baseballs that still lived in my bedroom closet and headed for the brick wall at the elementary school after work each day.

eighteen

Golden Gate Park
1980

"WHAT THE HELL HAPPENED TO YOU?"

Marino Paretti stood, arms crossed, fixing Conor with a curious stare. Conor had become accustomed to mound visits from coaches and teammates advising him through his struggles. This was a first, though.

Marino managed the other team.

The play at first base had been close, but not *that* close. Paretti charged from his dugout, alleged his runner beat the throw, kicked a little dirt, and, instead of returning to his own dugout, walked to the mound.

"Um... hi, Marino. I don't think you're supposed to be here."

"I knew my guy was out," Marino said. "I needed an excuse to talk with you. Last time I saw you pitch, you killed us. Like I said, what the hell happened?"

A baseball legend around the Bay, Marino Paretti had once been Billy Martin's roommate when he and Martin played for the San Francisco Seals. For as long as Conor could remember, Paretti managed teams made up mostly of players from the University of San Francisco baseball squads during the Golden Gate Park League's winter season.

On more than one occasion, that league was the salvation of Conor Nash's pitching career. People called it a Sunday beer league. Indeed, guys gathered below the bridge and shared a beer or two after the game. That image, though, vastly diminished the league's true stature.

Most area university teams played there during the winter. In an era before major league teams formed working relationships with Caribbean and Mexican League squads and sent players south of the border for winter ball, professionals kept their skills sharp through the off-season wherever they could.

For Northern California, that place was the Golden Gate Park League.

Conor's first season there was the winter of his freshman year at Cañada. He pitched for the San Mateo Loggers, easily the league's worst team. They went 0–22. Conor started every game and took every loss. Rosters of the other teams included names like Dennis Eckersley, Mike Norris, Willie McGee, Ricky Henderson—all local kids who, like Conor, aspired to the majors.

Lloyd Christopher, the Angels scout who signed Conor a year later, attended most of those games. Conor feared Christopher would lose interest. Christopher, though, did not become discouraged. "I saw you grow up that winter," Christopher told him later. "That experience fostered a maturity I hadn't seen before. Smart guys learn when they suffer."

Conor stared into the searching eyes of Marino Paretti,

then scuffed at the pitching rubber with his shoe. "It's that obvious, huh?"

Paretti nodded.

"Well... I had a pitching coach who messed with me and—"

"Which pitching coach?"

"Wilbur Spalding is the minor league pitching coordinator for—"

"Stop," Paretti said, raising his palm like a traffic cop. "Just stop right there. You don't need to say anything else."

"You know Spaldy?" Conor asked.

"Yeah, I know him."

"I guess you could say he and I had issues."

"Yeah, you and about a thousand other people on this planet."

Over Paretti's shoulder, Conor saw the home plate umpire striding toward them.

During his exchange with Paretti, Conor had shut out the ballpark noise around them. Now, though, he heard the leather-lunged bellows from the stands behind home plate.

"*Get off the field, Paretti! Go back where you belong, old man! You don't know anything, anyway! You're the worst...*"

"Marino, what are you doing here?" the umpire asked.

"I'm having a conversation with Mr. Nash, if it's any of your business."

"Conversation's over," the umpire ordered. "We got a game going here."

"Talk to me after," Paretti said, squeezing Conor's shoulder for emphasis.

"*Get off the field, ya' bum! Quit bothering the kid! Get off the field!*"

"Goddam," Paretti said. "That old broad's been on my case the whole fuckin' game."

"I know," Conor said. "That's my Aunti Di. She hates University of San Francisco sports teams. And she doesn't like you much, either."

Paretti laughed, turned toward his bench and yelled over his shoulder, "Shut up, you old bag! Get back in the kitchen!"

Paretti found him after the game.

"First of all," Paretti said as the grounds crew raked and watered and players headed for the parking lot, "you're giving Spalding too much credit. I didn't like the guy. And I've heard stories about his limitations as a pitching coach. But he got in your head because *you* let him do it. You have to accept *your* responsibility for this and stop blaming anyone else. Because if you broke it, you can fix it. Now, here's what I remember about your mechanics and the way you used to throw . . ."

"WHY ARE YOU YELLING AT YOUR ARM?"

Kate sat cross-legged on the elementary school lawn drinking a coke, watching Conor throw at the brick wall. Periodically, he shattered the beautiful summer evening with a minor meltdown.

"Stupid crappy frickin' arm!"

His criticism would have been harsher, except he knew Kate didn't like hearing him curse. He emphasized his disgust by smacking his left bicep with his glove.

"I'm yelling at my arm, because it's stupid and worthless, and it won't do what it's supposed to do."

"Does it listen?"

Conor threw a fastball and missed the chalk square by a foot. "Apparently not."

"So, it's your arm's fault?"

Conor sighed, bent, and took another ball from the bucket. "No. It's my fault, but you wouldn't like hearing what I think about myself."

"You're getting better," Kate said. "You still throw really hard. When you throw it over the wall, it goes a long way."

"Yeah, well, I'm not trying to throw it *over* the wall, though, am I?"

"What kind of things do you tell yourself?"

Conor dropped his glove and sat beside Kate. "I'm pathetic. I'm weak. I let some old guy goad me and shred my confidence. What kind of person is so short of guts and character to let that happen?"

"That sort of thinking is a big part of your problem," Kate said.

Conor gave her one of those *you just don't understand* looks and started to say something dismissive. She didn't let him.

"You are not weak. You are not pathetic. You are a talented athlete. And you *are* getting better." He looked away. She put a hand to his cheek and made him face her. "Did you like it when Mr. Spalding made fun of you? When *he* called you pathetic? When he said you'd fooled people into believing you were a pitcher?"

Conor dropped his chin to his chest. She clasped both of his hands.

"Then why say those things to yourself? What's the difference between him berating you and you berating yourself? You threw well in Tucson. What was different?"

"Spalding wasn't there," Conor said.

"He's not here, either. Besides that, what was different?"

Conor shrugged.

"Every pitch," she said, "a professional catcher was encouraging you. Someone you respected offered encouragement and validation."

Kate rose, dusted grass from the seat of her shorts and walked to the bucket.

"I married a pitcher," she said, flipping a ball to him. "So, go throw at your wall and be a pitcher again."

Well, it wasn't that simple. With Marino Paretti's tweaking of my mechanics, though, and an adjustment of my mental approach to both the game and myself I began to slog out of the quagmire. Along the way, I found another weapon. Never again would I allow someone to convince me I am not who I am. Never again would anyone's opinion of Conor Nash's ability outweigh Conor Nash's opinion of himself.

As I continued my journey, somewhere on the wall of some minor league clubhouse along the way, I found a framed quotation that spoke directly to my heart.

> When others don't believe in you, you just have to believe in yourself that much more.
> —Jackie Robinson.

nineteen

*A*LMOST TWO MORE SEASONS PASSED BEFORE I REALIZED with no small amount of amazement that I no longer questioned my ability to throw a strike when I needed to.

As the Golden Gate Park League continued the winter of 1979 and 1980, I progressed from throwing only an occasional strike to being effectively wild. I was back where I started. Being effectively wild made me a successful pitcher in the second grade. I threw hard enough to scare the pants off other second graders. Strike or not, they were happy taking three cuts and returning to the safety of their dugout. A survival imperative far outweighed any need to get a hit.

Same thing. Yips be damned, I still threw the shit out of the ball.

I'd uncork a couple of ninety-plus fastballs that might be a foot high or right at someone's ribcage. The hitter would duck and dodge and count himself lucky to reach first base with all his limbs attached. Other times, though, the jigsaw pieces fell into place, *and he'd be caught in mid-duck by a fastball painting the inside corner, or a curve ball nipping the black at his knees.*

Professional scouts were not strangers to Golden Gate Park. Someone from one team or another was almost always there on a Sunday, because the league's talent level was so high. My sheer velocity, combined with the fact of my left-handedness and my not-too-distant standing as a prospect, should have piqued someone's interest.

"We can teach people to pitch," *Carlos Estrada had told me.* "But we can't teach ninety miles an hour."

Still, our phone remained silent.

"I don't know," he finally told Kate. "I'm guessing word got around about the fight. I'm afraid I've been blackballed. Nobody will offer a contract to the guy who fought Wilbur Spalding."

"No," Kate said. "You're too good. You'll get back. It's just one more thing to overcome."

Conor smiled, amazed at the confidence his wife and brothers and friends still displayed.

"Well, okay. If this is over, though, you know what's going to piss me off the most?"

"What?"

"I didn't have enough fun. No matter what else it is, baseball's supposed to be fun."

"Well," Kate said, "you stole a bus."

Conor grinned. "Yeah. That was fun."

"I CAN GET YOU A JOB ON THE PIPELINE," BASIL SAID. "YOU'D love Alaska. And the money's good."

The money, in fact, was incredible. A.J. planned to be a

millionaire by twenty-five, but he'd just gotten his sandwich shop off the ground. Conor believed his wish in a tunnel destined him for a rich major league contract. Basil graduated high school and ran off to Alaska to become a welder.

As Basil turned twenty-five, he made sixty thousand dollars a year. He owned a house and land. He had a pickup, Harley and snowmobile. Vacationing, he showed up unannounced at Conor's door.

"No, I like it here," Conor said. "I like working at the Filoli estate, and I can play baseball Sundays. I'm considering going back to school. Maybe study grass and horticulture, things like that."

"Naahh," Basil said. "You're not a gardener or a student. You're a pitcher. The call's gonna come."

"Spring training starts in three days," Conor said. "If they haven't called by now—"

The phone rang.

"Conor Nash? My name is Norm Kasulke. I'm Farm Director for the Athletics . . ."

Oakland, under the waning ownership of Charles Finley, held the distinction of being the cheapest operation in professional baseball. The organization needed lefthanders—cheap ones—for their minor league system, Kasulke explained.

"I heard from a couple of guys at Golden Gate Park. They said I should sign you. Are you talking to anyone else?"

"Um . . . a couple of teams have expressed some interest," Conor lied.

"Okay, if you don't have anything else going, we'll offer a minor league contract at a thousand dollars a month if you can get to Phoenix by Monday."

Conor stood and indulged himself with an elaborate stretch that dissolved into laughter.

The Oakland Athletics. Charlie Finley, Norm Kasulke, Fred Tuttle... God, what a trip.

I drove east the next day. First thing I did when I got there was ask for Mr. Kasulke. I wanted to thank him one more time for offering the opportunity.

"You're looking for Norm?" the clubbie said. "Well, that's a problem."

"Oh?"

"He got fired yesterday."

Baseball people are fired all the time, and I didn't think much more about it. The following October, I took Kate to dinner at Fisherman's Wharf. We rode a bus into the city to avoid the hassle of parking. We stood holding hands at the bus stop for our return trip. The bus arrived, its brakes hissing. The door slid open.

I stepped in behind Kate and was shocked.

"Mr. Kasulke?"

The driver studied Conor for a moment.

"Mr. Kasulke, I'm Conor Nash. You're... you're..."

"Oh, yeah, I remember you."

"Why are you driving a bus?"

"The A's fired me. I didn't know I wasn't supposed to sign you. You gotta have exact change."

So, I guess I had been blackballed. Mr. Kasulke's mistake, though, is one more of those miraculous threads spun by... a baseball angel?

Conor couldn't quite bring himself to toast his angel so he

drank to the threads, absent any of which the whole cloth would have come undone. He followed with memories of Singin' Fred Tuttle, Darryl Clay, and one of the most woebegone teams in minor league baseball history.

West Haven, Connecticut
Double A Baseball
1980

THE WEST HAVEN WHITECAPS SERVED AS OAKLAND'S 1980 Eastern League affiliate. By August the White Caps were closing on a hundred losses, and I'd taken all I could stand.

Since learning that first day of spring training the Oakland organization really didn't want me, I'd been overlooked and underused every step of the way. I never pitched in a game that wasn't already a lost cause. I was the guy who came out of the bullpen the last two innings with the Whitecaps behind eleven to two. In fairness to you, though, Rita, lack of expectation became the greatest favor I might have wished for. The A's anticipated nothing from me. I never faced the pressure of blowing a lead. If I threw a fastball and missed by a foot, nobody came unglued because nobody paid much attention. And while they weren't watching, I worked my ass off.

During spring training in Scottsdale, Conor saw Camelback Mountain looming above the Phoenix landscape on the near horizon.

Camelback rises from the desert as a geologic structure of Precambrian granite and red sedimentary sandstone. Its name is derived from its shape, which resembles the hump and head of a kneeling camel. The route from desert floor to top of the hump gains 1,300 feet in a little more than a mile.

Camelback is popular among hikers. Local search and rescue squads do a thriving year-round business retrieving those who have collapsed, fallen, heat-stroked, heart-attacked or otherwise tuckered out somewhere along the way. Two main trails are carved into the mountain, one on each side. Railings or rope handholds help hikers negotiate some of the steeper ascents.

When Conor saw the mountain, he thought of Cañada and Mt. Vial.

"Hey," Conor said to a couple other minor leaguers, "let's go run Camelback."

That afternoon, Conor and two other brave souls stood at the foot of the Cholla Trail, a progression of gradual climbing switchbacks cutting their way upward.

They set off at a jog. Where he could, Conor abandoned the trail for a more direct route, straight toward the top, meeting the trail again where it doubled back on itself. When direct ascent was too steep or blocked by desert vegetation, he returned to the path, keeping a steady pace until an opportunity to climb more quickly presented itself. The others struggled after him.

Pain the ordeal inflicted—burning thighs, aching lungs, a throbbing rush of blood pounding his head, leaden arms pumping for balance—he dammed behind a firewall of single-minded focus: *I cannot fail, because I will not quit.*

When he reached the summit, he allowed himself a moment of respite as he bounced lightly on his toes, shaking feeling into his arms, hands and fingers as he did a slow, 360-degree turn, capturing all of Phoenix and the surrounding desert displayed below him.

He made the run four more times that spring, accompanied by different companions each time. No one else suffered the torment more than once.

Despite his hard work, as spring wound down, Conor fully expected his release. Which was okay. He was a pitcher again. He'd reclaim his job at the Filoli Estate. He'd throw balls against his wall. He'd play at Golden Gate Park. Someone would find him.

Tuttle, though, told him he'd be going to West Haven.

"Charlie Finley is a cheap bastard," Tuttle explained with a shrug. "We need another lefthander."

Not exactly a ringing endorsement.

Tuttle added, "I'll give you a chance."

He got a start the season's first week. His warmup felt fine, but his first game pitch flew a foot above the strike zone.

Focus, dammit!

He felt panic rising with each subsequent delivery of a four-pitch walk. He stepped off the mound, rubbing furiously at the baseball, staring into center field. *You are a pitcher. You can beat anyone here. Relax and do what you've done all your life.* Although he didn't win the game, he found positives in his progress. Rather than berating himself for his failures, Conor became his own biggest fan. He embraced and cheered every step as he rebuilt his confidence.

Although he didn't see much game action, every bullpen session he threw provided a step forward, until finally, he took the mound during a blowout that July, realizing the yips had become an afterthought. Now, he needed to prove the truth of Conor Nash.

He'd driven to the ballpark early and taken the long walk from the clubhouse to Tuttle's Airstream trailer parked by the right field foul pole where he confronted Tuttle concerning his lack of playing time.

"Fred, you told me you'd give me a chance to pitch. But you've had me buried for—"

"Yeah," his manager said, "because you suck."

Conor came to this meeting determined to rationally plead his case. Tuttle's curt judgement blew the doors off that plan. "Fuck you, I don't suck. Any more than anyone on this team sucks. We've lost ninety games, and I've pitched in damn few of 'em! Everybody sucks!"

"Including you!" Tuttle yelled back.

"Twice I've gone twenty-one days without pitching. What kind of performance do you expect under those circumstances?"

The argument deteriorated from there.

Finally, Tuttle said, "All right, fucker, I'll give you the ball. And you'd better damn well be ready to take it!"

Tuttle proved true to his word. The next night, he summoned Conor with no outs and bases loaded in the ninth inning, at which time the White Caps held a rare 3-2 lead.

Gee, thanks, Fred.

Conor threw three fastballs past his first hitter. The next batter hit a towering pop up. Conor's catcher handled it at the backstop.

Two gone. Just throw the shit out of the ball. The third batter flailed at a fastball. Adrenalin coursing, Conor humped up to bleed a couple more miles per hour from his arm and watched with horror as the little comet cut to the heart of the plate. The sound of bat on ball told him everything. The runner at third came skipping and clapping home, the player who would score the winning run dashing close behind.

With sinking stomach, Conor turned to watch his centerfielder begin a futile chase. *Headed straight toward the fence*... The batter had hit it so hard, though, the ball's topspin caused it to sink... *at least it will stay in the park*... The outfielder made a final, desperate leap at the warning track, his body fully extended, head craned back over his shoulder and . . . *Oh, my Good Lord, he caught the fucking ball!*

THE 1980 WEST HAVEN WHITE CAPS WERE THE ARMPIT OF Oakland's farm system. The A's themselves were no prize, having finished the 1979 season sporting a 54-108 record, worst in the Majors. The White Caps 1980 season record was a miserable 47 and 92. Our opponents outscored us by two hundred and nineteen runs.

Suffering through his last throes of ownership, Charlie Finley tried everything possible to move or sell the Oakland franchise and save every dime as he did so. The White Caps actually wore blue hats that clashed spectacularly with the garish hand-me-down green and gold uniforms Finley sent us.

At first, Kate was excited about going there. She knew about Yale University, and she envisioned a serene campus setting. We didn't realize while spring semester was still in session, every decent apartment would be taken. A place in a slum is all we could find. She cried when we moved in. It didn't help that she had to stay there alone the first week while the team left for a road trip.

We played home games at Quigley Stadium, built in 1947. The bleachers were some kind of war surplus and by 1980, were so badly rotted that big blocks of seating were closed. The outfield light standards stood inside the field of play, just waiting to coldcock any outfielder who might forget they were there.

Our manager was known as Singin' Fred Tuttle, because he liked karaoke. He called a team meeting about a month into the season, and we figured he'd ream us for being so bad. Instead, he told us he was singing that night at the fish place across the street, *and he expected us there. Most everybody showed up, and Fred, who had an extraordinary voice, performed three Sinatra songs, then went back to his Airstream.*

Finley's cost-cutting caught up to us that August when an outfielder wrecked his knee. We waited a week for the organization to send a replacement who never appeared. Our roster dwindled as injuries sidelined a couple more guys and, finally, the White Caps ran out of position players.

"They gotta send us someone, don't they?" infielder Marco Slagel asked Conor.

"Well, yeah. I mean, we have to finish the season."

"Besides pitchers, we've only got seven guys to play defense tonight," an outfielder said. "Somebody's gotta do something."

Catcher Darryl Clay volunteered. "I can do a rain dance."

"What qualifies you to do a rain dance?" Conor asked.

"I have Native-American lineage."

"And you can make it rain?"

"Well . . . what's the worst that could happen?"

Darryl said he needed two things—a tomahawk and a full headdress.

"What kind of headdress?"

"You know, like Indian chiefs in movies."

"What about a feather and a headband? Tonto just wears a feather and a headband."

Darryl remained adamant about the headdress.

They found a tomahawk easily enough. Conor and Marco located a hardware store, bought a cheap hatchet, and dressed it up with some ribbon and a couple of feathers from a pigeon nest near the right field fence. Finding a headdress proved more problematic.

An hour before game time, Conor finally located a costume

shop across town and snuck away during infield practice. He returned as Darryl walked toward the plate to handle our starter's warm-up pitches.

"Hey, Darryl!" Conor shouted as he raised the headdress.

Darryl grinned and dropped his mask at home plate. "Give me a minute," he said to the umpire.

He put on the headdress and trotted back to the plate. There, he raised the hatchet high in one hand and his catchers' mitt in the other. He began bouncing from foot to foot while twirling slowly and emitting a sing-song chant.

The crowd of four hundred initially offered curious applause. The faster Darryl whirled and chanted, though, and the more viciously he waved his hatchet, the more they got into it. Soon everyone in the place chanted along with Darryl.

In fairness, the sky was already overcast. Still . . .

"Tuttle, what the fuck is . . ." The home plate umpire stood scowling, mask in hand.

Tuttle rose to the top step, then went no further. At that moment, a few fat raindrops began to pound dimples onto the infield dirt.

The crowd screamed its approval. Daryl stopped for a moment, looked skyward, threw back his head and gave a mighty war cry. His bouncing and whirling gained renewed enthusiasm. Chanting filled the stadium. The heavens opened.

With his headdress drenched and sagging down the sides of his face, a grinning Darryl Clay retreated to the dugout.

"Told'ja," he said.

twenty

H AVING PRODUCED A MIRACLE THE NIGHT BEFORE and the weather forecast calling for sunny skies, Darryl didn't want to press his luck. So, the White Caps found no reprieve.

"Conman, I'm gonna need you to start tonight," Tuttle said.

As the season wound down, Conor was no longer an afterthought. Tuttle gave him regular work. His fastball dominated. The curveball and change-up continued their improvement. Conor hadn't expected a start, though.

"Great! What happened to Keith?"

Keith Abelard, the White Caps' ace, if a team claiming only forty-seven wins could be said to have an ace, was scheduled.

"Nothing. He's pitching. I need you to start in left field."

"Left field?"

"Hey, it's not because I don't value you as a pitcher. And it's not because the organization doesn't care if you get hurt. Well, maybe that's partly it, since they didn't pay you a signing bonus, but I've watched you shag during batting practice. You're the pitcher most likely to actually catch a fly ball. And you can run a little bit."

"Gee, I don't know, Fred..."

"Look, Conman, I need you. I'm forty-one years old, for Chrissake, and I'm gonna be the designated hitter."

So, for three of the final four games of the 1980 season, Conor played left field and hit ninth, behind Tuttle.

"Got any advice?" Conor asked Dodd Morris, who played center.

"Yeah. Don't run into a light pole and don't run into me."

Like every pitcher who'd ever played, Conor considered himself a hitter. He went zero for eight at the plate, though, his only success a walk during his second game.

Like many left-handed pitchers, Conor hit from the right side to protect his throwing arm. He stood in the on-deck circle for his second at-bat of the season's penultimate game, studying a left-hander on the mound. As he approached the plate, though, the opposing manager called to the bullpen for a righty.

Conor stepped into the batter's box. The pitcher fired a fastball Conor couldn't touch.

"Streeeee!" screamed the umpire.

Conor stared at the label on his Louisville Slugger, and figured, *what the hell*. He walked behind the umpire and catcher and resumed his at-bat left-handed.

The umpire raised his mask to his forehead. "What are you doing?"

"If I bat left-handed, my baseball card will have to say I'm a switch hitter."

Tuttle out-performed Conor offensively by managing one

hit. Batting in the ninth inning of a tie game, he dribbled a twelve-hopper through the infield, thus setting the stage for a storied moment in West Haven White Caps history.

Conor stepped to the plate. The pitcher's offering skipped past the catcher. Tuttle jogged to second. The next pitch was too wide for the catcher to get a glove on. Tuttle chugged into third.

Visions of a game-winning RBI danced in Conor's head. He swung and missed. He stepped from the batter's box, gathering his focus. The next pitch darted toward his knee. He dodged backward. The ball tipped the catcher's glove and caromed along the backstop, where it hugged the fence like a hockey puck skidding along the boards behind the goal.

The first baseman and pitcher sprinted after the ball.

"Come on, Fred!" Conor screamed and waved frantically.

Tuttle broke for the plate.

"Yeah, Fred! You got it!"

Fred didn't have it. Two-thirds of the way home he collapsed, landing spread-eagle on the foul line.

"Aaaagghhhh," he screamed, and grabbed at his right leg. "Hamstring! Hamstring!"

The ball continued its roll.

"Get up, Fred," Conor implored. "Get up!"

Tuttle rose to one knee, planted his right foot, then fell again. Still holding his bat, Conor ran along the baseline in foul territory where he stood, waving his bat like a curler sweeping his broom to smooth the ice.

"You can make it! You can make it!"

Tuttle began scooting along, somewhere between a slither and a crawl, his right leg dragging behind him.

"You're almost there, Fred! Keep going. We're gonna win! We're gonna . . ."

Tuttle's final collapse left his outstretched arm inches from the plate. The catcher received the ball from the first baseman and reached for the tag

"Yerrrout!" screamed the umpire.

"Mother fucker," wheezed Tuttle.

AS A REWARD FOR HIS WILLINGNESS TO PLAY OUTFIELD, Tuttle granted Conor the season's final start against Buffalo, a team headed to the Eastern League playoffs. Conor allowed one run and pitched a complete game for the win. Kate vaulted the railing along the third baseline and hugged him.

"You're back!" She grinned.

"Well," Conor said, "I'll be back somewhere. I don't think I figure into the A's plans, though. My numbers for this year are pretty bad."

She kissed him, and repeated, "You're back."

Conor had packed most of his stuff. He only needed to shower. Anxious to get home, they planned to embark on their cross-country journey from the parking lot. As Conor shut the trunk lid, he looked along the right field fence toward Tuttle's Airstream trailer. A light glowed through the windows.

"Give me a minute, Kate," he said. "I need to say thanks to Fred."

Tuttle stood, his back to the door, telephone in hand. "Yeah, let me talk with Walt. Yeah, Conor Nash. He threw great tonight. I know his numbers aren't good. That's mostly my fault. I misjudged this young man. I didn't give him a chance."

Conor slipped beside the door and leaned against the trailer.

Tuttle fell quiet for a moment, listening to A's Farm Director Walt Jocketty.

"No," Tuttle said. "We should keep him. I've watched how he's handled this all year. He worked his ass off. Nash deserves another shot. Yeah. Thanks, Walt. I appreciate it."

Conor stepped into the shadows and headed for the parking lot.

"You're right," he said to Kate, opening the drivers' side door and sliding inside. "I'm back."

They headed west, towards home.

I pitched at Golden Gate Park, this time playing for Marino Paretti's team. Aunti Di regarded it as a betrayal. About halfway through the season, though, she came to accept my choice, although she and Marino still screamed at each other every game.

Financially, we were against the wall. We lived with Kate's parents that winter. I worked mornings at the Filoli estate. Kate started a house-cleaning business. I mopped and swept and scrubbed during afternoons. At night, I supervised bingo games at a Senior Center for the Parks and Recreation Department.

Although Conor felt comforted by Tuttle's recommendation, he still held his breath each time their phone rang. Typical of Charlie Finley, the A's existed in a constant state of flux. Anyone might be gone tomorrow.

The call came on a January afternoon.

"Conor, it's for you," Kate's mom said.

"Conman? This is Walt Jocketty."

Conor's heart sank. A call like this in January couldn't possibly be anything except . . .

"Charlie hired Billy Martin today, and Billy wants to see all our left-handed pitchers. So, we're bringing you to big league camp. We'll re-sign you to a double-A gig and see what happens."

"I'm . . . what?"

"So, are you driving again? I got a note here from one of

Norm Kisulke's old files that you got room to carry some equipment."

And there they were, Rita—a few more critical threads stitched into this ever-more unlikely tapestry: Billy Martin, a guy named Gordon Schuller, and a diabolical, life-changing pitch called the screwball.

Scottsdale, Arizona
1981

MAJOR LEAGUE CAMP CONVENED EARLIER THAN MINOR *League camp. Uniforms were newer, the food better, and the meal money a godsend. Major League camp is restricted to players on the forty-man big-league roster and non-roster invitees. For this camp Billy Martin invited every left-hander he could find.*

Most of the invitees stayed at a cut-rate minor league motel.

I was napping just after noon when the sound of Susan Lucci screaming at her half-sister, and the acrid smell of marijuana smoke, woke me. I rolled over to see a blond-haired surfer-looking guy sitting cross-legged on the other bed, wearing jockey shorts and sucking at a bong.

"Gordon Schuller," he rasped without exhaling. "Nice to meet you."

"Um . . . same here."

Gordon expelled a blue cloud and raised the bong. "You mind?"

"Um . . . no."

"Right on." He drew deeply from the bong. "You watch All My Children?"

I nodded. Most baseball players watch All My Children because most baseball players have nothing else to do early each afternoon.

"I can't believe," Gordon said, "that Erica's hiding out as a nun!"

Gordon and I never pitched during a game that spring. Never. Not once. All we did was toss batting practice to the Major Leaguers and throw in the bullpen.

When minor league camp started, we thought we were screwed. Everyone there competed for a place on one of the teams. Martin sent the other left-handed invitees down. Finally, only a week remaining before the season started, Martin called us over. He hadn't said a word to us all spring.

"I kept you guys here because our hitters tell me you two throw the best BP," Martin said. "I appreciate your patience. I know you're probably wondering about making a team once we break camp. Don't worry about it. Schuller, you'll be our fourth starter at Double A. Nash, you're the fifth starter. It's all arranged."

twenty-one

West Haven A's
1981
Double A Baseball

"Mark Brouhard says you're a good pitcher and a good guy."

Bob Didier, at thirty-one the youngest manager Conor had ever encountered, had met Mark the previous year when he'd worked in the Milwaukee system. Brouhard's career skyrocketed when the Rule Five Draft sent him from the Angels to Milwaukee, where he spent the 1980 season with the Brewers.

"Billy says to give you a chance," Didier continued. "So, you're a starter. Show me something."

The West Haven White Caps, so miserable the year before, were history. They'd been renamed West Haven A's. Sixteen guys from that 1981 roster eventually played in the majors. Conor Nash had the opportunity to be a solid contributor on a good team.

So did Gordon Schuller. Sporting a mediocre eighty-two mile-per-hour fastball, Gordon, whom the Giants released the year before, consistently struck out eight to ten hitters every game. In particular, right-handed hitters struggled against him, which made no sense at all.

"What are you doing with that change-up thing you're throwing," Conor finally asked his roommate.

"It's not a change-up," Gordon said. "It's a screwball."

I like talking about the physics of baseball. Explaining to Kate's co-workers at Christmas parties why curveballs, sliders, fastballs and, yes, screwballs, do what they do is fun.

I don't know where the name screwball comes from. Like many baseball terms, its etymology lies buried in the pre-historic mists of our sport. I call it that because if I throw it right, you're screwed.

Conor raised his bottle and whispered a toast to the screwball.

The physics lecture, Rita, goes like this: the natural rotation imparted to a baseball thrown by a right-handed pitcher causes the ball to move away from a right-handed hitter. Same for lefty against lefty.

One reason hitting a baseball is so difficult is because any object thrown with considerable velocity at your head scares the crap out of anyone who has even a shred of common sense. A curveball or a slider thrown by a right-handed pitcher to a right-handed hitter leaves the pitcher's hand along a perceived trajectory to impact some part of the hitter's body. The hitter's primordial fight-or-flight instinct tells him to duck. He has only fractions of a second to decide whether this is, indeed, a curveball that will break harmlessly away from him and into the strike zone, or whether it's a fastball that might kill him.

Managers like to send left-handed hitters against right-handed pitchers, and vice-versa. With this matchup, because the ball does not threaten decapitation as it leaves the pitcher's hand, the hitter has precious extra fractions of a second to decide that he is safe and can hit this ball into next week.

Hitters spend their lives trusting this science. Then, along comes a screwball and screws up everything. I think there's a Bible verse, someplace in Leviticus or Deuteronomy, forbidding it as an unnatural act.

As a lefty throwing a curve ball, I rotate my hand with a counterclockwise motion, as God intended. To throw a screwball, I must rotate my hand the opposite way, putting extreme stress on my elbow. Few pitchers even attempt the screwball, much less master it, because their elbows are their friends.

Hitters, however, don't know what to do when a ball moves the opposite direction it's supposed to. Take a lefty who can throw ninety-plus, then arm him with a sixty-five-mile screwball, and you've created all kinds of possibilities.

EACH STARTING PITCHER CHARTED THE PERFORMANCE OF the guy preceding him in the rotation, so Conor charted each of Gordon's outings.

"You've got those guys falling all over themselves," Conor told him as Gordon racked up his strikeouts. A groundball out or a long fly ball might produce the same result. Strikeouts, though, captured the attention of farm directors and GMs.

"Show me one of those," Conor asked Gordon as they played catch between starts. Gordon's offering dove down and in so sharply, Conor didn't get his glove on it. The ball smacked onto the top of his left foot. Visions of Fat Brad's bloody teeth danced in Conor's head.

"Will you teach me?"

"Okay," Gordon said, "here's the first rule. From now on when you open a door, turn the doorknob the opposite way."

Right-handed people turn doorknobs clockwise. Left-handed

people turn them counterclockwise. This is the natural order of the universe. From that moment on, Conor Nash violated this rule. And, just as he'd thrown baseballs against a wall with single-minded purpose since second grade, Conor became obsessive about doorknobs. When confronting a doorknob, he seldom contented himself to twist it once and walk through. He counted three or four or five turns, as the person behind him—usually Kate—anticipated the actual opening of the door with the first turn and ran into him.

At parties, or waiting to be seated at a restaurant, Conor backed himself to a door, reached his left hand behind him, and twisted the doorknob with a vengeance.

"What are you doing?" Kate would ask.

"Nothing."

"Yes, you are. You're doing the doorknob thing. Stop it. People think you're weird enough as it is."

Conor worked on his screwball every day as he played catch before games. He integrated it into his bullpen routine. Finally, he began to get the movement he wanted, though the ball seldom came anywhere close to the plate.

"Try it in a game," Gordon told him.

"I can't," Conor said, recalling the hell he'd put his catchers through when he suffered the yips. "I don't think I can get it close enough for Darryl to catch it."

"Ask him about it. Darryl's good at blocking stuff. Sooner or later, you're gonna have to do it."

The next evening, Conor worked a no-ball two-strike count facing Buffalo's clean-up hitter. The A's held a five-run lead. *So why not?*

Darryl asked for a curve ball. Conor nodded—the prearranged signal that he'd try and make the ball go the other way.

Conor knew when it left his hand the ball wouldn't reach home plate. It dove down and into the hitter, as Conor intended, but it bounced a good twelve inches short. It landed hard and caromed off Darryl's chest protector.

But the guy swung at it! He missed it by at least two feet, then dragged his bat to the dugout, muttering and glaring at Conor the whole way.

An inning later, Conor threw a screwball again and produced the same result. The ball smacked short of of home plate, bounced high, and the hitter almost fell over swinging at it.

"We'll call it your drop-rise," Darryl told Conor. "First, it hits the ground, and they miss it on the bounce."

KATE AND I HEADED HOME FOLLOWING THE '81 SEASON, comfortable that an Oakland job waited for us. And for the first time, I'd get paid for pitching during the winter.

"Bob Didier is managing a team in Mazatlan and he asked me to go," Conor told Kate.

"In Mexico? All winter?"

"Two months. They'll pay me fifteen hundred a month."

Kate was pregnant. They would miss each other. Considering they'd made only six thousand for the whole of last season, though, the money seemed too good to pass up.

Their separation didn't last as long as they'd anticipated. Kate received his call a month later.

"They released me," he said.

"I thought you were pitching well."

"I was. They fired Bob, though. And I'm the guy he brought with him, so they fired me, too. I'm leaving for the airport now. My flight lands at ten."

"Senor Conman! Senor Conman!" shouted someone behind him. A man he recognized as some sort of team official trotted toward him.

"Aqui esta su dinero." The man handed Conor a stack of U.S. hundred-dollar bills.

"Um . . . gracias?"

On the taxi ride, he counted two thousand dollars.

They gave me two thousand dollars to go away! When the Angels released me, I didn't even get a bus ticket. So, I spent the rest of that winter pitching for Marino at Golden Gate Park, throwing screwball after screwball, trying to master a pitch that would rescue my career.

twenty-two

Scottsdale, Arizona
Spring Training
1982

"JOHN WAYNE IS A HORSE-SHIT ACTOR."

Darryl Clay sat across the dinner table from Conor, his statement the next salvo of a day-long argument.

"How can you say that?" Conor demanded for the twelfth time. John Wayne held god-like status in the Nash household. Hugh Nash revered the Duke and preached Wayne's celluloid divinity to each of his sons. "He won an Oscar, for Chrissake!"

"The Oscar was a sympathy thing because he was dying. John Wayne couldn't act his way out of a paper bag!"

Conor pointed his index finger. "I'm tired of this. You disparage John Wayne one more time, Darryl, and I'm gonna come across this table!"

Conor and Gordon Schuller were assigned to Major League camp for Spring Training of 1982, again a part of Billy Martin's ongoing search for left-handers. And, like the year before, they roomed at the minor league motel.

Which was fine with them because they were on a major

league schedule, making major league meal money. They threw bullpens early, completed their workouts, and could play golf the rest of the day. Charlie Finley had sold the A's during the off season, and the new owners didn't pinch pennies. Each player in major league camp received a hundred and fifty dollars meal money per day—a veritable fortune for minor leaguers who earned a thousand dollars a month for the six-month season.

Conor and Gordon both sent the meal money home to their wives and ate at the Ramada Inn. The motel provided players a buffet spread in a room adjacent to the main restaurant where civilians dined.

Darryl folded his arms across his chest, gave Conor an *I-dare-you* glare, and said with exaggerated deliberation, "John Wayne Is A Horse-Shit Actor."

Conor measured the distance across the table. He looked at his plate, scooped a handful of mashed potatoes, and flung the glob into Darryl's face. "Say it again, and I'll stick asparagus up your nose."

Darryl, temporarily blinded, groped for his meatloaf, missed Conor and hit the guy next to him. The battle was on. A room full of minor league baseball players emptied their plates, then scrambled for the buffet table to reload and began pelting anyone who crossed their path. Including the motel manager as he ran screaming into the room, threatening dire consequences. This meat and vegetable mayhem extended for ten minutes, until the buffet table ran out of ammunition.

The main restaurant patrons held front row seats. Some of the children cheered before their horrified parents squelched them.

As he walked to his room, plastered with supper, his head tilted to one side while he thumped gravy from his ear, Conor felt pretty sure he was in trouble.

"I WANT EVERY MOTHER-FUCKING MINOR LEAGUE GUY ON the third baseline right now!" Billy Martin's angry voice rang through the empty stadium.

Conor, Darryl and others tentatively withdrew from the group stretching ritual that began workouts each day. Exchanging sheepish glances, they made their way towards the infield.

"Now!" Martin screamed.

The collective mosey became a sprint.

They formed a neat row, shoulder to shoulder, toes touching the chalked foul line, Conor and Darryl separated by three guys.

"Who started it?"

They met Martin's demand silently. No one wanted to rat out a teammate. On the other hand, Conor didn't want everybody punished for something he'd instigated. He leaned to look at Darryl. Darryl returned a grim stare. *Okay, if you go, I'll go, but I'm not . . .*

And Darryl deked him. Darryl gave a little twitch, the slightest twist of his shoulder. Conor took a big step forward.

Martin was immediately in his face. "You started this?"

"Well, yeah."

Darryl did the right thing. He stepped forward. "Me, too."

Martin skewered them with a glare, said, "In . . . my . . . office . . ." and stomped away.

"Shit," Darryl said as they walked together. "We'll get released for sure."

They followed a dozen paces behind Martin into a building housing the executive offices. They entered a foyer with chairs along one wall. Martin pointed to the chairs. Conor and Darryl sat. Conor's chair stood directly facing the door marked *Manager*. Darryl chose a chair off to one side. Martin opened the door, entered, then closed it again, giving Conor a clear view of Martin's desk.

Conor smiled, turned to Darryl, and said, "You are fucked."

"What do you mean?"

"You are soooo fucked."

"You're just as fucked as I am."

"No, I'm not."

"Yes, you are."

"No, I'm not. Trust me."

Martin opened the door and waggled a finger, summoning them inside. "Wait here. I'll be right back."

As they entered, Darryl gasped. His shoulders sagged. His face drained of color. On the wall directly behind Martin's desk was an almost life-sized oil painting of John Wayne. Hanging next to the painting, a framed eleven by fourteen photo of Billy Martin and John Wayne. Conor made a slow, three-hundred-and-sixty-degree turn. Atop a cadenza along the wall sat a pair of boots, autographed by John Wayne. A rifle mounted in a wood and glass display hung on the opposite wall, the rifle's stock inscribed with a flowing script: *To my great friend, Billy. The Duke.*

Darryl turned to Conor, his eyes begging.

And Conor decided he couldn't volunteer the information. That would sound too much like whining, or tattling. If Martin asked, though . . . well, he couldn't lie, could he?

Martin ripped into them with a vengeance. How could they be so stupid? This wasn't some locker room prank. Civilians had been present. Didn't they realize they represented a Major League Baseball organization and not the slipshod, cut-rate carnival show operated by Charlie Finley.

"This is bullshit! I don't care what started it! Nothing excuses..."

Conor's heart pounded. He saw relief flow through Darryl's face. Conor said a silent prayer. *Ask me. Please, please just ask me.*

"... I don't even want to know... Fuck. Yes, I do. What stupid, fucked-up reason would you—"

Conor pointed at Darryl. "He called John Wayne a horseshit actor."

Martin's tirade screeched to a halt, eyes wide and unblinking. His mouth formed a neat O, as if he'd been told gravity was only an illusion, or God didn't make little green apples. Silence draped the office like a shroud until Martin finally pulled himself together.

"Excuse me?"

"He said John Wayne was a horseshit actor. He'd been saying it all day, and it really pissed me off. He must have said it twenty times. Finally, when he said it while we were eating, I was gonna punch him, but I couldn't reach all the way across the table. So, I hit him with my potatoes."

Once again, silence descended. Conor wasn't sure anyone was even breathing.

Martin again struggled to find his voice. "I... I can't even... In the first place, what would ever possess you to think John Wayne was a horseshit actor?" He looked at Conor through imploring eyes, as if he might find the answer there.

"Yeah, Darryl," Conor said. "Why would you think that?"

Darryl opened his mouth and wheezed a couple of times. He found no words.

"Nash," Martin said, "get out of my office."

Conor did not hesitate. He hurried away, leaving Darryl to his fate.

During the next afternoon's game, Conor watched Darrel run along the outfield warning track from foul pole to foul pole. Twenty times.

Both Darryl and I continued our employment with the A's. And Gordon and I continued throwing batting practice. Miraculously, though, following my defense of John Wayne, Martin granted me an inning during a morning B game—a game not on the official spring training schedule.

At every step of Martin's managing career, Art Fowler served as Billy's pitching coach and sidekick. Art was a Louisiana good-ol'-boy who matched Billy drink-for-drink in bars all across America. He'd noticed my bullpens, had complimented my fastball and the weird little change-up I'd developed, and decided I deserved a look-see during actual competition.

Spring Training, consisting of two or three weeks of workouts followed by a months' worth of baseball games, exists primarily for pitchers. Hitters and position players need a couple of weeks to get ready. Pitchers, however, must be brought along slowly. Occasional B games are arranged, because scheduled games don't provide enough innings for us to get the work we need.

The remainder of the B squad is typically a mixture of minor league prospects and major league vets who feel they need some extra at-bats. Occupying the opposite dugout this day was a group from the Giants—the team I'd dreamed of playing for as a kid.

Fowler attended—a surprise because he didn't rise early, having spent most evenings drinking until one or two in the morning with Billy.

Given these circumstances—Fowler, the pressure of a single inning to impress everyone and playing against the Giants—I surprised myself by remaining relatively calm. Until, as I finished my warmups, I looked into the outfield. I spotted Martin himself, trudging along the warning track towards the farthest reach of center field. Very likely hung over, Billy walked deliberately, eyes hidden behind sunglasses, head down, hands tucked into his back pockets until he reached the 408-foot sign high on the green padding of the outfield wall. Once arrived, he put his back against the fence and, ever so slowly, slid to a sitting position. He leaned his head into the padding, sunshine bathing his face.

Okay, the manager's watching. Maybe. Who knows what's happening behind those sunglasses. Maybe he's asleep?

CONOR DID HIS BEST NOT EVEN TO SEE HITTERS. He narrowed his vision to the catcher's glove, so the batter became only an indistinct presence. That accomplished, he took a deep breath, tried to dismiss Fowler and Martin from his mind, and see only the single index finger catcher Mike Heath extended.

Ball one. *Okay, focus.* Ball two. *Relax, dammit!* Ball three. *Shit. Don't walk the first . . .* Ball four! *Fuck, fuck, fuck, fuck, fuck! Ok. Start over. Check the runner. Throw over? No, I walked him on four straight pitches. He'll wait to see if I can throw a strike before he tries to steal. Deep breath.* Ball one. Ball two. Ball three. Ball four. *And here comes Fowler. Well, no one's warming up yet, so I should get at least a couple more hitters.*

Art Fowler walked with a fat-man's side-to-side roll. He displayed a bulbous drinker's nose and spoke from somewhere way down south. As he reached the mound, Heath and the infielders arrived as well.

"Ah don' need you otha' fellas heah," Fowler grumbled. The infielders dispersed, leaving only Conor and his catcher. Conor waited for a demand to *throw strikes*. Instead, Fowler unlimbered his thick neck with a little crick from side to side.

"Ah got home 'bout two-clock this mawnin," he said. "My wife's waitin' and she says, *Yew been out drinkin' with Billy, ain't ya?* I told 'er I was, and she said, *how much money yew spend?* I thought 'bout it, and I told 'er, *Oh, 'bout two hundred dolla.* So, she says, *Yew know how long it'd take me to spend two hundred dolla?* I thought 'bout it fo' a minute and I said, *Well, ya don't drink ... and ya don't smoke ... and ya got ya' own pussy ... so, I guess two hundred dolla' last yew just 'bout ferever.*"

Conor and Heath nearly fell over laughing as Fowler waddled away.

Conor struck out the next two hitters, then induced an infield pop-up for the final out.

"GUESS WHAT?" CONOR WALKED INTO THE WEST HAVEN apartment and wrapped his arms around his very pregnant wife.

"Okay. What?"

"No, no. Guess."

"You saw some woman naked—who wasn't fat and pregnant."

"No, of course not."

"A.J. and Basil and Brad are visiting and you're gonna get beat up in a bar fight."

"Nope. Better."

"Hmmmmmmm. No. No. Not Tacoma?"

Conor grinned.

"Gotta be there day after tomorrow."

Kate jumped, as best she could, fisted her hands above her head, and cheered. It didn't matter that she must pack the apartment and drive a Chevy Cavalier cross-country by herself—a week-long process. They were going to Triple-A!

Tacoma, Washington
Triple A Baseball
1982

FRED TUTTLE WELCOMED CONOR ENTHUSIASTICALLY, inserted him immediately into the Tacoma Tigers starting rotation, and Conor sucked. His fastball got hit. He didn't throw the screwball with any conviction and his curveball stunk because Conor devoted his bullpen time to the screwball.

"I wanted Triple-A too much," he told Fat Brad by phone following his second start. Once again, he'd been knocked all over the park.

"I thought the screwball was working," Brad said.

"Well, at Double-A it was. I don't know, these are Triple-A hitters, and I'd get behind and, well, I just didn't want to throw it."

"Wait a minute," Brad said, "most of these guys were Double-A hitters last season or the year before, You got them out then."

"Yeah—"

"They didn't turn into Superman because they moved to Tacoma. Trust your stuff."

Kate arrived two days after his second start. They unpacked into the apartment Conor had leased. Kate loved the cool Northwest weather. She loved that they were on the West Coast and closer to home.

She didn't make the Vancouver trip for Conor's third start.

"I pitched much better," he told her during his post-game phone call. "The screwball was working. I didn't win, but my numbers were good. Oh, wait, I've gotta go. Fred wants to see me."

"Conman, we're sending you back to West Haven. You're not ready. I know you pitched good tonight. To stay here, though, you had to pitch good three nights. So, I don't want you to feel like you didn't get a fair chance."

Conor stood in the visiting manager's cubicle. Everything about the place was dreary and grey.

"No, Ed. You gave me an opportunity and I blew it."

"Go to West Haven and take care of business. You've got the ability to pitch here. You're just not ready."

Conor plodded into the locker room, out to a hallway running under the grandstands, and the pay phone.

"Back to West Haven?" Kate asked, her voice quavering. "Conor, I... I can't do all that again... pack up and drive three thousand miles. I'm sorry. I just can't"

"I know. It's August. The season's almost over, and then we've got playoffs. I'll be done in a month. Go home and have a baby. I'll do my best to get there."

twenty-three

CONOR HAD BEEN ON THE MOUNTAIN FOR HOURS. He didn't know for sure what the time was, but he'd started his climb about three that afternoon. Now a grey dusk spread shadows across the valley below. He enjoyed a pleasant buzz and with a half bottle of champagne left, wasn't concerned about the passage of time.

I really sweated it when West Haven made the 1982 playoffs. The last thing I wanted was Kate giving birth without me. On her due date I started the opening game of the Eastern League Championship series against the Lynn Sailors.

Turns out I shouldn't have worried. She remained pregnant until I got home two weeks later, and then two more weeks after that.

As each day passed, Kate became more prone to snarling. Entirely too many people were patting her stomach and saying how much pregnancy became her.

"The apple will fall when it's red," an elderly aunt told her day after bloated day.

"This frickin' apple is so red, it's purple," she said. "And I'm gonna strangle the next person who touches my tummy!"

Jessica's birth occurred a full month late. Kate swore the baby must have weighed north of twenty pounds.

Conor enjoyed the complications of fatherhood but he could not escape a growing anxiety as Spring Training neared without an invitation to major league camp. Even though he screwed the pooch at Triple-A, his West Haven performance had been outstanding. He'd walked only sixty-four batters while striking out a hundred and fifty-four. The yips had died a lingering death while the screwball matured. He'd established himself as a starter.

This, however, was a different A's organization.

Young talent drafted when Martin and Jocketty took over began to mature. The A's didn't need an endless parade of lefties for Martin's perusal. At twenty-seven, no longer a young man in baseball years, Conor didn't know where, or if, he fit into Oakland's plans.

As, so often the case throughout his career, though, he performed best when his survival was at stake.

Having put polishing touches on the screwball during his winter appearances at Golden Gate Park, he tore up Spring Training. He cherished the day Billy Martin strolled through the minor league workouts and watched Conor throw batting practice.

"I need work on off-speed stuff," the hitter told Conor. "Give me a few of those changeup things you've been throwing."

Conor obliged. The hitter whiffed at four straight deliveries and said with a sheepish smile and a shake of his head, "That's a pretty good pitch."

"Ya' think?" Martin said, leaning against the turtle behind

the batter. "You knew it was coming, and you still couldn't hit it."

As Conor left the mound, Martin waved him over.

"That pitch looks a lot like a screwball," he said.

"Yeah, I've been working on it."

"Well, Conman, keep working. That thing's gonna make you some money."

Conor's high slumped to a corresponding low the morning rosters were released, and he found himself West Haven-bound for a fifth straight season.

"Here's the thing," he told Gordon Schuller, who'd been elevated to Tacoma, "I'm twenty-seven years old. I'm like an actor who gets typecast. They only see me as the Double-A guy."

He discovered the truth of that statement a week before the A's broke camp when Walt Jocketty summoned him.

Scottsdale, Arizona
Spring Training
1983

"First thing I want to make clear," Jocketty told Conor, "is how much we respect the effort you've given us. Everybody in the organization, Bob Didier, Fred Tuttle, hell, even Billy, says you're a good man with talent."

Conor's knees felt a little wobbly. Jocketty's statement sounded like a preamble to release if Conor had ever heard one.

"It's not that we don't want you, because we do. It's a matter of space. Since Charlie sold the club, we've been doing a better job of stocking the minors. We have a lot of hot young lefties at A ball who'll be knocking on the double-A door pretty quick this season. And at the same time, you're bumping up against some real good lefthanders above you."

If they kept Conor at this point, Jocketty explained, a mid-season release was probably inevitable.

"So..."

So, Conor picked up the thread mentally, *you're releasing me now with a few days left in Spring Training when everyone else's rosters are set and there's no way I'll find a job?*

"... we sold you to Detroit."

"Um... say what?"

"We sold you to Detroit. A guy over there is a friend of mine, and we talked yesterday."

The Detroit guy told Jocketty they had a slew of young pitchers at Double-A Birmingham and needed a mature lefthander to solidify that group.

"I told him I knew just the guy. So, we sold you to Detroit."

"Sold me? How much did you get for *me*?"

"A hundred dollars." Then he added quickly, "That's no reflection on you. It's the standard price for a transaction like this."

Conor wasn't sure what to say. After all, they could've released him and been done with it. He couldn't, however, keep his disappointment from showing.

"Hey," Jocketty said. "You've still got a uniform."

Conor stood and extended his hand. "You're right. And I appreciate it. Everyone here has been fair. I've learned a lot."

*Jocketty reached to take the offered hand.

Conor turned to go.

"There's one other thing," Jocketty said.

"Yeah?"

"Remember Charlie's orange baseballs?"

Conor did remember. The season before Conor signed with Oakland, Finley had tried to convince other Major League owners that baseballs should be orange. He'd argued that fans could see them better and would find the game easier to follow. So, he'd had all these orange baseballs made, and the A's were stuck with thousands of them.

"We thought we'd never get rid of 'em. Turns out, though, now everybody wants some of Finley's orange baseballs as collector's items."

"Okay..." Conor said.

"So, my friend wants a dozen. It's part of the deal."

"A hundred dollars and a dozen orange baseballs?"

"Yeah, and I've got 'em right here. Would you mind delivering them when you get to Florida?"

"They sold you?" Kate's eyes glistened a little. Pregnant again and caring for an infant, Conor sensed that things were beginning to pile up for his wife.

"Yeah."

"Didn't the Civil War resolve all that?"

"Not for baseball."

"Do we get any of the money?"

"No."

"Was it a lot?"

"No."

"You don't want to tell me, do you?"

"A hundred dollars and a dozen baseballs."

Her eyes glistened a little more.

Not once had Kate hinted he should quit. She genuinely loved baseball. True, they were always broke. They lived winters with their parents. They pieced together off-season jobs to achieve any semblance of financial solvency. She seldom complained, though, rarely gave any indication she didn't love this life they shared. But Conor sensed she was on the edge this time.

"I've still got a uniform," he said.

Kate took a deep breath, blinked and found a smile. "Yes. Yes, you do. So where are we going?"

"I'm going to Florida and finish Spring Training. You'll be meeting me in Birmingham."

"Alabama?"

"That's the one."

twenty-four

Birmingham Barons
Double A Baseball
1983

Conor scanned his Savannah, Georgia hotel room, looking for something to break. A mirror offered the most satisfaction, but mirrors were probably expensive.

He needed to break *something*, though. He needed to scream. He needed to curse the baseball angel. He needed to curse himself. And he did yell a couple of times. Without anyone to bear witness, though, a tantrum seemed kind of pointless.

If he had a bat, he could smash a lamp. He could probably afford a lamp. Pitchers didn't have bats, though. He hefted the lamp. Its weighted base made the thing feel awkward in his hand.

With my luck, if I throw it I'll probably tear my rotator cuff.

He slammed it onto the nightstand hard enough to shatter the bulb, casting the room into darkness.

The guy I delivered the orange baseballs to in Florida repeated what Walt told me.

They had a bunch of nineteen and twenty-year-old pitchers. They needed someone with experience, a good clubhouse guy. Walt told him I'd done everything the A's asked. That I understood my role.

Roy Majytka managed Birmingham. He apparently believed my role was to sit. He put me in the bullpen where, once again, I found myself going days at a time without getting the ball. And when I did pitch, I wasn't particularly effective.

I'd invested myself completely in the screwball. As a lefty out of the pen, though, I didn't find many opportunities to use it. The screwball is a weapon wielded primarily by a left hander against right-handed hitters. Bullpen lefties mostly face left-handed batters. My fastball still sizzled, but this wasn't A ball or college. At Double-A, most guys can hit the snot out of a fastball unless you have a second pitch to keep them off balance.

I hadn't pitched for ten days when the Barons arrived in Savannah. Earlier that evening, Roy had called on me to protect a ninth-inning one-run lead.

Everything collapsed around me. I walked the bases loaded. This time, no one rescued me with a funny story. The fourth batter hit a fly ball to our right fielder, scoring the tying run. I walked the fifth batter on a full count to give up the win.

Roy, a tolerant guy who treated his players with respect, didn't chew me out. I saw that he wasn't happy, though. So, I sat in this hotel room, looking for something to break, wondering why my fucking baseball angel had deserted me. Things got worse when the phone rang.

"Gordon Schuller pitched in the majors tonight!" Kate said breathlessly. "I saw it on TV!"

I wanted to feel good for my buddy. I should have gone somewhere and celebrated a good man's realization of the dream we all played for. Gordon's success, though, only underscored my own failure.

"Conor?"

"Yeah, I'm here."

"What's wrong?"

"I stunk tonight. I don't know how much longer they'll keep me."

"Well," Kate said after a brief silence, *"you've stunk before. And trust me, I know how good you really are. You'll live to stink again."*

"CONOR, THIS IS WALT JOCKETTY. HOW'S IT GOING?"

Momentarily surprised, Conor recovered quickly. "Well, this season's been a tough one," he said from the Birmingham apartment.

"Yeah, I saw the minor league reports. You don't seem to be getting a lot of innings. Team's doing well, though."

Indeed. The Barons cruised toward Southern League's first-half title, Conor's ninth-inning disaster only a minor setback.

"The reason I'm calling," Jocketty said, "is to ask if you might be interested in a coaching job."

"SO, YOU WOULDN'T BE PLAYING ANYMORE?" KATE ASKED. "You couldn't do this and then try out for some other team later..."

"No, I'd be finished as a player."

Kate frowned.

"But..." he said, the Savannah disaster fresh in his mind, "I may be done as a player anyway."

Jocketty told Conor the A's would try something new. Instead of a single roving pitching instructor touring minor league franchises, the A's planned to assign each minor league team its own pitching coach. And they wanted young coaches, closer to the players' ages.

"We're impressed by the things you did to improve yourself," Jocketty told him. "We love your work ethic, your approach to team and the game. Those things are what young pitchers need to understand."

Conor's contract provided him the princely sum of $1,100 a month for the six months of the year he played. Jocketty offered $1,500 a month for a full-year's employment. The deal included benefits and greater job security than an itinerant minor league pitcher would ever see. With a second child due by season's end, money and stability weighed ever more heavily on Conor's mind.

"We wouldn't' be packing halfway through a season heading somewhere else," Conor told Kate. "And this might be how I finally make the majors. If this idea works, if other teams adopt it, this first group of young pitching coaches will have an inside track for Major League coaching jobs."

Kate crossed her arms and stared out the window above their kitchen sink. "You said *we*."

"What?"

"You said *we* wouldn't be packing up. I'm the one who packs up and moves. You just kind of show up."

Conor didn't know how to reply. He thought Kate would embrace this new possibility with welcome relief.

"What did you tell them?" Kate asked.

"Well, of course, I said I needed to talk to you."

"When would you go?"

"The short A season started a couple of weeks ago. They want me now."

She took both his hands. "Your goal has always been to *pitch* in the major leagues, not coach there."

Conor felt his stomach churn. *She gave voice to the nagging thing that didn't feel right. Still . . .* "Kate, this is my fifth year of double-A and my third organization. We can hardly even *see* the major leagues from here."

KATE KNEW HER FISCAL FANATICISM SOMETIMES FRUSTRATED Conor. She hoarded their meager income like Scrooge McDuck. She insisted on off-season jobs for both of them, so they at least had *some* money in a savings account.

Deeply religious, Kate did her best to reconcile the sometimes diametrically opposed secular and spiritual worlds in which she lived. She knew when she married that baseball at whatever level it's played is a profane and bawdy carnival. She could only rationalize so much, though. For the first two years of their poverty-stricken marriage, she faithfully recorded each dime they earned, and finally, when they arrived in West Haven, told Conor something must be done.

"We owe God five hundred dollars," she said.

"Well, before we pay God," Conor said, "I think we need to pay the light bill."

"And that's what we do, but it's wrong."

Conor suggested she talk to their priest. Kate showed the priest her record of earnings and was near tears when she said they hadn't found a way to tithe. The cleric hugged her and smiled. "Kate, given the purity of your conscience, I think God will be all right."

And even though they were off the hook with God for the moment, Kate insisted the obligations of wordly debt they were forced to incur, like car payments, must be met promptly and according to the agreement they'd made with the bank.

"When would you get paid?" she asked him. "If you take the coaching job, I mean."

"Well, probably not until the middle of next month."

"You can't do it."

"Why not?"

"Because if you leave now, we won't get next week's check from the Tigers until who knows when. And we've got a car payment due."

"But we could—"

"No, we can't. Let's hang in here a little longer, at least long enough to make the car payment."

She smiled as she saw the relief printed on Conor's face.

The game that evening lasted eighteen innings. Majytka used every pitcher except Conor. As the game ended, a gentle rain began to fall. The shower became a downpour, canceling the following night's game. The Barons would play a doubleheader the final day of the season's first half.

"Conman," the trainer called from across the clubhouse two hours before the first game was to start. "Skip wants you."

Fuck! Conor hoped it wasn't too late to call Jocketty and ask if the coaching job was still available.

Majytka waved Conor into his office, leaned back in an ancient chair that squeaked a protest, then rubbed both eyes with his fists. He pointed at a metal folding chair.

"Conman," he said, leaning forward on both elbows, "I've got a problem."

Okay. Wait . . . he didn't tell me to close the door.

"That sounds kind of like," Conor said tentatively, "your problem is about to become my problem?"

"Yep." He waved toward the clubhouse. "I'm fresh out of arms. With the eighteen innings and now the double-header, I've got no one to start the second game. Ward's gonna start the first one, and I already told him I've got one guy available to relieve him—Moya. Roger Mason was scheduled for the second game. He's sick. That leaves you. And absolutely nobody behind you. If you give it up, I'll see if one of the outfielders can throw strikes. I'm sorry . . ."

"What do you mean, sorry? This is what I've wanted all along."

Majytka smiled the kind of smile that said *I appreciate the sentiment, but we both know the water's over your head here.* "Okay. You got the ball."

"Thanks, Skip. And, for the record, I won't give it up."

As Kate beamed her confidence from her seat behind home plate, Conor threw a complete game shutout, striking out ten.

Majytka summoned him back to the office.

"Wow! You're a totally different pitcher as a starter. I've made a big mistake."

"No problem. You're not the first manager to tell me that."

"Yeah, well, I've gotta make some calls. See if we can get you into the rotation."

Conor grinned and stood to leave.

"Oh, yeah," Majytka said, "I almost forgot. You threw a complete game shutout. You won a suit."

"A suit?"

"Yeah. The men's shop advertised on the right field fence? Any Barons pitcher throws a complete game shutout, they give 'em a suit. I got the certificate right here."

Conor walked out of Majytka's office carrying his certificate.

"You gonna use that?" Outfielder Mark Manchester pointed to his certificate.

"Because if you're not," Manchester continued, "I'm going to a wedding over the break, and I need a suit. I'll give you three hundred dollars for it."

Conor slid into the car and handed Kate three hundred dollars.

"I sold a suit," he said.

"You don't have a suit."

"I know. And I still don't. It's enough money for the car payment."

Kate grinned. "So, do you want to call the A's and go be a coach?"

He returned her smile. "Let's hang around here a little longer and see what happens."

AS A BRAND-NEW MEMBER OF THE BIRMINGHAM BARONS starting rotation, Conor made the third start of the second half. He threw another complete-game shutout. He struck out ten more. He won another suit.

"You want to sell the suit?" an infielder asked.

He handed Kate another three hundred dollars in the parking lot.

"Are you doing something illegal?" she asked. "Is this some scheme of A.J.'s?"

"Nope."

"Then where's the money coming from."

"I sold another suit."

I won ten straight over the season's last half. We ran away with the Southern League Title. I made my second straight All-Star team and was named left-handed pitcher for Birmingham's All-Decade team.

"I played basically two months, and I'm All-Decade," I told Brad.

As the season wound down, I overheard a group of sportswriters seeking comment from Roy, concerning the likelihood he would be named Southern League Manager of the Year.

"Boy, what a joke," Roy told them. "I had my best pitcher sitting the whole first half of the season. How smart does that make me?"

twenty-five

CONOR LEANED HIS HEAD BACK AND POURED A SMALL stream of champagne from the bottle to his mouth, gradually increasing the distance like a fancy restaurant waiter. He quickly discovered this skill requires practice. He tried to blink the sting of champagne from his eyes as he considered the happenstance of right place and right time.

During the strike of 1981, the major league season stopped for two months while owners and players hammered out a new collective bargaining agreement. One of the throw-ins was minor league free agency. Major League players won the right to become free agents in 1976. Minor leaguers, though, remained bound to the team that signed them forever, if the team chose. Over the winter of 1983-84, though, the rules changed. Any player under minor league contract for six years could declare his free agency.

And guess what? I'd been playing for seven seasons.

"Obviously, Conman, we want to sign you for next year."

Detroit's minor league pitching coordinator, Billy Muffitt,

called soon after Conor and Kate returned to San Carlos. Again, they lived with Conor's mom, arranging their winter jobs, securing a spot on the roster of a Golden Gate Park League squad.

During the final weeks of the 1983 season, a parade of Detroit executives and coordinators saw Conor pitch. Through the final games and into the playoffs, they saw him win duels against Jose Rios, Mark Langston and Bret Saberhagen. They saw a mature, one hundred-seventy-pound lefthander who threw harder in the ninth inning than he did in the first and augmented his stuff with a screwball that turned right-handed batters inside out.

Both A.J. and Brad greeted Conor when he and Kate arrived home, eager to know what he planned.

"Well, I can't imagine Detroit won't offer me a contract—"

"Yes," A.J. said, "but what kind of contract? You've done everything you can at Double-A. You want a Triple-A contract and an invitation to Major League camp."

"Yeah, that's what I want. It doesn't mean they have to give it to me."

"Yes, they do," Brad said.

"They do?"

"I've been looking at the minor league free agency agreement taking effect January first. You can declare free agency and sign with anyone you want. You've got the leverage, now."

"You're assuming anyone else will want me," said Conor, who hadn't been *pursued* by anyone since he signed his first Angels contract.

"A.J. and I did a study of lefthanders your age and with similar stats," Brad said. "Trust us. Teams will want you."

So Conor and Kate faced a dilemma. Should they travel the

safe road and accept whatever Detroit offered, or put their faith in a guy who lost his front teeth to Conor's knuckle curve, and another guy who chased him around the diamond with a baseball bat when they were seven years old.

Muffitt called a few days later.

"That's great, Mr. Muffitt," Conor said. "And I'd like to sign with Detroit. What sort of contract do you have in mind?"

"We'll do a two-year minor league deal. We'll invite you to Major League spring camp."

"Where will I stay?" Conor asked.

Muffitt seemed taken aback. "Well, our minor league hotel is across the street from—"

"I won't be at the main Tiger Town complex?" Conor drummed his fingers and heard another moment of silence.

"Well, no. We only offer housing there for the Major League guys..."

Conor took a deep breath. *Now, or never.*

"I want to stay at the Major League complex and go into the season as a member of the starting rotation at Evansville."

"Our minor league hotel is very nice..."

"I understand, but I've stayed at minor league hotels for seven years."

"...and we can't guarantee a spot in the triple-A rotation before Spring Training even begins."

Conor closed his eyes and felt sweat bead across his forehead. He took another deep breath. Kate rested a reassuring hand on his shoulder.

"I appreciate your offer, Mr. Muffitt," he said, hoping he'd kept the quaver from his voice. "Under the circumstances, I'll declare free agency and see what else is out there."

Another moment of silence.

"Well, Conor, you're twenty-eight years old. Every club is drafting younger talent—guy's they can hold onto for six years. You might not find free agency as attractive as you think." Muffitt had stated the scenario keeping Conor awake the past few nights as he struggled with Brad's and A.J.'s advice.

He closed his eyes again. He saw his father seated at this same table, telling Lloyd Christopher he'd tear up the thirty-thousand-dollar Angels contract if Christopher didn't allow Conor to pitch against the College of San Mateo. His father had every confidence that, if the Angels walked away, Conor would find other suitors.

"Thanks for the offer," he told Muffitt. "I owe it to myself and my family to explore the options."

CONOR APPRECIATED THEIR SUPPORT. HE COULD HAVE done without the added pressure, though. The day his free agency became official all his brothers crowded into their mother's kitchen. Basil came home, taking a break from the Alaska winter. Brad and A.J. were present, as well. Kate and Conor's mom made coffee and snacks. They anticipated a long day of hold-your-breath tension.

The phone rang at nine a.m.

"Yes, this is Conor Nash. Yes. Thank you. I look forward to talking, too. Yes, I'll be sure we go over details before signing with anyone else."

He disconnected the call, reclaimed his seat and picked up his coffee cup.

Nine sets of eyes riveted him. Conor drank, set the cup down, scratched his chin.

"All right," brother Sam said, "if you don't tell us right now,

I'm gonna haul you outside and kick your scrawny ass!"

Conor grinned. "The Yankees."

A cheer reverberated through the kitchen, so loud they nearly missed the ringing of the phone for the second time.

By day's end, Conor wasn't answering. A.J. took over, taking notes, making observations, dropping hints about calls they'd already received, making tentative appointments for meetings.

"I've never seen anything like this," his Mom said over and over.

"After all the years, worrying about being released or sent down or . . ." Kate said. "Everybody wants you!"

They fielded a dozen calls, the only disappointment being that neither the Giants nor the A's were included. Conor still dreamed of playing near his hometown and offers from either of those teams would make his choice an easy one.

"So, what are you gonna do?" A.J. asked.

"I have no idea. I have to think about it."

"This is a different sort of contract than you've ever dealt with," A.J. said. "You need an agent."

"Who, you? A.J., you don't know anything about being a sports agent. I can handle this."

"At the very least," Brad said, "sign nothing until I look at the contract."

A.J. nodded.

Basil concurred, and said, "Okay, let's go out for a drink."

A.J., Brad and Conor's brothers shouted their agreement.

Kate rolled her eyes. She cornered Basil the lover and Sam the brawler.

"Sam, he's your brother. Don't start anything tonight. And you, Basil, stay away from the scotch. The last thing we need is Touchy Teddy making an appearance. I want Conor returned in the same condition as when he left."

CONOR AND A.J. WERE BOTH SURPRISED WHEN GEORGE Brophy, farm director for the Minnesota Twins, called a third time. They thought the ball remained in their court.

"Have you decided?" Brophy asked

As a matter of fact, Conor had.

He planned to accept the Twins' offer of $3,500 a month, an invitation to Major League camp for Spring Training, and a Triple-A contract. Other interested teams made the same offer, for a thousand dollars less each month of the season.

"Well, I think so..."

"Before you say anything else," Brophy said, "let me update our offer."

"Um... okay."

"Instead of $3,500 a month, we'll make it a split contract. And offer you a two-year deal."

Conor looked across the kitchen table where Brad and A.J. had set up camp. He covered the receiver, and he whispered, "What's a split contract?"

They both shrugged.

Okay, so much for playing the cool negotiators.

"I'm sorry... what's a split contract?"

Brophy explained that, rather than being paid $3,500 for each month of the season and Spring Training, roughly $21,000, Conor would earn a salary of $25,000 for the year. If he should be called to the majors, he'd go onto the forty-man roster. He'd make major league minimum salary of $40,000, pro-rated to the amount of time he spent at the major league level.

"Well, your offer sounds good, Mr. Brophy," Conor said.

"If you'll give me a few minutes to talk with my . . . advisors, I'll get right back to you."

He replaced the phone in its cradle and grinned. "I'm rich, and I'm a helluva' negotiator."

"They upped their own offer?" A.J. asked. "Just think how much you could've made if you'd let me do the talking."

"So," Brad said, "a split contract. What else did he say?"

"Oh, yeah, it gets even better. They offered a two-year deal."

"No," Brad said.

"What do you mean, no?"

Brad tapped his index finger for emphasis. "You never again sign a minor league contract for anything longer than one year."

Conor didn't understand. "Why wouldn't I want—"

"Is the contract guaranteed?" Brad asked.

"Well, no. I have to make the team."

"What if you hate it there and they want to keep you? What if someone like Wilbur Spalding wants to bury you? On the other hand, what if you like it and you're good? Won't they give you another contract?"

"Well, I suppose."

"You're a free agent. As long as you're signing minor league contracts, you can be a free agent every year. And if you're good, you'll get other teams bidding for you."

A.J. slapped the table. "See, this is why you need an agent."

"SO, YOU'RE STILL GOING TO VENEZUELA?" KATE ASKED.

"Yeah," Conor said. "I signed a contract. And don't forget, they're paying me three-thousand a month."

When Birmingham's season ended, a representative of the Caracas Tiburones had approached Conor to play winter ball for two months. Conor jumped at the chance. Besides the money, the deal offered an opportunity to prove himself against major league players who wintered in the Caribbean and Central America.

"What about the Twins?" Kate asked.

"I told them I'd made this commitment. They didn't say anything one way or the other."

Venezuela also meant he wouldn't have to do house-cleaning this winter. Conor had decided he disliked scrubbing other people's toilets. Despite Venezuela's deteriorating economy and political chaos, he looked forward to playing ball in a Latin country again.

Roughly halfway between Miami and Caracas the phone built into the seatback in front of him trilled. Conor had never heard one of these phones ring. The phone chirped again. Conor cautiously answered.

"Conor, this is George Brophy. We don't want you to go to Venezuela."

"Well, I'm on the airplane, and we land about an hour from now. I don't think I can *not* go to Venezuela at this point."

"Yes, yes, I understand. We don't want you to stay there."

Conor looked at the Caribbean Sea below. "Okay, is there a particular reason?"

"The Twins and the Sharks, um, I guess they're the Tiburones, had a working agreement a couple of years ago. We had some serious disagreements. We don't like them, and they don't like us."

"Well, nobody said anything—"

"We *really* don't like them, and they *really* don't like us. We're concerned you might be in some jeopardy."

"What, like somebody might shoot me or something?"

Brophy laughed without further comment.

Conor lifted his cup, hoping the stewardess patrolling the aisle might take a hint and bring him another drink. "Well, here's the other thing, Mr. Brophy. My wife and I are counting on this money to get us through this winter."

"We'll compensate you," Brophy said. "We can't pay for the full amount of time you were supposed to be there, but we'll will send you a check for three thousand. Even though the Tiburones people aren't very happy about it, they'll compensate you for your time thus far."

The plane landed at Simon Bolivar International Airport.

Walking toward baggage claim, Conor waved above the crowd to a man wearing a black suit, narrow tie, white shirt, and black fedora. He held a sign reading *Senor Nash*. The man met his wave with a frown. He gave a nod to a pair of bearded men clad in military uniforms holding automatic weapons. They stepped away from the wall.

"You are the one they call the Conman?" the man asked.

"Um... yes, I—"

"The cancellation of this contract is an unfortunate matter," the man said darkly.

"Well, yes. Obviously, there's been a misunderstanding—"

"I've been told to give you this check for six hundred and twenty-two U.S. Dollars."

The soldiers stepped a little closer.

"Um... you folks don't need to—"

"We insist. Our president is an honorable man. He believes we should keep our agreements. Your return flight departs ten minutes from now. They are holding the plane. These gentlemen will escort you."

Flanked by soldiers, Conor turned to go when the man

added, "Our president is a great fan of baseball, particularly Tiburones baseball. You are well advised not to return to Venezuela."

Safely beyond Venezuelan air space, Conor used the seatback phone to call Kate. "Guess what?" he said. "I'll be home tomorrow. They paid me to go away again."

THE 1983 TWINS HAD BEEN MEDIOCRE. ENTERING 1984, though, their Major League roster included a host of young unknowns who, three years later, would win a World Series. Even before they started negotiating against themselves, Conor had decided on the Twins. First, because they were bad, and jobs might be more available. Second, because he knew several players within the Twins organization, including Kenny Schrom. Kenny had appeared briefly in the majors for Toronto in 1980 and 1983. He would become a starter in the Twins rotation for 1984.

"I signed with you guys, because I wanted to check on the champagne," Conor told Kenny when they met at Tinker Field, the Twins' ancient spring training facility at Orlando. "I understand Brouhard gave you custody. You haven't lost it or broken it or anything?"

"No, Conman. It's sitting in a wine rack at home, waiting for the last survivor."

Twins manager Billy Groves wanted Len Blanco, who'd had a solid season the previous year, as his bullpen lefty. Blanco, though, struggled through the spring. I came to camp to prepare for a spot in a Toledo Mudhens' rotation, but I found myself mopping up the major league spring training games because of Blanco's ineffectiveness.

I appeared late in games, facing triple-A and double-A guys who took over after the major leaguers had their two or three at-bats and were taking their showers. Major league coaches saw what I could do. Pitching Coach Johnny Podres seemed friendly enough. Groves, the manager, appeared unapproachable and indifferent. He didn't speak to me. Every day, though, pitchers departed for their minor league assignments while I stayed until finally, only Blanco and I remained. With a few games left before opening day, I still hadn't allowed a run. I'd pitched a dozen innings, giving up only four hits with thirteen strikeouts.

"*I don't want to get your hopes up,*" *I told Kate,* "*but I've got a shot at making this club.*"

twenty-six

Minnesota Twins
1984

TWO ROOKIES LEFT SPRING TRAINING ON THE Minnesota Twins 1984 opening day roster. Conor Nash and Jeff Rasher, who was promoted because catcher Tim Laudner suffered an injury during camp's final week.

Conor called everyone he knew. Kate cheered and cried. His mother cheered and cried.

Brad's voice wavered as he said, "I always knew you'd get there." Basil, who was not a crier, admitted to tears running down his cheeks. A.J. bawled, and through his sobs, reminded Conor he needed an agent.

Sam said, "Just remember who made you a pitcher in the first place, you little snotweasel." Then, he added, "Can you imagine how proud Dad would be today?"

Conor walked into the Florida evening and remembered his father's voice as clearly as if it had been yesterday.

Conor, you've only got one basket. For the other boys, that would be a weakness. Not you. That's your strength.

CONOR STEPPED ONTO THE METRODOME FIELD AND FOUND Kate and his brothers Sam and Mike a dozen rows above the home team dugout. His brothers traveled to Minnesota for a Twins-Angels series. So far, Conor hadn't pitched.

Usually, Conor imposed a rule. He'd impressed upon Kate not to attempt to attract his attention while he was on the field. He wouldn't acknowledge her or others while he was working. He granted an exception, though, in deference to his brothers' patience. He offered a discrete wave, validating the story they were telling everyone within hearing distance.

Every time he'd stepped from the dugout the past two games, his brothers stood and announced, *Hey! Hey, there's our brother! Conor Nash. There's the Conman!*

Here they were, playing the Angels—the first organization to say Conor Nash wasn't good enough. So, what if they were playing at a stadium with a plastic bag for a roof? Conor was about to do what he'd promised since he was seven years old.

Conor imagined his Major League debut about a thousand times. He pictured a holy moment steeped in ceremony. His original vision, of course, painted himself as a starter for the Giants. Knowing his debut would come as a reliever, he made the appropriate adjustments.

First, the call. A shrill ring of urgency. The bullpen coach answers, his grave visage reflecting the true extent of this emergency. He names the Conman. Conor rises, nods his assent and begins a precise ritual of quick shoulder stretches, short, easy tosses, backing up with each throw until he feels the bullpen mound rise against his heels. A determined climb to the rubber. Then a studied acceleration of fastballs on each successive pitch until the pop of the catcher's glove rings through the stadium.

Beyond, the rest of the world stops as his manager breaks the news to Conor's predecessor. Conor waits, unmoving, towel draped over his shoulder as a symbol of availability. Like a king anointing a champion, the manager lifts his left arm high, a gesture twixt summons and plea. Conor enters, his pace determined and deliberate, his arrival greeted with thankfulness. And in the manager's outstretched hand, a baseball. *Please, Conman, smite thee down thine enemies.*

A man rendered faceless and nameless by Conor's power of concentration steps into the batters' box. The umpire invites Conor to proceed and the message is delivered as a blazing strike clipping the plate's outside corner.

The Conman has arrived.

Yeah, right.

This guy *definitely* had a face. And a name. *Reggie Fucking Jackson* stood there, waving his bat like a toothpick, offering not even an iota of concern.

Bases loaded.

Conor had taken so many deep calming breaths, he feared he'd hyperventilate. He received his catcher's sign, then glanced once, twice, three times to the runner at second.

"Time!" The call came from a base umpire who stood between the mound and second.

This was nowhere in the script.

The umpire extended his hands, a symbolic request for the ball.

Conor obliged with a gentle, underhanded toss.

The umpire massaged the baseball and nodded for Conor to meet him behind the mound.

"Son," he said, "I understand this is a big moment—major league debut and all—but if you can't control the way your knees are shaking, I'm gonna have to call a balk."

The demise of Conor's grand scenario began during the second inning when Twins starter Pete Filson nailed Angels' catcher Bobby Gritch with a fastball to his ribs. Conor learned later that Filson's assault resulted from a grievance incurred last season when the Angels and Twins had brawled. Filson chose the first opportunity to settle his vendetta despite runners already occupying first and second.

Conor picked the interval before the start of this inning to stroll to the dugout and get bottles of water for his bullpen mates. He had a clear view while the drama unfolded.

As Gritch sagged to one knee, Conor experienced a stark realization concerning the sheer size of the Angels. Brian Downing was a beast with a hat on. Reggie Jackson best resembled a Coke machine with biceps. Gritch was huge, Don Baylor and Doug DeCencies bigger still.

Like a sprinter leaping from starting blocks, Gritch shot toward the mound where he met Filson with a full tackle. Both benches and bullpens emptied.

Conor learned during the brawl marking his first professional game to carefully time his arrival. As a rookie, his presence was mandatory. He wasn't, however, required to be quite as engaged as those who had a more personal stake. Etiquette required finding someone near his own size—or better yet, someone he knew—on the outskirts of the battle and engaging in pushing and shoving while asking after the wellbeing of family or catching up on events since they'd last seen each other. At the same time, Conor must be wary of someone preparing to sucker-punch one of his teammates. If that happened, he'd be obligated to intervene.

The skirmish required a full dozen minutes to run out of gas. Conor and his teammates, breathing heavily and sporting a few lumps and bruises, some untucked jerseys or torn pants, returned to their dugout. Threats and epitaphs were still exchanged, although now from a safer distance. Filson, who along with Gritch had been ejected, bled from a scratch across his face and disappeared down the stairs leading to the clubhouse.

As Conor congratulated himself for remaining unmarked, he heard a voice over his shoulder shout, "You!" He turned cautiously. He found Billy Groves, two buttons missing from his jersey and his hat still askew, pointing an accusing index finger. "You!" Groves repeated. "You're pitching!"

The next few moments dissolved into a blur. First problem, he'd left his glove at the bullpen bench, so he sprinted to get it. Next, Umpire Rich Garcia, who had apparently taken a couple of glancing blows as he separated combatants, screamed for a pitcher. Conor sprinted to the mound.

An adrenaline overload left him shaking with each warmup pitch as the ball flew blindly from his hand. Every few seconds, Garcia yelled, "Two more! We've gotta get this thing going." Teammates Kent Hrbek and Gary Gaetti intervened on Conor's behalf. "No, no, Richie, you've gotta let him get ready. It's not his fault there was a fight!"

CONOR CLOSED HIS EYES. WHEN HE OPENED THEM, HE found Sam, Mike and Kate. She stood, hands together as if in prayer. Sam and Mike jumped and cheered, pointing at their brother for all to see and hear.

Given the umpire's warning of an impending balk, Conor slowed himself. He looked first to the depths of center field. He scanned the infield, realizing only now that the bases were full. He toed the rubber, staring at his feet. *Maybe... just maybe...* He cautiously raised his eyes. *Nope. That's Reggie Jackson, all right.*

He found some inner reserve quieting his trembling legs, saw catcher Dave Engle extend an index finger and set at the outside corner. *Right. Gotta pitch Jackson away.* His fastball screamed shoulder high, tailing inside, then further inside. Jackson ducked, then confronted Conor with a glare. Shouts of protest erupted from the Angels' dugout.

Shit. Fuck. You can't hit Reggie Jackson. Especially right after we hit Gritch. The guy will come out here and tear your arm off!

Engle called for another fastball, this time emphasizing the outside corner with a stab of his mitt.

Conor took another deep breath. *Okay... you can do this...*

Again, the fastball tailed. Just enough to put it cock high, dead center of the plate. Conor grimaced in anticipation of the impending disaster. Jackson, his black-rimmed glasses gleaming, his afro poofing from under his flapless batting helmet, took one of *those* swings. The one where he uncoils with a force taking him to one knee after the ball has been struck, his bat extended majestically in his right hand behind him.

Jackson hit the ball so hard, Conor swore he saw a contrail along its path toward the right-centerfield bleachers. *Wait!* Second baseman Tim Teufel made a leap—a full-body extension—of which no human should be capable. The ball's velocity nearly took his glove off. He rolled on the artificial turf, righted himself in one athletic flow of motion, and flipped the ball to shortstop Ron Washington at second base.

Double Play! Double Fucking Play!

Conor suppressed the urge to give a little punch of victory as he bounded off the mound, skipped over the foul line, and trotted into the dugout. He buried his face in a towel to hide his smile.

"What the fuck do you think you're doing?" Grove's growl held a malevolence Conor hadn't thought possible. He peeked from behind the towel, past Grove's glare, past snickering teammates, past disdain on the face of Richie Garcia, to the mound, occupied now by Hrbek and Gaetti, the latter flipping a baseball in and out of his glove while shaking his head.

"That's only two outs, numb nuts," Groves said.

"Oh… um… I…" Conor fleetingly considered making an excuse. Something about his glove, or his shoe or… Even facing humiliation, he had the presence of mind to realize what a mistake that would be.

He retrieved his glove and retraced his steps, enduring sarcastic cheers and jeers of the home fans. He glanced quickly toward Kate and his brothers. Sam sat with his Twins cap pulled low over his eyes. Mike shielded his face behind both hands. Kate offered a shrug.

Gaetti handed him the ball. "Two cases of Molson for the clubhouse."

"What?"

"Two cases of Molson. That's the Kangaroo Court fine."

Conor induced DeCencies to pop up the next pitch. Groves told him he was done. Conor presented Gaetti two cases of Molson beer the next morning.

twenty-seven

Almost a decade removed from those events, Conor understood his Minnesota failure.

He rose stiffly from the sandstone bench. His leg muscles had begun to tighten. The last thing he wanted was to suffer the paroxysm of a hamstring cramp. He took a few careful, shuffling steps.

Here's how it was, Rita. To make the 1984 Twins roster Len Blanco only needed to be a little bit good. He was Grove's guy. A 5.00 ERA, and he owns that last roster spot. Not with a 10.00.

Groves used me as Blanco's wake-up call.

Happens all the time—some rookie's career dangled as bait for an underperforming veteran. Bottom line, though? I didn't take advantage of it. I made four appearances, three of them against Detroit, which opened the 1984 season thirty-five and five on their way to the World Series. I delivered a mediocre performance.

I failed my first major league attempt because, once again, I wasn't ready. I let myself be intimidated by the legends. Jackson, Cal Ripkin, Alan Trammel, Kirk Gibson. I didn't pitch to the catcher's glove. I pitched to the back of baseball cards.

I came prepared to play in Toledo. Ken Schrom and Dave Engle bought me two sports jackets when we flew to Baltimore. Their generosity helped me meet the big-league dress code. No one, though, could buy me a Major League frame of mind.

Conor stood in the baggage claim area at the Minneapolis-St. Paul International Airport, waiting for a carrousel to disgorge his luggage the first week of May. He worried about Kate. Before the Twins left for the road trip, the wives arranged an Easter get-together for players and their families. Except Kate hadn't been invited. Len Blanco had been among the most popular teammates. When Conor replaced him, the wives reacted by shunning Kate. Minor league wives had always embraced each other, formed a mutual support group to lift each other during times of disappointment and celebrated any success they could find. Kate didn't give the Twins' wives the satisfaction of displaying her hurt, but Conor knew she felt frightened and alone.

Conor saw Billy Groves weaving toward him, tipsy as a result of his encounters with the drinks cart during a somber flight from Seattle.

The manager regarded him for a moment, one eye displaying a half-squint.

"Um . . . you need help finding your bag, Skip?"

Groves ignored the question. Instead, he said, "Here's how it is, Jeff. We've got some guys finally getting healthy, so we're sending you down."

Groves turned and walked away.

Conor suffered a moment of stunned paralysis, disrupted as

Jeff Rasher approached and cleared his throat.

"Um, Conman," Jeff said. "I might have bad news for you. I . . . I think you're getting sent down."

Conor was still trying to understand being demoted under the wrong name in baggage claim. *And now . . . what?*

"Who told you?"

"Well, a couple of minutes ago, Billy called me *Conor*, and said *we're going to make a move*."

Conor slung an arm around Jeff's shoulder. "Well, then I've got bad news for you, too, Dude . . ."

Toledo Mudhens
Triple A Baseball
1984

JEFF AND I REPORTED TO THE MUDHENS THE NEXT AFTERNOON. Kate packed our stuff in Minneapolis. She and the kids would arrive in Toledo a few days later. I'd already informed my mom and brothers, along with A.J., Basil and Brad. Everyone offered encouragement. Everyone said I'd certainly reach the pinnacle again. I would not, they assured me, be one of those thousands teased by a brief taste of nirvana, never to find my way back.

By now, I'd been hardened to the shuffle of players, like pieces on a game board, by executives who regarded so many of us living at the cusp of the majors as tokens easily sacrificed. Any illusions I might have held about justice or simple fairness had long since been ground into the dirt of a thousand pitching mounds.

Success at any level requires a player to cling with every molecule of his being to his passion for the game. This game is too difficult, the everyday grind too demanding, to approach with any degree of indifference. The irony, though, is that executives who manage players' fates remind them at every opportunity that "it's a business." And business has little regard for passion.

The trick, I found, is to build a fortress where your passion is safe from cynicism and disappointment. In that small place I could live in awe of a Reggie Jackson or a Wilbur Spalding. I could tingle at the thrill of putting on a baseball uniform. But only there. I must construct a separate room for my professionalism. Failure and success co-exist in that room. Neither can overwhelm the other. Emotion is checked at the door. Bad calls, bad breaks, bad bounces must become as insignificant as hotdog wrappers twisting through a windy stadium. I needed to resist forever more the temptation of blame. I could hold only one person accountable—myself.

My angel blessed me with a major league fastball. Hard work and tenacity produced a devastating screwball. These other things, these mental disciplines, were what I had to master during my time at Toledo, so at the next opportunity—if my friends and family were correct and I earned another chance—I would finally be ready.

"SON, YOU GONNA START FOR ME. I LOOKED AT YOUR STATS, and you ain't no bull-penner. You're a starter. Get yourself settled. Throw a bullpen. Then, three days, you gonna start the Pawww-tuckett series."

Cal Ermer's words wafted over me like poetry.

Somewhere in his seventies, Cal labored for dozens of years as a minor league player, coach or manager. He's one of a handful of men who, like W.P. Kinsella's Moonlight Graham, earned their way into the Baseball Encyclopedia by virtue of a single major league appearance. He started at second base and went zero for *three for the Washington Senators on a day in 1947. He played second base and had seven defensive chances. He made four putouts and contributed three assists. By the time I met him as manager of the Toledo Mudhens, I saw a spare, white-haired man with a perpetual tobacco stain tracking from his mouth to his chin. Throughout a ballgame, Cal's distinctive chatter rang. "Hey, segasegachigachigasegasega . . . Shu!"*

I never understood what any of that meant, but I loved playing for Cal.

APART FROM THE DISAPPOINTMENT OF HIS DEMOTION, Conor thrilled at being a Toledo Mudhen. Who could escape the image of Corporal Klinger holding a cigar, wearing a dress and a Mudhens' cap, behind him the grim theater of the Korean War? Several times that season, Klinger himself—actor Jamie Farr—appeared at the ballpark. He and Conor traded autographs.

The Mudhens' park, though, was a nightmare. At Lucas County Stadium, hitters stared into the setting sun and every pitcher became Nolan Ryan for four innings. When the sun set, though, the wind picked up and blew straight out to center field.

All that would come later, after Pawtucket, the Red Sox's Triple-A entry in the International League, where, in his first appearance, Conor faced a young pheenom named Roger Clemens.

"So?" Kate began their post-game phone call.

"We won," Conor said.

"Wow. Clemens is supposed to be pretty good. How'd you throw?"

"I blew their doors off. Cal took me out after five. I struck out ten."

The relative significance of his performance fell into perspective the very next day.

"Phone call for you," the clubhouse guy told Conor.

"Can you take a message?" Conor asked. "I need to—"

"I don't think so. It's the owner."

"Of the Mudhens?"

"No. Owner of the Twins."

As Conor hustled for the phone, his mind raced. *They heard about last night's game and they're calling already? Maybe somebody got hurt.*

Calvin Griffith, a patriarch among Major League executives, served as both Twins owner and general manager. His father, Clark Griffith, the club's original owner when they'd been the Washington Senators, willed the team to his son Calvin and daughter Thelma when he passed away in 1955. Calvin's tight-fisted ways made him notorious among Major League owners.

Conor took a deep breath.

"This is Conor Nash," he said brightly.

"Nash! When you went to Toledo last week you left without paying your clubhouse dues. I'm taking it out of your paycheck."

Click.

At Toledo, I won twelve and lost six as a starter, including six complete games. My earned run average totaled 2.79. I struck out a hundred and sixty-four, while walking only fifty-six. I remained on the forty-man Major League roster, so wasn't eligible for minor league free agency. I'd made the adjustments, though. My Triple-A performance could not be ignored. Both mentally and physically, I felt ready.

What could possibly go wrong?

"The Twins want me to play winter ball in Puerto Rico."

"Oh, good," Kate said.

Conor studied her face with a hint of suspicion. "You said you were glad I was staying home this winter."

"I am."

"I'll be in Puerto Rico."

"So you say."

"What, you don't believe me?"

Kate smiled. "I believe you *think* you're going to Puerto Rico."

When she kissed him goodbye at the airport, she said, "Have fun. Call me when you're on your way home."

Halfway across the Atlantic, the seatback phone rang. Conor's chin dropped onto his chest. *No. This is not possible . . .*

"Conor? George Brophy. I'm sorry to bother you . . ."

"Oh, that's okay. I'm on an airplane. It's not like I've got anything else to do."

"Yes, well, here's the thing. We've had contacts from some Japanese teams, who've expressed interest in a number of players from our system. Your name came up . . ."

"Japan?"

"Don't worry about it. The possibility of us doing a deal is unlikely. Still, with you being part of the discussions, we don't believe Puerto Rico is a good idea for you."

"I'll be in Puerto Rico two hours from now. I can't just jump out of the window."

"It's not only the Japanese thing," Brophy said. "You threw about a hundred and sixty innings last year. The more we considered it, the more we believe pitching in Puerto Rico would not be in your best interest."

"What about the Puerto Ricans? What do they think? I might want to take a vacation there someday."

"Oh, they're fine with releasing you from your contract," Brophy assured him. "We're sending them someone else."

"Okay. Once again, we've got an issue of money. My wife and I were counting—"

"We'll pay you a thousand dollars for the inconvenience. Some people there will give you a check."

"Will they have guns?"

twenty-eight

CONOR, KATE AND THEIR TWO CHILDREN WERE staying at his mother's house for the off-season when Rocky Horano called.

"Conor, for you." Kate passed the phone across the kitchen table.

"Mr. Nash?" The voice had a distinct Japanese accent. "I am Rocky Horano. I am American liaison with the Yomiuri Giants, and we are interested in talking with you."

Conor had told A.J., Brad and Basil about Brophy's statements concerning the Japanese. He put his hand over the receiver and told Kate. "It's A.J. He's screwing with me."

Kate rolled her eyes.

"Okay," Conor said, sarcasm dripping from each word, "what can I do for ya' Mr. Herrr-ah-nooo?"

A brief silence ensued, followed by, "We have studied your record, and would like to discuss your playing baseball in Japan."

"Well, I ain't goin' to Japan for anything less than a million bucks, Mr. Herrr-ah-nooo."

A longer silence.

"And... would that be for three years? Or... we cannot pay so much for one season, because you are not top of our list."

"Why wouldn't I be top of your list, Mr. Herrr-ah-nooo?"

"Several big-leaguers are on our list as well..."

His mother, working at the kitchen sink, offered a quizzical glance.

"Hey, I've played in the majors."

"Yes. Most of your records have been in the minor leagues, Double-A. Only recently Triple-A."

Conor felt a moment of panic. A.J. didn't seem to be coming out of character. A.J. could carry one of these fake calls only so long before collapsing in laughter.

"Um... I'm sorry, who are you again?"

Kate heard Conor's half of the conversation thus far with an indulgent smile. Her smile quickly shifted to a look of alarm.

"I am Rocky Horano. I am American liaison with the Yomiuri Giants." The voice offered not a hint of annoyance at having to repeat itself. "Representatives of our organization will be in San Francisco soon, and we would like to meet with you and your agent."

Okay, it's A.J. after all, giving me another dig about this agent thing. He met Kate's concern with a shake of his head and a wave of his hand.

"Well, there's this schmuck who *wants* to be my agent, but I don't think he knows shit about what he's doing."

"Ahhhhhh... I am... sorry for your misfortune."

Uh, oh.

"Um . . . A.J. Is this you?"

"Mr. Nash, I am Rocky Horano. I am American liaison—"

"Oh, my God. Mr. Horano? Is . . . is this for real? Because I have a friend who likes to mess with me . . ."

"I assure you, Mr. Nash, our interest is genuine."

Conor felt a little light-headed as he ended the call.

"I don't think," he said to Kate slowly, "that was A.J."

Kate's mouth dropped open. "What was that thing about a million dollars?"

If Conor thought the million would impress Kate enough to excuse him from cleaning houses that off-season, he was mistaken. Apparently, the Japanese contingent set their sights on some other American pitcher, because when Rocky Horano called again, the Japanese option had been relegated to one more pipe dream they'd encountered along this journey.

"Conman-San? I am Rocky Horano. I am American liaison with the Yomiuri Giants . . ."

"Mr. Horano," Conor said, commanding Kate's attention from across the kitchen.

"My associates are in San Francisco. We would like to meet you for dinner this evening if it is convenient."

"Yes, Mr. Horano. It would be very convenient."

He gave Kate a thumbs-up. She pumped her fist.

"And will Mr. Schmuck accompany you?"

"Mr . . . who?"

"Your agent?"

"Oh. Him. He is Mr. Cohen, and he *is* a schmuck, but I'm not sure he would—"

"My associates are more comfortable talking if an agent is present."

"Yeah, okay. He'll be there. Um ... you do realize I'm under contract with the Twins organization. I can't just—"

"Oh, yes. The process is this. Initially, we must reach agreement with you. If we are successful, we would reach a separate agreement with the Twins for purchase of your contract. They are aware."

"The Twins would sell me to the Yomiuri Giants?" Conor said, mostly for Kate's benefit.

"Yes. Shall we say eight o'clock?"

"So, the Twins would sell you?" Kate asked.

"Yes."

"I still don't think people should be sold."

"Well, I've been sold before."

"This time tell the Twins to hold out for at least *two* boxes of baseballs."

CONOR AND A.J. STOOD AT THE RESTAURANT ENTRANCE and collectively took a deep breath.

"Okay. Let me do the talking," A.J. said.

"You're not registered as my agent," Conor said. "You're not registered as anyone's agent. I can't let you do the talking."

"I have one thought for you," A.J. said. "Arizona land deal. Which one of us failed to make a killing?"

"Yeah, yeah." Conor opened the door.

They were ushered to a private space off the main dining room. Conor suffered a jarring memory of John Wayne and the Ramada Inn food fight. As Conor and A.J. entered, a host of five elderly Japanese gentlemen and a sixth younger man, stood.

"Conman-San," the younger man said. "I am Rocky Horano.

I am American liaison for these honored elders who represent the Yomiuri Giants."

The five men bowed and, one at a time, handed Conor a business card.

Conor returned the bow. The Japanese men appeared expectant.

Conor did not have a business card. A.J. rescued him. He stepped forward and distributed five of his own cards, shaking each man's hand. "A.J. Cohen. Howyadoin? Goodtameetcha!"

The Japanese men smiled awkwardly. Conor hoped none of them read English, because the card they'd just received said, *A.J. Cohen, Land Baron*.

"And Mr. Cohen is your representative?" Horano asked.

Carefully wording his response, Conor said, "Mr. Cohen is my advisor and my friend."

"Ah, then we should proceed. Initially, I've been instructed to convey we cannot offer the sum you have requested."

"What sum?" A.J. asked.

"In our first discussion, Conman-San suggested one million dollars."

"May we be excused for a moment?" A.J. asked a half hour later. As Rocky Horano translated between the parties, Conor and A.J. did their best not to appear stunned—or offer each other high fives—when numbers were revealed.

"We need Fat Brad on this right now," A.J. told Conor as they stood side-by-side, staring into the men's room mirror. "We have to nail this thing down before anyone changes their minds."

Apologetically, Rocky Horono said Yomiuri could offer Conor Nash only a two hundred thousand dollar signing bonus, and two hundred and fifty thousand dollars a year for three years. The first two years guaranteed. The team would hold a $50,000 option to buy out the third year.

Conor found a pay phone and called Brad, who practiced law in Fresno.

"Do not sign anything until I've reviewed that contract," Brad ordered. "Set up another meeting. I'll be there."

FAT BRAD.

Conor drank. He wished he could somehow set aside his anger.

The world below clung to dusk. Shadows deepened as Phoenix became a vast panorama of sparkling light. Endless slithering lines of cars crept along freeways. The perpetual stream of jetliners descending into and departing Sky Harbor International Airport became a parade of blinking white and red stars.

My dad was right. Brad was the steady one, the voice of reason. But Hugh Nash never saw the full extent of Brad's goofy sense of humor.

"Conman-san, we do not require the presence of an attorney. The contract is generic. We are anxious to finalize—"

The group met at a Los Angeles airport hotel. Conor and A.J. arrived the day before, anticipating closure of a deal that evening. A court hearing ran long, though. Fat Brad hadn't been able to get a flight until morning.

"I'm sorry," Conor said. "I can't sign a contract my attorney hasn't approved. He'll be here any minute, I'm sure."

Conor and A.J. had returned to Conor's mother's house following the initial meeting, repeatedly asking each other if they'd actually heard what they heard.

"Well," Kate called with a touch of skepticism as they walked through the door, "did you get the million?"

"No," A.J. grinned, "but we came damn close."

His answer stunned Kate almost beyond comprehension.

As she heard details, she kept repeating *Japan?* Until they got to contract's term. Her ongoing response became *three years?* Conor admitted to himself that until this moment, reality hadn't registered for him, either.

A.J., though, clearly sensing their uncertainty, laid out the facts.

"Listen to me," he said. "It's almost a million dollars. Connie, you've been a minor leaguer for eight years. Eight years of being broke. Eight years of working your asses off. Eight years of living with your parents. You've got two children. You've got debts. You *have* to do this!"

A knock came at the door. Conor breathed a sigh of relief, anticipating Brad's arrival. Instead, a bellman entered bearing more tea and coffee. Conor, A.J., Rocky and five elderly Japanese sipped silently.

"A.J.," Conor said, "Maybe we should call—"

No knock. Just a click of the latch, a whoosh of the heavy door as it swept across the carpet, and Fat Brad Grady burst into the room.

He wore a too-small white T-shirt, his belly protruding below. His pale, hairy stomach hung over loud Bermuda shorts. He wore black socks, one of which was pulled to his knee. The other drooped around his ankle and spilled over a brown sandal.

He strode confidently to the table separating Conor and A.J from the Japanese contingent, reached into his mouth, laid his two front teeth on the table and said, "All right fellath, leth get down to bithnethh. Thombody thaid thomthin about a million dollath?"

Conor covered his face. As he began quaking with suppressed laughter, he hoped the Japanese gentlemen would think he was crying. He glanced at A.J., who bit hard on his upper lip to keep from guffawing. His shoulders quaked, and tears seeped from the corners of his eyes.

An absolute silence from the opposite side of the table dissolved into quick indecipherable murmurs, punctuated by many *aaaaaaahhhhs*, cleaning of glasses and shrugging of shoulders. Eventually, the eldest, likely in his eighties, rose and with a hesitant bow, offered his business card. The others followed suit. Brad gravely accepted and studied each one before placing them alongside his teeth.

BRAD EXCUSED HIMSELF, SAYING HE'D RETURN MOMENTARILY. The five elderly Japanese continued muttering and declaring among themselves. Conor sidled next to Rocky Horano. He whispered, "Can you give me a rough translation?"

Rocky, his complexion a little pale, glanced from Conor to his employers, then back again. "I . . . I'm not sure that would be . . . appropriate . . ."

"Well," Conor whispered, "I don't speak a word of Japanese, but I'm guessing it comes down to something like, *what the fuck?*"

"Yes, you've gotten the gist."

The door opened. Fat Brad returned, wearing a three-piece suit, carrying a briefcase Conor estimated to have cost about five hundred bucks. Brad bowed deeply, then reinserted his teeth. He leaned across the table handing each man a business card and said, in carefully memorized Japanese, "My name is Brad Grady. I am honored to be here acting as legal representative of Conman-San during these negotiations. I apologize for the actions of my evil twin."

The Japanese stared for a moment, shared another round of *ahhhhhhhhhhs* and muttering, then rose and bowed as one.

twenty-nine

"No."

Brad scratched the contract with his pen.

"Noooooo." More scratching. "We'll just change this *and* to an *or*. Maybe. Oooookay. Change this *or* to an *and*. Okay. Page two."

The Japanese sat patiently as Brad worked his way through the document. Finally, he pushed it to Rocky. The Japanese contingent retired to a couch and two chairs across the room. More mumbling, interrupted by an occasional searching glance toward Conor, A.J. and Brad.

They retaliated and returned the document.

"Um... nope." *Scratch, scratch, scratch.* "Oh, no. This whole page has to go now." More reading. More scratching. Brad returned serve. They muttered, stared, muttered, directed Rocky to scratch on their behalf.

They volleyed back to Brad.

He read, pen hovering.

"Brad-San, we've met most of your terms," pled Rocky. "What is left to change?"

"Well, for one thing, we'll change this *or* back to an *and* because of the period you inserted on page five." Rocky sighed. Brad adopted a grim expression. His pen hung perilously over the page. Conor heard a collective intake of breath.

"Weeeeelllll..." he lowered pen to paper. "... okay. I guess that one's okay."

The match lasted three hours. Brad authored twenty-two changes. Originally, the Japanese offered Conor *fight money*—a bonus for each time the team won—only when he pitched. Under Brad's modifications, he received a thousand dollars for every Giants victory whether he played or not. The team's original offer of a thousand-dollar monthly utilities allowance was negotiated to two thousand five hundred. Given her penchant for turning out lights, turning the heat and air conditioning down, Conor knew Kate could probably limit their bill to about two hundred. Conor received a five-thousand-dollar monthly allowance for limousine service. Kate would bank the money and make him ride the subway.

Finally, Conor sat, contract before him, his own pen hovering. The Japanese contingent leaned forward with fearful anticipation. As pen touched paper, Brad slapped himself on the forehead and said, "Tickets."

Conor withdrew the pen.

"Tickets?" asked Horano.

"Yes, plane tickets."

"The contract specifies the team will supply plane tickets for Conman-San's family," said a puzzled Horano.

"Ah," Brad said. "It doesn't specify how many. Conman-San has a big family. Let's say, for Conman, four for 1985, um...

eight for 1986, eight for 1987, that's the option year, and if the option isn't exercised, we will be compensated for the ticket value in cash."

Horano translated. The weary Japanese nodded their assent.

Again, the pen hovered. Again, Brad interrupted.

"For me and my family, two for 1985 and four for 1986. Um . . . A.J., what about you?"

"Well, I'm pretty busy. Just one for 1986."

"Then there's Basil," Brad said. "Basil needs two tickets for 1986. He'll bring a friend."

The Japanese assented. The pen hovered.

Until Brad added, "No coach."

The oldest Japanese gentleman stood. "No coach?"

"No coach," Brad repeated. "First Class."

Horano didn't need to translate.

"No First Class!" the patriarch shouted. He stared daggers from Brad to Conor. "Business Class."

Brad leaned across the table and shook the man's hand.

As the celebratory cups of iced sake were raised, Rocky whispered to Conor, "My employers wonder how much your agent and attorney are paid."

Conor smiled. "Nothing."

"Nothing?" Rocky's voice displayed his astonishment.

"They are my friends. They work for plane tickets."

"My employers," Rocky said, "are glad our other players do not have friends like yours."

Now Conor's deal depended on the Twins. He waited a week and heard nothing. He placed a call to new Twins general manager Andrew McMillain.

"We're having difficulty coming to agreement with the Japanese," McMillain told him. "They aren't offering us enough."

"Well, my Twins contract would pay me $47,000 next year. So, I can't be worth all that much."

"We think you are. We've got plans for you."

"What plans?" Conor clamped the receiver in a death grip and promised himself he would hold his temper.

"You're penciled in as our sixth starter."

"Teams don't have six starters," Conor said. "What you're saying is I'm still an insurance policy. I'm still on the Triple-A staff. How much have the Japanese offered?"

"I really can't..."

"Look, you know I'll find out one way or the other."

"They've offered a hundred thousand."

"What's wrong with that?"

"We believe you're worth two hundred."

"Then why," Conor demanded, "are you only paying me forty-seven?"

"Look, we have a lot of things to consider..."

"Okay, who else can I talk to?"

"I'm the GM," McMillain said. "The only person I answer to is the owner."

"All right. Transfer me to Mr. Griffith."

McMillain chuckled. "Sure, why not."

"Mr. Griffith? This is Conor Nash..."

Dead silence. Until Conor heard Griffith whisper, "Who is Conor Nash?" Someone whispered in reply. "He's the guy we're talking about with that Japanese team."

"Oh, yes, Mr. Nash. How can I help you?"

"Mr. Griffith, I'm appealing to you to get this deal made. This is an extraordinary opportunity for me and my family. And you folks really don't have any plans for me . . ."

"Um . . . one moment, Mr. Nash." Another overheard whispered conversation. "Do we have any plans for him?" *"Yes, he'll be our sixth starter."* "Since when do we have six starters?" *"We don't. That's just the way we say it. He's going to Toledo."*

"Mr. Nash, we do have plans for you. You'll be our sixth starter."

Conor placed his hand over his eyes and shook his head.

"Mr. Griffith, I've been in the minor leagues nine years. I'm broke. I live at my mother's house. I've got two kids. Finally, here's an opportunity to make some money, to pay my bills. And for you, I'm a contingency. Please, can you find a way to make this deal?"

More silence. Not even a whisper. Then finally, "Yes, Mr. Nash. I'll see what I can do."

The Twins sold Conor Nash for $150,000, half of which, as per his contract, was deducted from his $200,000 signing bonus. Conor, Kate, daughter Jessica and son David were off to Japan.

IF I HAD TO CHOOSE AGAIN, WOULD I GO TO JAPAN?

Conor checked his champagne. A third of the bottle remained, and he'd acquired a pleasant buzz.

See, Rita, the Twins made a mistake. As soon as they got their money from Japan, they removed me from their forty-man roster, and I became a free agent. The Japanese still hadn't sent me a check. So, technically, I could have walked away from that deal. An hour after Minnesota posted my release, the calls began. A dozen teams wanted to offer me a job.

Yeah, I promised to accept the Japanese offer. I knew by bitter experience, though, baseball promises were broken every day. I could have signed with someone else. The Twins would have to give the money back.

I was tempted. But no one else would offer me $250,000 a year, would they?

I tell you, I pitched great over there. The fans loved me. Most American players kept to themselves. They rejected Japanese conditioning routines. They lived in American compounds. They fled during the off-season. Not Conman-San. I embraced Japanese training methods. I studied so I could speak Japanese for interviews. We lived in a Japanese neighborhood. My kids attended Japanese schools. Although Kate and the kids flew home for the off season, I stayed two full years.

The business of baseball isn't any kinder there than here, though. Going into 1986, the Yomiyuri owners became infatuated with a different American player. Conman-San became old news. And since each Japanese team was limited to two foreigners, Conman was no longer wanted.

They offered the $50,000 buyout. No. I trotted out my copy of Brad's contract. "That's for the third year. You owe me $250,000."

Of course, a conscientious angel would know all of this, but I guess I'm operating on the assumption that my angel suffers from some sort of angel attention deficit disorder. And from time to time, something shiny came along and you forgot all about me.

They sent me to the minors. I didn't know they had minor leagues over there.

Experience had shown them that Americans took the quickest path home they could find. They believed no American player would suffer the inconvenience and indignity of such a demotion.

I did. I commuted hours to the minor league park on game

days, where I'd sit and watch—until the great Sadaharu Oh intervened. Oh remains the most revered player in Japanese history—Japan's Babe Ruth, the undisputed star of the Giants. He liked me as a teammate and was pissed off when I got sent down. When he learned I wasn't getting any mound time there, he talked with team owners. I remained a minor-leaguer, but I pitched regularly from then on.

When the 1986 season ended, the team exercised its release option for $50,000 and my unused plane tickets. I went home. We finally had money in the bank. The whole winter remained to sort out what I would do next.

thirty

Golden Gate Park
1987

"Maybe I should wait until next week," Conor said into the phone, carefully rotating his upper body, exploring the pain in his lower back and legs.

"A half-dozen teams are sending scouts," A.J. protested. "The game's this afternoon. You know you'll feel better when you get up and around."

"What will you do?" Kate asked as they lazed in bed early on the morning of the 1987 Super Bowl. At A.J.'s urging, Conor had agreed to pitch at Golden Gate Park that afternoon, his first game appearance since returning from Japan. A.J. worked the phones all week, recruiting teams to send scouts, who would be grumpy because they'd miss the football game.

Conor stood and took a few painful shambling steps toward the bathroom.

"You look terrible," Kate said. "What happens if you play today and you're awful?"

"You make a good point," Conor said. "Maybe the best point anyone's made this week. I'll say I can't make it today. Maybe next Sunday. The Giants aren't sending a scout anyway."

Hugh Nash had established a holiday football tradition. Without fail, the family played football games on four occasions: Turkey Bowl Thanksgiving Day, Claus Classic Christmas Day, Hangover Bowl New Year's Day, and Super Saturday. Ostensibly, they played touch football, but Hugh didn't urge anyone to give any slack. Occasionally, A.J., Basil or even Brad joined the game. They soon learned, though, in the interest of survival, absence might be the better part of valor.

"Okay, Connie, wear this," Sam declared before opening kickoff of the 1987 Super Saturday game. He handed Conor a bright red t-shirt.

"Why do I—"

"Because you're pitching tomorrow. Scouts will be there. We don't want you to get hurt."

"Shoulder pads would do me more good than a red T-shirt," Conor said.

"So, take it easy on the Conman," Sam ordered his brothers.

The sides were Sam, Mike and Brandan against Conor and Dylan. Which might seem a mismatch. Conor had that left arm, though, and Dylan was the best athlete among them. He ran like a blue dart, starred as a football player at San Carlos High, and scouts from several major league organizations showed up every time he pitched.

Conor's red shirt privilege lasted about two plays before the afternoon devolved into the usual scratching and biting Nash riot.

SINCE OUR RETURN FROM JAPAN, RITA, I FOUND MYSELF victim of a troubling and persistent ambivalence. *I finally had a choice. I didn't have to climb back onto this particular ride. I said I'd pitch in the majors, and I did. We'd made good money overseas. Our financial backs were no longer against a wall. We wouldn't live with our parents. I could find a normal job—maybe even work again at the Filoli Estate—come home every day and see my kids.*

I knew A.J. sensed this uncertainty the first time we talked.

"We're going to a Giants game," A.J. said. He'd gotten game tickets during the final home stand of the 1986 season.

"I haven't paid to watch a baseball game in twelve years," Conor said.

"Yeah, yeah, I get it," A.J said. "I'll buy the tickets, big shot. I can afford it."

Indeed, A.J. could afford it. While he never revealed a specific number, Conor's boyhood buddy enjoyed a personal worth of millions.

They sat behind third base, hunched into their jackets against the Candlestick gales. Maybe 17,000 spectators sat scattered about the park at the close of a lackluster season. Conor recalled how intimidated he'd been by the 17,000 fans who'd watched him at the Metrodome. He'd played before 70,000 raucous Japanese fanatics game after game in Tokyo.

He watched the Giants' pitchers struggle against hitters he'd routinely retired a few years ago playing Double-A or Triple-A ball. "Why'd you throw him a fastball?" Then, "This guy can't hit a curve to save his... throw him a damn curveball!" Or, "This guy will fall over if you give him a screwball... oh, wait. You can't throw a screwball, can you?"

A.J. wore a perpetual smile during the drive home.

A month later, Conor scheduled a dental appointment and haircut the same day. His dentist—not the one who pulled the wrong tooth, but his regular guy—asked, "What about next season?"

"'Ell," Conor said, his mouth stretched by clamps, "I 'hink it 'ight 'e 'ime 'o 'ink a'ow 'oing 'othig else."

The dentist's eyes grew wide under the glare of his lamp. He aimed the needle point of the pic in his hand. "You can't do that. You're our hometown guy. You can't quit until we see you play for the home-town team. Your dad wanted you to play for the Giants."

A few hours later, his barber, holding a straight razor at Conor's throat, said essentially the same thing.

Although his dad never said so, Conor knew Hugh had hoped his son would play for the Giants. And while Conor never offered his father any verbal promise, he did make an emotional vow that he would not surrender until he'd succeeded. Did six innings of relief for the Minnesota Twins constitute success?

CONOR SOAKED IN A HOT BATH, DRANK COFFEE AND READ the newspaper. He had to admit he felt better. Still . . . he kept remembering the Giants weren't coming. Two hours before the game, though, he still hadn't called to tell his team they needed another pitcher today.

He could take some aspirin. He knew he'd get an adrenaline jolt erasing most remaining aches the moment he stepped on the mound.

What if I suck, though?

Wait a minute.

What if I do suck? Sucking makes the decision for me, doesn't it? Maybe the best thing is putting the whole issue onto the shoulders of the damned baseball angel.

"You look like you're getting ready to go," Kate said.

"Yeah, I told them I'd be there. So, I'd better play."

WAS THE SONG AN OMEN?

Conor stared through chain linked wire enclosing his dugout, past the pitcher's mound, past the parks department guy prepping the infield, past teammates he barely knew who played catch or jogged across outfield grass.

At first, the song echoed as indistinct background noise. As he tugged his shoelaces tight, though, its lyrics took shape.

"Hey A.J., you hear the music?"

Sitting beside Conor on a worn metal bench, A.J. smiled.

"Yeah, man. That's the Dead."

"Somebody's got a boom box?"

"Well, maybe. Maybe not. Look where we are."

The baseball field lay in shadows of the Golden Gate Bridge. A cloudless sky behind the looming towers anchoring the bridge on the San Francisco side of the bay a crisp blue, although January's sun didn't cut an early afternoon chill.

"What, you think it's really them?"

A.J shrugged. "Who knows? Jerry Garcia lives somewhere around here."

Conor shook his head.

"Gotta be a boom box."

One more bit of irony. The Grateful Dead.

If, indeed, Conor's career *was* dead, six innings in the Major Leagues certainly wasn't enough to make him grateful. At the very least, Jerry Garcia and Bobby Weir were offering a neat summation of the Conman's career.

. . . Sometimes the light's all shinin' on me,
other times I can barely see,
and lately it occurs to me what a long strange trip it's been . . .

The music faded. Conor tied his shoelace. A.J. gasped.

"My, God. I think that's Al Rosen."

Conor followed his gaze toward a paved path coursing through the park behind them.

"Where?" Conor asked.

"The tandem bicycle."

Conor saw a yellow two-seater being peddled at a leisurely pace by a fairly non-descript middle age couple—a man steering, a woman on the rear seat. They were dressed more for the cool January sunshine than for serious exercise.

"You sure it's Rosen?"

"Well, if it's not, I'm gonna make a fool of myself."

"No, A.J. Al Rosen won't . . ."

A.J. sprinted across the grass. "Mr. Rosen!" he called. "Mr. Rosen! Stop! Stop!"

The bike wobbled and from the rear seat the woman's legs splayed like a wishbone.

Tomorrow's San Francisco Chronicle headline flashed through Conor's mind. *Giants General Manager Maimed in Bicycle Accident.* The man managed to get both feet grounded, though, and sort of run the bicycle to a halt despite the dead weight of his spouse shifting unexpectedly behind him.

Rosen turned halfway to calm his wife, then considered his pursuer.

Slowing to a trot, A.J. waved. At least the gesture made him look less like a mugger, although Conor saw Mrs. Rosen reach into a hip pocket and produce something that might have been a can of mace.

A.J. raised both arms high as a demonstration of supplication.

WHAT NOW? ROSEN THOUGHT.

"I'm sorry... I didn't mean to... um... startle you," said the man approaching them. "I just... well, there's a guy over here you need to see pitch..."

From the seat behind him, Rosen's wife said, "Oh, my good Lord."

"No, really. He's been in Japan the last two seasons and..."

Rosen's expression conveyed neither understanding nor sympathy.

"... and he pitched for the Twins. He'll be throwing here this afternoon..."

Rosen shook his head, making preparations to get underway. Before he and Mrs. Rosen coordinated their efforts effectively enough to gain any momentum, though, A.J. added, "He's left-handed."

Rosen stopped again.

"Oh, why did you tell him that?" Rosen's wife glared at A.J. and reached again for the mace.

As they peddled on, Mrs. Rosen spoke to the back of her husband's head. "You said we'd have a nice, quiet ride by the bridge. It's Sunday. I should've sprayed him."

"Yeah," Rosen answered over his shoulder, "but the guy's a lefty."

Conor watched the bicycle continue on its way. Even though he didn't expect A.J.'s gambit to succeed, if indeed the guy pedaling away was San Francisco Giants general manager Al Rosen, his hopes fell just a little.

Then he heard a snippet of conversation behind him. "... so that's him, huh? Fuckin' Major Leaguer thinks he's some kind'a hot shit..."

Conor remembered another team was here today. He finished tying his shoe, then looked to the opposite dugout. He saw fifteen hungry kids stealing glances his way, most of them wearing their game-face scowls. They'd shown up today knowing they would face the guy from Japan, the guy who'd been to the summit. They, too, knew scouts would be on hand this Sunday afternoon. They were gambling, just like him. Betting they could make their bones by kicking his ass.

Adrenaline coursed through Conor's blood. Ambivalence fled. He stood and met every eye that dared challenge him. He felt the weight of an unblemished baseball nestled in his glove.

Time to pitch.

With two outs in the third inning, Conor saw the yellow tandem bike leaning against the backstop. He shook away his catcher's request for a fastball and snapped off a screwball the batter flailed at for strike three. The hitter cursed himself, then glared at Conor as he trudged to the dugout.

The bike remained as Conor dispatched the game's final batter.

"I missed the first two innings," Rosen said. He stood behind the dugout as Conor changed his shoes. "How many hits you give up today?"

Conor banged his cleats together, dislodging clumps of red mound clay.

"None."

"That's what I thought. You got an agent?"

"Well. Sort of. I guess. You met him before the game."

"Come by my office tomorrow," Rosen said.

Conor smiled.

Indeed, *what a long strange trip it's been.*

thirty-one

THE NATURAL SANDSTONE BENCH OFFERED ENOUGH length for Conor to lay on his back if he pulled his boot heels close. He stared at emerging stars. He found Polaris, the North Star. From there he followed a curving line of lesser stars and held the bottle at just the right height and angle, as if he might pour champagne into the Big Dipper.

So, at the start of Spring Training, 1987, my career remained alive, and Kenny finally surrendered. That's when I took custody of this bottle.

Conor heard a sharp whistle from behind him. A man standing at the dugout rail, waving a hand high overhead.

"Kenny?" Conor called and trotted over.

Ken Schrom embraced Conor, then offered the bottle. Its label had peeled a little at the edges. Foil covering the cork showed tearing here and there. The wire bale, though, still held everything together.

"What's this?" Conor asked.

"I'm done," Schrom said. "Shredded my shoulder. They tried to put it back together, but ... I'm done."

Conor took the bottle, cradling it between his chest and forearm.

"Can you believe," he asked Kenny, "how young we were?"

"Well, take care, and when the time comes, when you finally quit, enjoy your champagne," Kenny said. "Not for a long time, though. And get your ass out of here. You should be pitching in the bigs."

CONOR DRANK.

The Giants never made it easy.

All six teams with scouts at Golden Gate Park offered me contracts. The Giants did, too. Their offer wasn't the best. I guess I felt an obligation, though, to my dad, my family, my hometown and—in a lapse of judgement—my frickin' angel. And like magic, everything clicked. Pitching in relief, I didn't allow a single run until my last outing. I didn't let any inherited runner score. I don't know what the spring training record is for saves, but I had six of them.

Roger Craig said he'd keep one lefthander for the pen. By the last week, only I remained. And it's not like he went out of his way to give me a break. As my last test, Roger put me into a game in Yuma against the Padres—bottom of the ninth, bases loaded. One-run lead. I smoked 'em. Three up. Three down.

When spring training began, I was a two-paragraph back-page story for the home-town papers: Local Boy Long Shot at Giants Training Camp. *With each passing week, though, the story became more dramatic. Rosen talked about a gem he'd discovered at Golden Gate Park. Craig said he liked the guy from Japan as well as any lefty he had. Now, the San Francisco papers were writing about* a thirty-one-year-old rookie, released seven times, once traded for a box of baseballs. *Nobody got it exactly right. I realized, though, the myth sports writers were building helped my cause. You want me to be the inept guy who's been released seven times? Okay, I'll be that guy.*

Finally, after all the years, Conor Nash actually became The Conman.

Being an angel and all, I don't know if you'll appreciate this, but I also reached legendary status with my manager and coaches.

That was mostly Basil's doing, though.

"I met a couple of girls who may show up tonight," Basil told Conor as they visited during batting practice at the Angels Spring Training park in Palm Springs.

"What, already?" Conor asked. "We just got here."

"No, I showed up a couple of days ago. Alaska's cold. I told the girls if they can't find me, they should go to the dugout and ask for you so you can tell them where I'm sitting."

"Where did you meet these girls?"

"At a club."

"What kind of club?"

"A strip club."

"So, they're strippers."

"You say that like it's a bad thing. Everybody has to make a living. I told them you're on the team. They're impressed."

Conor began his pre-game routine, forgetting about strippers.

As the game began, he took note of Basil's seat a few rows behind home plate. By the fifth inning, a woman occupied the seat next to Basil. When Conor gathered his stuff and headed to the bullpen at the start of the seventh, both seats were empty.

Okay, I'll be having dinner alone tonight.

"Conman, you're up," bullpen coach Norm Sherry called as

the Giants took their at-bats during the top of the ninth.

Conor entered the game with a two-run lead. He was halfway through his warm-up pitches when his tunnel vision failed. Every male eye, including his, felt something like the tidal pull of the moon as a pair of women descended the aisle toward the Giants' dugout.

Their steep platform shoes accentuated legs that seemed to go up forever, merging into the tightest, tiniest cutoff jeans legal in a public setting. They had waspish waists below breasts spilling over the thin line of their tank tops. One blonde, one brunette, their luxuriant hair spilled down their backs.

Conor caught himself just in time to avoid being clocked by the return throw from his catcher. He forced his attention to home plate, executing one more delivery. Now the women stood right behind the row of folding chairs where the manager and coaches sat next to the dugout.

The blonde bent low, riveting the eyes of every player, including Conor, to cleavage rivaling the Grand Canyon among the world's natural wonders, although *natural* might be stretching it. She said something to . . .

Oh, no. God, no!

. . . Roger Craig.

Craig stood, fielded a question from the second woman, then pointed at the mound. Conor read Craig's lips.

He's right there.

The women waved.

Conor regained sufficient focus to retire the Angels in order. He skipped the post-game receiving line, making straight for the dugout without raising his eyes. He planned to hide in the training room long enough to discourage the strippers from waiting around.

He sat on a training table as the procession of coaches filed past.

"I'm proud of you," said Bob Lillis.

Next, Don Zimmer. "You're a better man than I thought. Way to go, kid."

Norm Sherry. "Are you shitting me?"

Finally, a grave Roger Craig approached, then extended his hand.

"Conman," he said, "a big part of me wants to say you made this club right here tonight."

Spring training of 1987 ended with a three-game series against the White Sox in Chicago, where Conor suffered his only failure. He let Chicago load the bases with two outs and a one-run Giants lead. Fly ball to left field where Jeffrey Leonard fought a brutal sun. Tying and winning runs scored on the error.

"Don't worry about it, Conman," Craig told him. "We can't make an official announcement yet but pack your bags for the Bay Bridge Series. You made the team."

Conor called everyone. His mom cheered. Kate screamed. Half the town—many of them die-hard Giants fans who would rather eat bark than watch a ballgame in Oakland—bought tickets for the first game of the Bay Bridge series at the Coliseum.

Conor drifted to sleep that night comfortable his dream had come true.

They pulled the rug from under him the next day.

Ben Cisco, an assistant general manager, gave him the bad news.

"We've decided not to keep a left-hander for the bullpen."

"Then what was this whole spring about?" Conor demanded.

Just a last-minute decision, Cisco explained. They'd planned to release a veteran who suffered a miserable spring. The money guys, though, decided they'd eat too big a contract. They'd give the veteran a few more opportunities to turn things around. They had no contractual investment in Conor Nash. He could start the season at Phoenix and be available should the veteran falter.

Conor thought he'd become immune to the brutal realities of baseball business. He thought he'd successfully cultivated a cynicism leaving him invulnerable to surprise and disappointment.

This insult, though, broke his heart.

"I... I already told people..."

"Well, you probably should have waited for the official—"

"Yeah."

"Look, you'll spend a few weeks in Phoenix and if you pitch well—"

"If I pitch well, what? Then I'll make the team? Pretty tough to pitch better than I did this spring. Pitching well didn't make me a Giant."

"Hey, I know it's embarrassing to tell people you made it and then say you didn't. Look, we'll have you travel for the Bay Bridge series. We'll get you into a game. And then we'll announce that something unrelated happened and we had to make an unanticipated move."

Conor's stare bored into the man. "Mr. Cisco," he asked, "have you ever been comfortable lying to your mother?"

CONOR FLEW ALONE FROM CHICAGO TO SAN FRANCISCO. He refused the offer to play in the Bay Bridge series. The

Giants granted his request for a few days before reporting to Phoenix. He didn't exactly hide back in San Carlos, although he spent a lot of time at home.

A.J., Brad and Basil offered encouragement. Just another setback. Big deal. He was pitching as well as he ever had. He'd been through disappointments before. Why stop now?

All valid arguments.

"I'm sick of it," he told Kate. "If all I needed to do was be good—be better than the other guy—then I'd jump back in. I'd take my chances. Because I am better. But I can't fight the politics. I don't have to *only* be better. If someone's got a million dollar contract, he can pitch like crap and hang on. I have to be *ten times* better. We can buy a house. I can get a normal job somewhere, just be a normal guy . . ."

"Well," Kate interrupted, "I'm not sure you have it in you to be a *normal* guy, no matter what you do for a living. If you want to quit . . ." She stopped in mid-sentence.

"I was going to say, if you want to quit, okay. But A.J., Basil and Brad are right. You're pitching as well as you ever have. You may think you can walk away, but I know you. You'd spend the rest of your life saying *what if?*"

"Kate, I'm serious. I don't know how much more failure I can stand—"

"It's not your decision alone," Kate said, a note of anger touching her voice. "Yes, you've had a rough time. But so have I. Did you know once, when were broke and I was pregnant, and you were on a road trip, I only had seven dollars? So, I ate tomato soup and green beans for three days. I took my kids to Japan for two years, following you. I've moved so many times . . . If I'm willing to put up with this a while longer, maybe you should be too!"

Conor rarely saw this side of Kate. He found himself balancing somewhere between shock and anger. She softened him with a kiss.

"Jessie has her T-ball game tonight," she said, "Come and watch. It's a hoot."

His five-year old daughter was a Giant. Her blond curls spilled from under the Giants cap that couldn't remain straight on her head. Her orange t-shirt jersey bunched and drooped over the elastic waistband holding up her white pants. He'd demonstrated how to fold the cuffs under so her orange and black stirrups showed above her shoes.

In truth, Conor wanted to stay home. The lighted four-field complex where Jessie played was three blocks from his mother's house. The t-ball game would be at one field. Three of his brothers would be playing softball at another. Half the neighborhood would be there.

He knew he should go.

Kate was right. The five-year-olds were a study in pure comedy.

Jessie approached the task of hitting with the grim purpose of a soldier heading to combat. From the left-hand batters' box, she pounded her bat on the ground behind the tee, then hoisted it onto her shoulder. Her tongue protruded from the corner of her mouth. She took one half swing, measuring her bat against the ball perched atop a tee, returned the bat to her shoulder, raised her left knee, Japanese style, and struck. As the ball dribbled toward third base, she ran giggling, her hair flowing in the wind, her t-shirt ballooning behind her. Reaching first base, she paused, assessing the state of the defense, then burst toward second base, little arms churning with effort.

Each time a five-year-old put a ball into play, the carefully ordered defense became a nine-player scrum fraught with arguments over who got to pick up the ball—*No, it's my turn! You threw it last time!* —then a careful reconnaissance determining the enemy runner's progress, and an overthrow followed by another nine-player charge in that direction.

After each play, a host of parents, including Kate, reorganized the group to their defensive positions, explaining patiently if the ball wasn't hit to them, they must stay and guard *their* territory. The children swore solemn promises forgotten with the very next batter.

Conor snickered through several innings then walked to the adjacent field where his brothers competed. The Nash boys were the best players, driving slo-pitch lobs into distant darkness, deftly handling anything hit toward them. The men here dug at each other over errors and outs, but laughed like the five-year-olds, anyway.

On a third field, elevens and twelves played. Here, the game stood at the cusp of respectability, players disciplined and drilled on where to go and what to do in any given circumstance. Hits and successful defensive plays remained joyous. Errors, though, elicited self-deprecation, downcast eyes, and apology.

Conor allowed himself to be amazed, once again, at the joy this game engendered in all its forms, at all its levels. And at how intricately it weaved itself into the fabric of his home, his neighborhood, his life.

And, he realized, *any one of a hundred people playing here tonight would trade places with me in a heartbeat.*

Back at the house, his daughter asleep, Giants cap hanging from her bedpost, he told Kate, "I guess I'm going to Phoenix."

thirty-two

San Francisco Giants
1987

Conor drank a toast to Candlestick Park and his precious few days as a Giant.

Rita, I played before friends and family, and I never once failed when they were there.

Except for weekends, Mr. Rosen told me I could leave a hundred passes for every home game. On the streets of San Carlos people pointed me out. That's Conor Nash. He's a San Francisco Giant!

Hard as it might be, I suffered my demotion to Phoenix without complaint. I behaved as a professional. I did what my manager asked and did it well. By mid-May, the veteran they'd hoped would come around suffered his release, and the Conman became a thirty-one-year-old rookie in the National League.

"Hey, Conman," the PR guy said as Conor slumped at his locker, "Ralph wants you to do his post-game show. What should I tell him?"

Conor sighed. They were in Cincinnati, and the Reds hadn't

been kind to the Conman. Tonight's game had been televised nationally—Howard Coselle, Monday Night Baseball. Conor gave up a walk-off home run to Dave Parker. Three nights before, closing the first game of the series, Conor had allowed Parker a game-winning double.

Conor was a favorite of Ralph Barbieri, who hosted the Giants post-game radio broadcast. Barbieri, a gravel-voiced curmudgeon, spared criticism for no one. "I like having you because you're a stand-up guy," Barbieri explained to Conor, "and because of the crazy calls we get from your hometown."

Conor sighed. He wasn't anxious to be on the radio tonight, but he would not hide from his failure.

"Well, that was a rough one, Conman," Barbieri said. "We'll get to that, but right now, we've got some phone calls. Okay, caller, you're on."

"Hey, Lefty, this is Foo. You remember me, dontcha?"

"Yeah, Foo, I—"

"Okay," Ralph broke in, "tell us who Foo is."

"Foo was my catcher at San Carlos High School."

"Why didn't you throw Parker the knuckle curve, Lefty? He ain't never seen nothin' like your knuckle curve."

"Um ... Dave Parker is better than the guys we played against in high school, Foo. I don't use that pitch anymore."

"Yeah, and that's the problem. You gotta throw em' the knuckle curve."

"All right, we've got a vote for the knuckle curve," Ralph said. "Here's another caller."

"Yeah, that you, Connie?"

Conor shook his head and put his hand over his eyes. "Yes. Why are you calling me, Mike?"

"Who's Mike?" Ralph asked.

"My brother."

"Where do you keep the spare key on your car?" Mike asked.

"Why do you want to know—?"

"I kind of lost the other key."

"My car is supposed to be at the players' lot at Candlestick Park," Conor said.

"Yeah, I left something in it. When I got there, I couldn't find the key. I thought I put it in my pocket. I had to get back to San Carlos, but if you'll tell me where you hide your spare key, I'll—"

"Mike, if I tell you where my spare key is over the radio, I think it's likely someone will come and take my car. Why don't we leave it like it is until I get home?"

"Well, the thing I was gonna get—"

"Mike, this is the Giants' post-game show. Why don't we confine our questions to baseball?"

"Okay. Why can't you get Dave Parker out?"

"And," said Ralph, "here's another call."

"Hi, Conor, this is Sarah Lester, do you remember me?"

"Yes, Sarah, I—"

"Don't worry, I'm not going to bring up that time in high school when . . . well, you know."

Despite Dave Parker, I was hot. My ERA stood at 2.05. I had two wins and two saves. I'd struck out twenty-one during my fifteen appearances. The Giants were winning, headed toward their first playoff appearance since 1971. Then Mark Davis sought me out as soon as he arrived at Candlestick the afternoon of July third.

"Conman, I think I'm gonna get traded."

"What? Why would you think that, Mark?"

Davis looked left and right, then said, "I got this call last night, after the game."

"Yeah?"

"Yeah. Some guy with this gravelly voice, like he smoked twelve packs a day. He says his name is Doc, and he's the Padres' traveling secretary. I said, Padres? He said, hasn't anybody talked to me yet? I said, about what? He said, never mind and hung up."

"I wouldn't worry about it," Conor said. "Sounds like one of the guys is pulling your chain."

On July fourth, the Giants and Padres pulled off a blockbuster. Maybe that deal was like the tradeoff when I was five, right, Rita? My sight rescued in exchange for the stutter.

To this very day, I haven't made sense of it. Everybody knew something big was coming. The Giants were seriously good—legitimate World Series contenders—and the trading deadline lurked at month's end.

The Giants got Kevin Mitchell, Dave Dravecky and Craig Lefferts from the Padres. Heading south down Interstate Five were infielder Chris Brown, pitchers Mark Grant, Mark Davis, and ... me.

Among every disappointment this game handed me, being traded from the Giants hurt the most.

"Why me?" Conor asked. A desk separated him and Rosen. Roger Craig occupied a chair next to him. "I mean, I'm sure the Padres didn't tell you they had to have Conor Nash. I must have been a throw-in."

"You're still in the big leagues," Rosen said.

"Why not Joe Price? He's *from* San Diego. He said he'd be thrilled—"

"I threw out lots of names. They said no. When I put your name out there, they said yes. Granted, Mark Davis was the keystone, and they wanted Chris Brown."

"Do they know about his eyelid?" Conor asked.

Brown had spent time on the disabled list a few weeks earlier with a sprained eyelid. He told the trainers it wouldn't stop blinking. During that particular training room consultation, Conor lay on a nearby table undergoing his third cortisone shot since spring.

Unfortunately, Conor and the others didn't drive down the road to San Diego. The Padres were in Montreal. So, four ex-Giants rushed to catch a red-eye that sped them across four time zones during the dark of night, slogged bleary-eyed through customs—the agent was NOT impressed that they were baseball players—then sparred with a French-speaking cab driver, who clearly regarded them as English subversives. They arrived at Olympic Stadium in time to change into their poop-brown Padres jerseys and rush onto the field for the Canadian national anthem.

Conor threw an inconsequential inning late in the game, then retired to the clubhouse in a jet-lagged blur of fatigue and disappointment.

Sitting at his locker, a stubby man who looked a little like Danny DiVito approached him.

"Nash?" the man asked.

"Yeah."

"Hotel's out of rooms. You gotta double up with Davis. We'll get it fixed tomorrow."

The man handed Conor a room key, then disappeared around the next row of lockers. "Who was that?" Conor asked the guy on the stool next to him.

"Our traveling secretary, John Mattei. Everybody calls him 'Doc.'"

"Doc?"

"Yeah, he's a legend in San Diego. Used to be a trainer for the Dodgers. Was the first guy Buzzy Bavasi hired when they started the San Diego franchise. Now, he's the traveling secretary."

"I once stole a bus from a trainer named Doc," Conor said.

CONOR AND MARK DAVIS STUMBLED INTO THE TEAM HOTEL lobby and gave their names to a French-speaking desk attendant, who handed them room keys with the hint of a smile.

He said, "Congratulations."

"What's that about?" Conor asked Davis as they waited at the elevator.

Davis answered with a weary shrug.

They entered their room as Conor fumbled for a light switch. The first switch he flipped produced only a soft hum. A second switch lit the room. Neither man spoke. Furnishings consisted primarily of a huge heart-shaped bed mounted to a turntable that spun in a slow circle on a floor covered by plush red carpet. Heavy red drapes covered windows along one wall. Atop the lone bedside table, a magnum of Champagne nestled in a silver bucket of ice.

While Conor watched the bed spin, Davis opened a second door. "We've got a hot tub, too."

Conor picked up the phone from a low-slung credenza along the wall. "Can you connect me with Doc Mattei?" He waited through a series of rings.

"Yeah?"

"Doc? This is Conor Nash. I hate to complain first night out and all..."

"Look, you can't get too picky. There's a convention, like I said. It's all they got. So, what's the problem?"

"Well . . . there's only one bed."

"I'll have them send up a roll-away."

Conor hung up.

Davis said, "So?"

"I'll flip you for the bed."

The Conman spent his first night as a Padre watching himself slowly rotate in the reflection from a ceiling mirror, wishing he was still a Giant.

San Diego Padres
1987

WE JOINED A PADRES CLUBHOUSE LOADED WITH TALENT. John Kruk and Joey Cora were the youngsters. Both Alomar brothers waited in the Triple-A wings. Veterans included Tony Gwynn, Gary Templeton, Goose Gossage, Bruce Bochy, Mark Parent, Benito Santiago, Storm Davis, Eric Show, Ed Whitson. And, during his final season of a stellar career, Steve Garvey.

I hated Steve Garvey.

I'd never met the man, but growing up an unrepentant Giants fan, I'd been indoctrinated from birth to hate everything Dodger. We allowed an exception for Sandy Koufax, because, well, he was Sandy Koufax. Garvey, though, his clean-cut image shimmering like heat waves rising from cars in a stadium parking lot, embodied the 1970's Dodgers who regularly squashed the Giants. Garvey was the first Padre who approached me as I unpacked at my locker.

"Hi, I'm Steve Garvey. Just wanted to say welcome and see if you need anything."

"Um . . . I'm Conor Nash. I . . . um . . ."

"Right. The Conman. I've heard good things about you. Are you moving your family down?"

"Well . . . yeah, that's the plan."

"If you need information about schools or neighborhoods, let me know. When your wife gets here, my wife will show her around."

Mark Davis arrived a few minutes later.

"Shit," Conor told him. "I just met Steve Garvey. Turns out the cocksucker's a nice guy. God, I hate that."

"Yeah, he talked to me, too. He's super, isn't he?"

Logan Vega, in his rookie year as a manager, became my main issue with the Padres. The transition from Roger Craig to Vega was like the difference between a rising and falling tide. Craig, ever the calming force who spoke only when he needed to, let his players play. Vega, pacing, growling, intimidating. With bitter experience as my teacher, I knew I should ignore his theatrics, keep my head down, and just pitch.

My teammates blew that strategy away when they elected me their union player representative

Two Months Earlier

"HEY, BUDDY, YOU WANT A THANKLESS JOB?" JIM GOTT put an arm around Conor's shoulder the day after Conor's call-up from Phoenix to the Giants.

"What?"

"I got a thankless job, and I need someone to help me."

"Um . . . you want me to help you move?"

"No. I'm the player rep, and I need an assistant. Somebody to pass out papers, make phone calls every now and again. Every team has to have a player rep and an assistant player rep."

Then came the trade.

Dave Dravecky had been the Padres player rep, Craig

Lefferts his assistant. Both were now Giants. Vega called a team meeting the day Conor and the others arrived. He told them they needed to elect a new player rep.

Tim Flannery said, "I nominate Conor Nash. All in favor of the Conman being our player rep raise your hand."

Conor's first confrontation with management occurred soon thereafter.

Joan Kroc, third wife of McDonald's magnate, Ray Kroc, inherited both the team and the company following his 1983 death. A week after Conor became player rep, she issued an edict banning beer from the Padres clubhouse.

Goose Gossage furiously voiced his disapproval in full hearing of sports writers. They quoted him as saying, "What is this? She can poison the world with her burgers, but we can't have a beer after the game?"

Mrs. Kroc suspended Gossage for his remarks. Goose appealed his suspension. The league and union appointed an arbitrator to hear the appeal.

Vega, concerned about losing his closer, cornered Conor.

"What do you know about being a player rep?" Vega demanded.

"Hey, get someone else if you think they'd be better."

"Yeah, right."

"Just to ease your mind, Logan, when they made me assistant at San Francisco, I studied. I'll know what I'm doing. I don't take this job lightly."

The arbitrator ruled in favor of Gossage.

A few weeks later, Benito Santiago suffered a bad game and assaulted his locker with a bat in view of the writers. A story appeared the next day.

"Hey, Conman," Santiago said, "how can they write this?

They aren't even supposed to be there. The rules say they give us twenty minutes."

Conor called a meeting. "Union rules say the press has to wait twenty minutes following a game before they come in. We haven't been enforcing it. What do we want to do?" The vote called for strict enforcement. Conor passed the news to reporters. One ignored the mandate. Conor saw him walk through the door immediately after the next day's game.

"You gotta wait," Conor said.

"I'm not here talking to players. I'm here to see Logan."

Conor blocked his path. "The rule is, you gotta wait."

The man threatened that Vega would not be happy.

"Why are you keeping the press away?" Vega demanded later that evening.

"It's not me. The players voted. They want the twenty-minute rule strictly enforced. Come on, Logan, you were a player rep. You know how it is."

"I was player rep after being in the bigs for fifteen years. You haven't even played a full season up here. That guy you kicked out is writing my book. We use this time right after a game to talk."

"Hey," Conor said, "if you meet him at the door and usher him in yourself, then I guess you can. But the players voted . . ."

Vega walked away.

Conor didn't pitch for ten days.

Conor knocked at Vega's office door.

"Yeah?"

"Hey, Skip, if this player rep thing is the reason I'm not pitching, then I'll resign as player rep."

"Being a player rep doesn't keep a pitcher from pitching," Vega said. "Bad pitching keeps a pitcher from pitching."

Conor's sparkling run had continued. He hadn't suffered a poor outing since joining the Padres.

"Okaaay... but I have to say I don't think I'm throwing bad. When I'm throwing."

"I'm not saying you are. I'm saying bad pitching is what keeps a pitcher from pitching."

"Well, I was throwing pretty well—"

"I know you were, but bad pitching is what keeps a pitcher from pitching."

Okay. Uncle.

"What did he say?" Mark Davis asked Conor.

"He said bad pitching keeps a pitcher from pitching."

"You're throwing great."

"Yeah, he said that, too. And he added that bad pitching keeps pitchers from pitching."

"God," said Davis, "I've been throwing like shit, and I'm pitching every other day. I wonder what *that* means?"

Conor and Vega never spoke again.

thirty-three

Off-Season
1987-88

"I'M NOT GONNA CLEAN HOUSES THIS WINTER."

"Okay, what will you do?" Kate asked.

"I may coach girls' basketball at the junior high school again. I like coaching. But I'm a Major League baseball player..."

"You won't always be a Major League baseball player. Someday, you'll retire. I'm investing our Japanese money. It won't last if we don't work during the off season."

"Well, I'm not cleaning houses."

"Take the coaching job. I'll ask at the junior high if they have anything else for you to pick up a few more hours."

Conor entered the school office to get some printing done for basketball practice.

"Oh, Mr. Nash, I'm so glad you're here," said Assistant Principal Mildred Baker-Finch. "They need you at the cafeteria right after lunch."

"Why would they do that?"

"Poor Mrs. Emmiger. We didn't know what we'd do until your wife called—"

"Why is Mrs. Emmiger poor?"

"She hurt her back."

"Who is Mrs. Emmiger?"

"She's the dishwasher."

Kate greeted him at the door with a kiss. "So, how was practice?"

"They made me wash dishes."

"Oh, good. You got the job."

"Look, I know I've told you my baseball experience over the last thirteen years has pretty much stripped me of my pride. I found out today, though, I've still got at least some of it left."

Kate kissed him again.

"Just think," she said, "how happy you'll be when you can buy Jessi and David cars as their graduation presents."

"Jessi is nine," Conor said. "David is seven. How do you know they'll even want cars?"

Las Vegas Stars
Triple A Baseball
1988

DESPITE AN OUTSTANDING SPRING, I REMAINED BURIED IN *Vega's doghouse. Still a member of the Padres forty-man Major League roster, I wasn't eligible for minor league free agency. I opened the season at Triple-A Las Vegas, where manager Steve Smith was glad to have me. Smith installed me as his closer, and I slammed the door every time out.*

"Man, I don't know what you're still doing here," Smith told me.

"Yeah. I wish they'd take me off the forty-man and give me my release."

"They won't do that. You're throwing too well. You're too valuable if something goes wrong up there."

As the Padres struggled in the National League West—Vega was fired in May—we were crushing Pacific Coast League competition. We had Joey Cora, Mike Brumley, Jerald Clark, Bip Roberts, Sandy Alomar, Roberto Alomar. The Las Vegas Stars won the PCL championship going away. Despite seventeen saves and an ERA of 3.14, I didn't get a September call-up. To make room for those who did, though, the Padres dropped me from the forty-man roster, restoring my free-agency. I obtained my release at season's end.

Off-Season
1988-89

"I'M NOT WASHING DISHES THIS WINTER. I'LL COACH basketball again. I won't wash dishes."

"Okay," Kate said. "I understand. What about driving around and making some deliveries?"

"What kind of deliveries?"

"Flowers. I met the nicest lady who runs a florist shop downtown. She needs someone to make morning flower deliveries."

Mrs. Bently, the flower lady, welcomed Conor into her office. Conor liked how the shop smelled. Mrs. Bently, though, seemed . . . wary.

"And you do have a valid driver's license?" she asked.

"Well . . . of course."

"It's not suspended, or anything?"

"Not that I know of."

"And you realize you must be prompt."

Each morning, Mrs. Bently welcomed him with a handshake, followed by a quick glance at his arms and a stern gaze into his eyes. Even though he appeared each time he was summoned, she always checked the clock and seemed surprised.

Finally, about a month into the job, she said, "I must say, Mr. Nash, I believe you may have turned the corner."

"What corner?"

"Your drug problem. You hang in there. You can whip this thing."

"My drug problem?"

"I gave you this job because your poor wife seemed so anxious for you to have it. I felt sorry—"

"I don't have a drug problem. Why do you think I have a drug problem?"

"Well... um... well, you were a Major League baseball player. Why else would you need a job at a florist shop?"

Scottsdale, Arizona
1989

THE GIANTS CALLED SOON AFTER THE 1988 SEASON ended.

"We see you're available, and we like your numbers," Rosen told him.

Conor pitched through the winter at Golden Gate Park, coached basketball, delivered flowers, and entered Spring Training of 1989 throwing as effectively as he ever had. One-by-one, other lefthanders were demoted. With four days remaining to opening day, Conor knew he'd pitched well enough to make the team. He also knew his performance didn't necessarily count for anything.

Roger Craig walked across the outfield grass where Conor shagged fly balls.

"Conman, we really like how you pitch, but... we've got no room for you. We've got all these young lefties coming up. I can't send you to Triple-A, because we don't have room there, either."

Conor knew the truth of Craig's statement. He'd been watching them. Mike Remlinger, Terry Mulholland, Dennis Cook.

"I can't create a logjam," Craig continued, "so we're letting you go."

This time, Conor felt neither surprise nor heartbreak. His mind simply raced ahead to the logistical difficulties caused by getting cut only a few days before the season opened. All the late spring releases would flood the market. Too many guys. Too few jobs.

"I understand," he said. "I appreciate the—"

"Here's what I *will* do," Craig added. "We play Seattle this afternoon. I've heard that Jerry Latham is looking for lefthanders. I'll tell him we just let a quality lefty go, and he'll give you a call. You should hear from him today."

The Seattle manager didn't call that evening. The Padres did. They told him they'd suffered a couple of injuries, and they needed someone to fill a short-term role in Las Vegas.

"I'm expecting a call from Seattle," Conor said. "Can you at least wait until the end of the day?"

Jackson hadn't called by midnight. Conor accepted the Las Vegas offer. Seattle called the next day.

"I told you," Fat Brad said, his index finger jamming down with enough force to rattle the silverware, "*never* sign a contract until I look at it."

"Well," Conor said sheepishly, "they needed an answer last night. And it's only a one-month deal. What can go wrong?"

"A one-month deal?" asked A.J.

They were dining at one of their old San Carlos hangouts.

"Yeah. They had an injury. They need a guy until they can get some people off the disabled list. They offered me six thousand dollars to play for a month. By then all the Major League teams will have an idea where they need help, and I'll be available."

Las Vegas Stars
1989

OF ALL THE TIMES YOU COULD HAVE GOTTEN INVOLVED BUT didn't, Rita, I understand 1989 the least. Once again, Smith made me his closer. I threw even better than the previous year. At the end of April, the Padres asked me to stay for another month. A.J. contacted team after team. No better offers had surfaced. So, reluctantly, I agreed to play until the end of May—when I got a call from Todd Rubenski, the Padres director of player development.

"Congratulations," Rubenski said, "We're keeping you the whole season."

I told him no, that wasn't our agreement. I signed a one-month contract, which I'd agreed to extend for a second month. Now, I had other opportunities.

Rubenski laughed at me.

"The month-to-month thing is only a verbal agreement on our part. You signed a standard contract. And frankly, you're pitching too well for us to release you."

"Is it bad that they want you?" Kate asked.

"They screwed me with the *verbal agreement* thing. Mostly,

I want to pitch at the big-league level. I know I can. I know I can be good."

"Okay. In the meantime, though, be patient. At least you're getting paid. Give A.J. time to find something else."

"Hey, Conman, this is Bob Didier. What's going on?"

"Bob. Nice to hear from you. I'm stuck here in Las Vegas."

"I know. I've been following your stats. You're rockin'. Get out of there."

Didier, Conor's manager at West Haven, had graduated to the Seattle Mariners' major league staff.

Conor labored through June with the Las Vegas Stars, racking up save after save and trying to calculate his escape.

"Ask for your release," Didier urged.

"I've asked. They've refused. I'll be a free agent at the end of the season—"

"Ask again. I can guarantee you a spot with the Mariners if you can get out of that contract. We've got no lefties. We're dying here."

"Well . . . okay. Um . . . isn't this *collusion*? Isn't this against the rules?"

"I won't tell anyone if you won't."

Conor drove to the ballpark that afternoon—July third, final day of the triple-A season's first half—more determined than ever.

Wearing his workout gear, still brooding, he shagged batting practice fly balls in left field. Returning to the clubhouse he passed an empty office. Hesitating, he checked the hallway in both directions, then stepped inside.

He knew Rubenski's phone number by heart.

"I want my release," Conor said without preamble.

"I'm not listening to this," Rubenski said. "We've been over and over—"

"Yes, we have. I'm not going out there. I'm done. You've taken advantage of me. I accepted this verbal agreement in good faith, and you screwed me. You're holding my career hostage."

"We have a contract—"

"My agent and my lawyer say we can get free of this contract. I'm not playing for the Padres or any of your affiliates again."

Nnnnnnnnnnuuuhh. "Yes, you are."

"No, this is ridiculous . . ."

Uhhhhhnnn. "We control you the" *Uhhhhhnnn* "rest of the year."

The grunting confused Conor until the reality occurred to him. "Hey, are you taking a crap?"

"Well, yeah."

"This is my future we're talking about and you're on the toilet, taking a fucking dump? I don't know why I'm even surprised."

"Okay, fucker, okay. I've had it. You've got your release. As of this moment. And you know what? You might find getting signed by anyone ever again very difficult! Clear your stuff out today!"

Exiting the office, Conor bumped into catcher Jeff Egret.

"Hey, Conman, what's the word?"

"Well, believe it or not, I just got released by a guy while he was taking a crap."

"No, you did not."

"Yes, I did. I'm a free man. I'm gonna have a beer and pack my bags."

As they ran off the field for the bottom half of the first inning, word spread among the Stars' players.

Conor packed his locker as guys ducked inside offering their goodbyes. By the time pitcher Todd Simpson stopped by Conor had enjoyed three celebratory brews. So, he was vulnerable to Simpsons' suggestion.

"You know what you should do, Conman? You should put on the Starman! costume."

thirty-four

THE STARMAN! DESERVED NOT ONLY A TOAST, Conor decided, but a moment of silence as well. He stood, stepped onto the sandstone bench, and raised the bottle high.

Boy, Rita, I hope you weren't off somewhere else when we resurrected the Starman!

The Las Vegas Stars' 1989 pre-season promotions centered on a new mascot: Starman! Always printed and spoken with an exclamation mark. In keeping with minor league mascot tradition, they billed Starman! as a wild and crazy guy who would commit shenanigans and hijinks, bringing raucous humor to Cashman Field that summer.

Starman! plastered billboards all over town. He was interviewed—although mascots are forbidden from talking—on local television channels. He appeared at pre-season grocery store openings. He visited a children's hospital where he scared the snot out of most of the kids.

The Starman! costume consisted of a giant five-pointed star. A cutout in the top point displayed his face. His arms extended from two more points, his legs from the others. The team hired a gymnast from UNLV, envisioning Starman! as a creature who would flip and cartwheel and somersault his way into fans' hearts.

So, on opening day, a packed house waited to welcome the Starman! He was supposed to make his entrance sprinting from the home dugout, cartwheeling his way to the foul line, ending everything with a full back flip leaving him standing at home plate.

The kid, who usually performed his acrobatics before a half dozen gymnastics fan and his parents, became so caught up by the roar of ten thousand fans, he forgot he had a good eighteen inches of star protruding over his head.

He spiked himself into the ground on his second cartwheel and became a rolling avalanche, star points flailing, until, mercifully, he came to rest—face down—in the right-hand batter's box.

We thought he might be dead. Trainers from both dugouts waved their arms at an ambulance parked just past the outfield fence. As the left field gate opened and two ambulance attendants rushed forward carrying a portable gurney, someone chanted Starman! Starman! Starman! Someone else joined in. Pretty soon ten thousand people added their voices.

The Starman! remained out cold as the ambulance guys arranged all his points to fit on a gurney and rolled him away. The crowd sent him off with wild applause, stomping their feet and screaming.

Starman! Starman! Starman! Starman!

"Hey," Simpson told Dave Lieper, "Conman got released. He's gonna wear the Starman! suit."

"Oh, man, that would be epic."

"I'm not putting on the Starman! suit. I'm packing."

"You've got to, Conman. They'd be talking about it forever. Here, let me get you another beer."

"We don't even know where the Starman! suit is," Conor said.

"I'll bet we can find out."

They located Don Logan, the Star's general manager.

Okay, Rita, businesspeople who own and run minor league baseball teams have nothing to do with the baseball aspect of their enterprise. They sign an agreement with their major league partners and provide a ballpark. The major league team provides and is in complete control of the players. To make money, owners and their representatives must convince people to attend. All manner of bizarre and tasteless promotions lure fans like carnival barkers. I've seen Toss A Midget Night, Mike Tyson Plastic Ear Night, Moses Bobblehead Night. Even Vasectomy Night at some ballpark in Arkansas where a lucky fan won a surgical procedure.

So, Don Logan, thrilled at the idea of Starman! making another appearance, said, "Yeah, I know where the suit is. I'll go get it."

Several minutes—and one more beer—later, the empty Starman! costume rested at my locker, along with a half-dozen members of our pitching staff.

"I told you, I'm not putting it on. I'd probably get in trouble."

"What are they gonna do, release you?" Everybody laughed,

and somewhere, bubbling through the snorts and giggles, I heard those three little words: I dare you.

EVERYTHING *SEEMED* TO FIT. A BAND OF ELASTIC CLAMPED the tight circle of fabric around his face. While his legs were flexible enough to run and jump, Conor found his arms more restricted. The star points were stiff and bringing his hands together took considerable effort, like doing bench curls with heavy weights.

"Okay, between innings, run onto the field," Simpson instructed.

"No, no. that's boring. He's gotta make an entrance!"

"What kind of entrance?"

"The Go-Kart!"

Conor's eyes, now floating on the surface of his sixth beer, lit up.

Yeah! The Go-Kart!

Conor and the other bullpen guys loved the go-kart.

Grounds crew guys used a go-kart, festooned with Stars logos, to drag the infield before and during each game. The go-kart sat locked in a cage under the bleachers at the left-field foul pole. A concrete ramp ran from this cage down to field level. A gate a little way from the Stars' bullpen seating area admitted the cart onto the warning track.

Conor and the other bullpen pitchers had plotted all season to get their hands on the go-kart. The cage, though, was kept locked. Before his release, Conor had been constructing an elaborate scheme to make a wax impression of the head groundskeeper's gate key so he could make duplicates.

Late during the sixth inning, the pitchers snuck Starman!

along a narrow concourse running under the stands.

"Starman! needs the go-kart," they told the cage guardian.

This slack-jawed kid looked Starman! up and down. Conor did his best to offer a reassuring smile, although a smile coming from the disembodied face of someone wearing a giant star is pretty creepy.

The kid took a couple of wary steps away from Starman! and protested, "Nobody told me anything about—"

"It's one of those things that just came up. Don Logan okayed it."

"Mr. Logan did?"

"Yeah. Call him if you want. He's in the owner's box with some really important guys . . ."

"And he said it was okay?"

"Who do you think gave us the Starman! suit?"

The kid produced a key.

Yesssss!

"THIS WON'T WORK. THE ARMS ARE TOO STIFF. I CAN'T bend them enough to keep my hands on the steering wheel."

Conor sat wedged into the go-kart. His Starman! feet were too big for the gas and brake pedals and his legs were bowed. His main problem, though, would be steering.

"No, no, we can fix it," Simpson said. "Hey, Pat, run into the clubhouse and get some tape."

As Simpson pushed the left arm, and Pete Labine pushed the right, they bent the suit enough to secure Starman!'s hands to the wheel with a roll of athletic tape.

"Okay, can you drive?"

"Yeah, yeah, I think so."

Conor, strapped into the golf cart and unable to rotate his head left or right without popping his face out of the cutout, asked for instructions.

"I'll get it started for you," the kid said, "from there it's easy. Push the gas pedal to go and let off to stop."

Conor found the gas pedal with his right foot.

"What about the brake?" he asked.

"You won't need it. Just back off the gas."

"One last thing," Simpson said. "Sunglasses."

Starman!, being a native of Las Vegas where the sun always shone and celebrities always hid behind shades, never appeared without sunglasses. Simpson carefully placed the darkened lenses over Conor's eyes, tucking the stems into the elastic band surrounding his face, and sliding them over his ears.

Simpson stepped back and examined his handiwork. "You *are* the Starman! Okay, we've gotta get to the bullpen. The kid will open the gate at the bottom of the ramp. What are you gonna do when you get out there?"

"I'll circle the field on the warning track. Then I'll stop at our dugout, say goodbye to everyone, and drive back here."

The kid started the go-kart with two outs in the bottom of the eighth. Conor sat idling at the top of the ramp. Given his limited range of vision, he could only follow the game on the center field scoreboard which stood directly in his line of sight.

He saw the light indicating third out wink on. The other lights and numbers reset themselves to zeroes. Stars' left-fielder Shane Mack entered Conor's vision, trotting to take his warm-up tosses between innings.

Okay. Here we go...

The kid waved and swung the gate open. Conor jammed his right foot onto the gas pedal.

"Aaaaaaaaaaaahhhhhhhhhhh!"

He slammed back against the seat with a force he estimated at about two G's. The go-kart screamed down the ramp. As he blasted past the kid and he heard something that sounded like *Noooooo ... Toooofaassst ... Toooofaasst!*

As his head snapped back, his chin became untucked from the elastic band framing his face. He stared at black sky as the go-kart's rear wheels bit into the warning track. He tried to slack off the accelerator, but his right foot was wedged solidly into place.

He forced his chin down to find Shane Mack, raw fear etched across his face, as a demonic, screaming machine driven by some multi-tentacled creature wearing sunglasses leapt from the stands and homed in on him like a heat-seeking missile.

The brake! Hit the brake!

Conor shoved with his left foot. The rear wheels kept grinding but the left front wheel locked. Conor saw a blurred and repetitive collage: *ShaneMackWallFans, ShaneMackWallFans, ShaneMackWallFans...*

Now, both feet were wedged. Conor fought, and finally the left one popped free.

As the kart tore from its spin, Starman! screamed toward the Las Vegas bullpen.

Cashman Field's bullpens consisted of a double mound and two home plates situated along each foul line. Pitchers occupied a row of metal folding chairs lined against the wall separating fan seating from the field.

The seven Las Vegas bullpen members roared with laughter as Shane Mack fled the spinning go-kart. Now, though, this bullet headed straight for them.

Conor couldn't free himself from the gas pedal, as,

one-by-one, pitchers bailed over the wall and fans helped pull them to safety. Conor cranked the steering wheel enough to avoid a fiery collision into the crowd.

Now his path took him directly toward the bullpen pitching mound.

He braced for a jarring collision. Instead, the mound's rear slope propelled Starman! and his go-kart gracefully into the sky. Time slowed to a crawl.

In his peripheral vision, Conor saw a blur of faces as he soared past fans. He saw the distant press box and grandstand, brightly lit against a horizon of glittering Las Vegas neon. He saw the opposing team's third base coach leap, performing a graceful, twisting slow-motion pirouette, worthy of any matador.

Conor's world began to tilt sideways as the go-kart's aerodynamics failed. His taped hands wrenched at the steering wheel to correct this slow roll. The go-kart, lacking ailerons, failed to respond.

The go-kart twisted a full ninety degrees as it began its descent. Conor smashed into the warning track on the cart's left side, plowing a furrow through the red clay, coming to halt fifty feet from his dugout.

Mercifully, the engine only whined for a moment before dying. One wheel spun silently. Someone yelled, "Get out! Get out! That thing might catch fire!"

Someone else yelled, "He can't get out!"

"Why not?"

"His hands are taped to the steering wheel!"

Lying sideways in the dirt, his sunglasses askew, Conor watched as a Stars trainer sprinted heroically, carrying a pair of scissors to cut him loose.

"Conman, Conman, are you okay?" the trainer demanded.

A single thought occurred to Conor. "Didn't your mother ever tell you how dangerous it is to run with scissors?"

They cut Conor free and helped him to his feet.

"Can you walk?"

"Yeah, I think so. I'm—"

The ovation sounded as if it came from a stadium of a hundred thousand.

Conor turned in a stiff, slow circle. From every part of the park, fans stomped and whistled and cheered. The chant began, spreading to both teams and even the umpires.

Starman! Starman! Starman! Starman! Starman!

Conor managed a small but triumphant leap. He raised his arms as best he could, ran to home plate, then executed a stiff-legged tour around the bases.

Finally, he bowed stiffly, squeezed his way down the dugout steps and into the clubhouse.

Conor decided to surprise Kate and the kids. He began the long drive north early the next morning, arriving home that afternoon. He encountered a state of chaos.

Kate yelled. David cried. Dogs barked.

"Why are you home?" Kate asked.

"I got released. What's going on?"

"David fell into the pool."

"He knows how to swim."

"He had his clothes on and I guess it kind of scared him, which scared me. I swear, I tell him time after time to pay attention to what he's doing. Sometimes, I think he's got no common sense. Where do you think he gets that?"

"Yeah, where do you think?"

"So, getting released is good, right?"

"Very good."

"Okay. I hope you took time to say goodbye to everyone."

"Yeah." Conor smiled. "Yeah, I did."

thirty-five

I EMBRACE THE CONCEPT OF KARMA. THAT'S ABOUT AS *Zen as I get, though. I hold a basic faith that what goes around, comes around.* When you struggled through as many manipulations and mistreatments at the whim of baseball executives, as a lot of us did, to survive without surrendering completely to cynicism you must nurture a thread of belief that somewhere, somehow accounts will be settled.

When the Padres released me, the Angels were embroiled in a pennant race. Neck and neck with Oakland and Kansas City as the second half began, the Angels blew a comfortable lead, ultimately finishing seven games behind American League champion Oakland.

I heard later the Angels manager made a specific plea to GM Mitchell Preston. *Get Conor Nash. Give him whatever he wants. He fits our needs perfectly. He might make the difference.*

Conor thought of his first release and the disputed dental bill.

He raised a toast to karma.

"So, will you finally get out of the way and let me do this? I must say, I'm not sure I could do a lot worse."

"Okay, A.J., you are officially my agent. The Mariners already told me—"

"Connie, stop right there. This is the problem. You're still ready to accept what someone tells you. We'll do it right this time."

A.J. rented a suite at the airport Marriott in Los Angeles.

"Why do we need a suite?" Conor asked. "You're just calling people. You can do that in a phone booth."

"Hey, I know money. I know deals. You must achieve a certain frame of mind—which requires a specific ambiance. George Steinbrenner will know if I'm calling from a phone booth."

A.J. explained his strategy. He'd call every GM or owner who'd listen. He would discuss three signing options: A package, Conor is immediately placed on the forty-man roster and assigned to the major league club; B package, Conor is on the forty-man, assigned to Triple-A, with a guaranteed call-up at some point during the season; C package, not on the forty-man roster, assigned to Triple-A, a guaranteed September call-up.

"A key to negotiation," A.J. said, "is giving people options. Of course, we want you in the majors. What we're really negotiating for, though, is the forty-man roster."

"We are?"

"Must I remind you, Kate is pregnant again? Ultimately, who will I have to answer to? Not you. You've been pissed at me before. I don't want Kate mad at me. We get on the forty-man, you've got medical benefits."

Conor waited and watched a *Days of Our Lives* marathon on the soap opera channel as A.J. worked the phones. Periodically, A.J. emerged from the bedroom for a drink or something from the fridge.

"Just talked to Lou Gormon with the Red Sox!" he'd announce. Or "Peter O'Malley says the Dodgers are interested!"

"In what?"

"They're getting back to me."

"What about the Mariners?"

"I left a message for Lee Petty."

"I know they want me."

"Hey, it's one thing for a coach to fudge the rules a little and say something during a phone conversation. A GM can't do that. He's got a procedure to follow. If they want you, we'll know soon enough."

As return calls poured in, everyone focused on the C package. A.J. said they would hold out for at least a B. The consensus response: "Well, if anyone offers a B, let us know. We like your guy."

A.J. emerged beaming from the bedroom. He'd begun the day wearing a three-piece suit. He'd shed his jacket and vest sometime around noon. His tie disappeared a couple of hours later. Now, he wore a t-shirt, boxers and black socks.

"The Mariners called back," A.J. said. "They offered a B package."

Conor jumped from the couch and punched the air. "Yesssss."

"They wanted to know if we'd gotten any B offers. I told them we had one other."

"Do we?"

"No."

"What now?"

"They're gonna call back."

"Okay. One other thing..."

"What's that?"

"Put your pants on. If George Steinbrenner calls, he'll know you aren't wearing pants."

Before A.J. retrieved his trousers, though, the phone rang again.

"A.J.? This is Mitchell Preston again. We've thought it over, and we'll bump our offer to a B package. We're in a pennant race here, and we believe one more solid lefthander could make the difference."

"That's good to hear, Mr. Preston. But we have a B package offer from the Mariners already."

After a moment of silence, Preston said, "We really want him. What kind of money are the Mariners offering?"

"Um... major league minimum—$68,000, prorated to time he spends in the majors. And they said the call-up will come pretty soon."

"We'll offer $80,000 if we can get this thing done tonight."

A.J. hesitated. "We'll need time for Conor's attorney to go over the contract."

"A.J., this is a standard contract. Oh, and please tell Conor I hope there are no hard feelings. I hope we can let bygones be bygones."

"Okay... okay. We'll... we'll get right back to you."

"... AND HE SAID KIND OF A WEIRD THING RIGHT AT THE end. He said he hoped there are no hard feelings and wanted bygones to be bygones."

"Yeah. I should have reminded you. Mitchell Preston is the

guy who screwed me by keeping me at A ball when other Angels coaches told me I was ready for Triple-A. He's also the guy who handed me my first release. He told people I'd never have the mental discipline to pitch at the major league level. Then he hung up on me. For him to bring it up at all tells me he hasn't forgotten any of it."

"Okay. What do you want to do? I mean, this is business, and twelve thousand bucks is twelve thousand bucks."

Conor didn't hesitate.

"Call Preston. Tell him bygones are *not* bygones. Tell him we're gonna sign with the Mariners. I hope I never need twelve thousand dollars so bad that I have to trust a guy like him again."

Calgary Cannons
Triple A Baseball
1989

"THE CALGARY CANNONS?" KATE ASKED. "SHOULD I FIND our passports?"

"They say I'll only be there for a week while I clear waivers and they make a spot on their forty-man roster."

"We've heard things like that before," Kate said.

"Yeah, I know. You guys sit tight. Hopefully, you'll be coming to Seattle."

Seven days later, Calgary Manager Rich Morales shook Conor's hand. "Go get 'em, Conman, you got the call."

I took a cab from SeaTac International Airport to the Kingdome, arriving mid-afternoon. Walking into a new clubhouse is always a deep-breath kind of a moment. These were people who, for the most part, I didn't know. People whom I'd live with as close as family for long months. People who, to a large extent, controlled my fate. Pitching well is only part of it. Your teammates have to catch it. And they have to put runs on the board. They carry you over the rough spots, and you do the same for them. Having a couple of people you know provides a kind of crutch while the others size you up.

The only guy I knew here was Jeffrey Leonard, but we weren't close during our time with San Francisco

I found my way through the Kingdome's shadowy catacombs to the home clubhouse. I took a deep breath and pushed open the door. Most players sat at their lockers, involved in their afternoon rituals. The clubhouse guy showed me my spot. I said a couple of polite hellos as I made my way.

There came a single voice, joined by another, then another, until half the clubhouse, it seemed, stood and chanted, Starman! Starman! Starman! Starman! *Baseball gossip travels fast.*

I waved and took a bow.

Finally, I was ready.

I allowed a run during my first appearance as a Mariner. It would have been more, except for Jeffrey.

When we were together on the Giants, Jeffrey Leonard was a looming, scary sort of presence. He preferred the nickname HacMan. Some sports writers, though—drawing on inspiration from Alcatraz's proximity to Candlestick Park—dubbed him Penitentiary Face. Like a lot of sluggers, Jeffrey didn't have much use for pitchers. When we'd all be on a bus driving to a ballpark on the road, I'd always sort of duck a little when he walked down the aisle.

On my first appearance as a Mariner, I had bases loaded with one out when the batter hit a shot into left field, too much out of the gap for Ken Griffey Junior to reach. Jeffrey was at the end of his career, and not the quickest of left fielders. His primary job with the Mariners was to mentor Griffey in his rookie year and keep the cocky nineteen-year-old out of trouble. But HacMan put on an all-out sprint and made a diving grab that limited to damage to one run.

After the game, Jeffrey found me on my clubhouse stool. He modified his scowl in his best attempt at a smile and presented a huge black fist for a bump. Referencing the sun ball, he lost all those years ago in Chicago, he said, "I owed you that one, Conman. Welcome to the team."

I allowed my second run twenty appearances later.

Seattle Mariners

SEATTLE. A FRANCHISE STEEPED IN FAILURE AND FRUSTRATION. Over its thirteen-year history, the Mariners had never finished above .500. This team, though, oozed with young talent.

At the trading deadline they sent Mark Langston to Montreal for Randy Johnson, Brian Holman and Gene Harris, bolstering a roster that already included Eric Hanson, Mike Jackson, Billy Swift, Ken Griffey, Jr., Jay Buhner, Jeffrey Leonard, Alvin Davis, Edgar Martinez, Harold Reynolds, Jim Presley and Omar Vizquel.

Most of my pitches were painted onto corners. When I missed, though, Omar would perform some sort of defensive miracle at shortstop, or Presley would smother it at third base. My screwball performed its baffling pirouette. When chance allowed the meat of a bat to find it, Griffey executed a circus catch in center, or runners were snuffed by Buhner's cannon from right. The Conman appeared thirty-one times, striking out twenty-two, walking ten, and posting a 2.81 ERA. If I'd sucked, the legend of the Conman would have been limited to dinner conversations with A.J. and

Baze and Fat Brad. The combination of being good and eccentric and old, though, attracted attention.

"Hey, can we do a story about the Starman! thing?" the newspaper guys asked.

"Sure."

"And you were released how many times?"

"Well, nine so far."

"And you were once traded for . . ."

"Yeah, a hundred dollars and a bag of baseballs. And they made me deliver the baseballs. That wasn't as weird, though, as when I drove from Phoenix to Connecticut with two pitching machines crammed into my back seat, because Charlie Finley was too cheap to rent a truck."

Sports Illustrated called me *the man who'd had more cups of coffee than Juan Valdez.*

"You got in a fight with Wilbur Spalding?"

"Well, I was young and stupid at the time."

"And they won't let you go back to Venezuela?"

"That's what they said . . . and they had guns."

"Al Rosen discovered you when he happened to ride by on his bike in Golden Gate Park and saw you throw a no-hitter in a beer league?"

"Yeah. Yeah. That's what happened, all right."

thirty-six

Phoenix
Off-Season
1989-90

"OKAY, WE'VE GOT A HOUSE. THE MARINERS WANT me back. A.J.'s working on a new contract. You don't know anyone in Phoenix, so you can't find people who want me to wash dishes or supervise bingo. I'm taking the winter off."

"Off from what?" Kate asked. "You're not planning to play?"

"Phoenix to Golden Gate Park is a long weekend commute. I'll work out at the Tempe complex. I'm talking about not having a winter job."

"So, what will you do?"

"I don't know. Sit around and watch the soaps?"

They lived in Scottsdale. A straight shot of just a few miles took him to Tempe, the Mariners Spring Training home. He didn't even have to get on a freeway. For the first time ever going into spring, his name appeared on a twenty-five-man roster. A.J. told him negotiations appeared promising.

Off-Season 1989-90

"Lee, you'll have to bear with me here. I'm just a neophyte at this agent stuff."

A.J. Cohen faced the Mariners assistant GM across a desk at the team's downtown Seattle offices located a couple of long-tosses of a salmon away from Pike Place Market. The windows looked west, the blue expanse of Puget Sound and snow-capped mountains of the Olympic Peninsula beyond.

A.J. presented Lee Petty with 1989 statistical rankings of major league pitchers. Conor's performance during the final three months placed him twenty-fifth on the list, just behind Cincinnati's Norm Charleton of Nasty Boys fame, and the Met's John Franco.

"Let me point out a couple of things," Petty said. "First, Conor is ten days short of being eligible for arbitration this season, so anything we provide beyond the Major League minimum is generosity on our part. Not that we don't want to compensate Conor fairly. He certainly performed beyond the minimum level, but Charleton is well-established..."

A.J. offered his apology.

"Look, we know Conor isn't Norm Charleton. We know he's not John Franco. We know he's got to prove himself longer than a half-season in the majors. And if Charleton enters arbitration, he'll get what? Four hundred thousand? We won't ask for that."

"Okay, what are you thinking?"

A.J. smiled. "Well, again, tell me if I'm out of line, because I'm just a neophyte here. Maybe $200,000..."

Petty's eyebrows lifted briefly, betraying his poker face.

"Well, A.J., $200,000 is probably doable."

"... and a few performance incentives."

The eyebrows drooped. "We have to be a little circumspect about performance incentives, A.J."

A.J. knew what Petty expected. Most players asked for $50,000 or $100,000 payoffs as they hit certain statistical thresholds over a season. Typically, those thresholds were weighted toward the final third of the year. Bonuses for making an All-Star team or being named to a major award were often tacked onto many contracts.

"Again, what do you have in mind?"

"How about five thousand dollars?"

"Come again?"

"Five thousand. At fifteen appearances. Or is that unreasonable? Again, I'm just a neophyte..."

"Well, sure."

A.J. offered a schedule. Five thousand dollars at fifteen appearances, five thousand more at five game increments up to fifty appearances. Ten thousand at sixty games, twenty thousand at sixty-five topping out at thirty thousand for eighty appearances.

"I won't get eighty appearances," Conor told A.J.

"We know that, and they know that. You have to put a big number at the end, though. A big number makes the little numbers more palatable. Especially when they know you won't hit that big one."

Petty looked at the incentives schedule and said, "Let me think about this. We'll get together next week."

"CHA-CHING!" CONOR ANNOUNCED AS HE WALKED INTO THE visitors' clubhouse at Cleveland Municipal Stadium late that May.

"What?" demanded bullpen mate Mike Jackson. "What cha-ching? There's no cha-ching in May."

Cha-ching was the code phrase a player used to announce he'd hit the threshold for a bonus payout. Conor made his fifteenth appearance, and the Mariners owed him five thousand dollars.

Conor grinned and repeated, "Cha-ching."

Players held modest clubhouse celebrations recognizing teammates who achieved a bonus. Soon several gathered at Conor's locker, trying to understand.

"It's what my agent negotiated," Conor said.

That impressed everyone. Granted, Conor didn't go out of his way to say the payoff was only five thousand. But cha-ching was cha-ching.

Two weeks later, Conor cha-chinged again. Now his teammates' curiosity became intrigue, which only deepened with each subsequent cha-ching. Again, he disclosed no dollar amounts.

"And your agent negotiated these bonuses?"

Conor shrugged.

"Tino Martinez talked to me while I was waiting for you last night," A.J. said a few days later. "He wants me to be his agent."

"Yeah, a couple other guys asked me about you," Conor said. "What did you tell Tino?"

"I told him no. I told him I'm just a neophyte at this. I said I'm not too worried about fucking up *your* contract, because I've known you since second grade, and you're not paying me anything. I said I'd feel really bad if I fucked up some real baseball player's contract."

THE BUZZARD CIRCLING THOSE CONTRACT NEGOTIATIONS *during the early months of 1990, though, was the sixth labor disruption of major league baseball since 1972. The previous five-year contract would expire at the end of 1989. The two sides argued about revenue sharing, salary caps and adjustments to the arbitration process. As talks stalled, owners decided not to wait for players to strike. The day pitchers and catchers were supposed to report for Spring Training, the owners locked us out.*

Conor laughed as he recalled his initial panic.

"Finally, I'm ready, and now this," he'd complained. "Why doesn't the damned angel just strike me with a lightning bolt and be done with it?"

Best not second-guess a baseball angel. The lock-out worked in my favor.

The lockout ended March nineteenth. The owners pushed the seasons start back to April ninth, giving us less than three weeks to prepare.

"We can't look at a lot of people," Mariners manager Jerry Latham told the twenty-five-man roster gathered before him. "This is our team. Do what you need to do and get ready."

Grinning, Conor told Kate, "I think I'm a lock. I don't have enough time to screw this up."

THOUGHTS OF 1990 BROUGHT A RUSH OF MEMORIES TO THE mountaintop.

Nolan Ryan pitching for the Rangers at the Kingdome. Me watching from the dugout.

"Look at him," Conor told pitching coach Paul Michaels. "Watch his back foot. He slides it forward. He's pitching four inches in front of the rubber!"

"Yeah, he does that sometimes."

"Why don't they stop him?"

Michaels shrugged. "He's Nolan Ryan."

I worked the seventh inning of the same game, two strikes on Rafael Palmeiro, a runner at second. If ever I needed an extra four inches on my fastball, this was it. I slid my left foot forward, came set, and delivered.

"Balk! That's a balk!" screamed two umpires in unison.

And Dave Parker.

Every pitcher has that one guy he can't get out. At least my guy wasn't some .200 banjo hitter, who couldn't get a ball past the infield. My guy played nineteen years in the bigs, 1978 National League MVP, three World Series rings.

Dave Parker hit the Conman like a speed bag.

The 1990 season brought Parker—at the end of his long career and not quite the force he once was—to Milwaukee. That same season the Mariners and Brewers fought one of the epic brawls of baseball history. Animosity rooted in Spring Training of 1989 exploded as the teams contested a pair of scuffles during each end of a doubleheader. Two months later, Mariners catcher Dave Valley suffered a broken leg when Brewer Bill Spiers took him out with an aggressive slide at home plate.

Finally, playing at the Kingdome the last day of June 1990, Brewers pitcher Bob Sebra hit Mariner Tracy Jones, who charged the mound. The resulting free-for-all flared, sputtered and reignited three times, taking the mass of combatants from home plate to first base and then right field over a span of twenty minutes.

Just like the Angels-Twins brawl on the day of my Major League debut, I couldn't help but be aware of the sheer size of our opponents. Yes, the Mariners had Jeffrey Leonard and a 6-10 Randy Johnson. The Brewers' behemoths, though, included Greg Vaughn, Don Baylor, B.J. Surhoff, Chris Bosio, Dale Sveum and . . . Dave Parker, a genuinely large human being.

Since Conor didn't know any Brewers well enough to recruit as a passive wrestling partner until order was restored, he floated on the fringes of the battle, keeping his head on a swivel, tugging at a jersey here and there. He hugged it out with the aforementioned Vaughn for a few minutes, then extricated himself during the first lull, adding, "Yeah, good meeting you, too, Greg."

Most disconcerting, though, everywhere he went over the course of the entire twenty minutes, Parker—nicknamed The Cobra—seemed to be stalking him. Conor conducted himself professionally in every phase of shoving and squeezing and shouting. At every turn, though, Parker loomed.

"I don't know," he told Kate after the game. "I must have done *something* to make him mad."

"Does it matter?"

"Yeah, it matters. I've never even met him. Maybe he's a friend of someone who doesn't like me. What bugs me is everyone says he's a good guy. I don't mind pissing off jerks, but a good guy..."

Conor brooded over the issue all night. He arrived early at the Kingdome the next day and watched for the big man to come from the visitors' clubhouse and begin his stretching routine.

"Um...Dave?"

Parker glanced up from his sprawl on the Kingdome turf, a pre-set scowl reserved for fans or media disturbing his preparation fixed on his face.

"I'm Conor Nash. We haven't met...I just want to clear the air here. Have I done something, somewhere, sometime, to upset you?"

Parker appeared genuinely puzzled. "Why would you think that?"

"Well, yesterday, during the fight, you seemed to be . . . sort of . . . following me around."

Parker smiled. "Well, I was."

"Okay . . . so what did I do to—"

"Nothin', man, you didn't do anything. I just had to make sure you were okay. You haven't pitched yet, and I can't afford to let you to get hurt."

Other conflicts marked the 1990 season, including bullpen wars between the Mariners and Rangers. The initial skirmishes involved little craft or guile. Lighting firecrackers by delayed fuse under the opposing team's bullpen bench. Or a well-tossed stink bomb.

When a television news crew interviewed members of the Rangers bullpen following one of these assaults, the enemy pitcher said the Mariners displayed no real creativity or imagination.

That didn't sit right with the Conman. So, he organized a bobsled race. The Mariners bullpen pitchers practiced under the stands. Then, between the second and third innings of a Rangers game, they took a long metal bench and placed it between the bullpen mound and home plate.

They lined up, carefully stepped over the bench in unison, and sat facing the grandstand. On Conor's order, they hunched forward and began to jiggle slightly.

"Okay," called Conor, who occupied the anchor position, "right turn on three."

As one, they leaned violently left, maintaining the jiggle. "Now, left turn." They jerked right.

Conor took them through a couple more turns before they

relaxed, raised their arms high in victory, and dismounted to cheers. "Let's see 'em top that," Conor said as they exchanged high fives.

The next day, between the second and third innings, the Rangers hauled their bench to the corresponding spot at their side of the field and sat facing the foul line. Initially, they leaned side to side in unison, then crossed left legs over right legs. Next, right over left. Finally, each pitcher removed his hat and placed it on the head of the player to his left, the last player jumping up and carrying his hat to the other end of the bench, placing it on the first guy's head as everyone slid down one spot.

The crowd went crazy.

"Why are they cheering?" one of Conor's mates demanded. "That's our crowd, cheering the other team."

"Shit," Conor said, "you have to admit, they were pretty good. Let me think about this. We'll get 'em when we go to Arlington."

"OKAY, HERE IT IS," CONOR TOLD HIS BULLPEN MATES A month later following the first of a three-game series at the Rangers new stadium. He held a tube like caulk comes in at hardware stores. The tube said, "Liquid Concrete."

"We hide here and wait until everyone's gone. I mean everyone. Then, we go to squeeze this stuff into the lock on the bullpen gate."

The architects of new stadiums locate bullpens behind outfield fences in left and right fields. The padded gates are part of the wall, swinging into the bullpen so people can enter and exit. In Arlington, the locking mechanism that secured the bullpen when the stadium wasn't in use during a game or practice was built into the gate.

The Mariners pitchers waited until the grounds crew left for the night, creeping along in the shadows of the warning track as they made their way to the home bullpen. Conor squeezed as much of the liquid concrete as he could into the keyhole. They carefully toweled away the excess and fled into the night.

"Won't they figure it out when they try and unlock it tomorrow morning?" one of the pitchers asked Conor.

"I don't think they lock it during homestands," Conor said. "If we're lucky, they won't find out anything until the starter goes to warm up. There'll be enough people in the stands to see it."

The bullpen crew maintained a wary eye. They expected a flurry of activity as grounds crewmen fought the frozen and inoperable locking mechanism. Nothing seemed amiss, though, as everyone calmly went about their pre-game routines.

"They probably got here early, and we missed it," someone suggested.

"Crap," Conor said, and then brightened. "Maybe not. Maybe no one's been there yet."

The time arrived for the Rangers' starting pitcher to begin his warm-up routine. Nothing. No one headed to the bullpen. Conor's heart sank. *Okay, they figured out they can't get in, and they won't give us the satisfaction. Their guy is throwing somewhere else.*

As the Rangers completed infield practice, Conor approached one of their coaches.

"Hey, Rusty," Conor said, "your starter's so good, he doesn't need to warm up today?"

"Oh, hi, Conman. No. When we designed the stadium, we had a bullpen mound installed under the stands by the home clubhouse. Some starters prefer to get ready there."

"Okay, guys," Conor told his bullpen mates, "this is either going to be a bust or really good."

Typically, neither relief corps occupied the bullpen during the first few innings, because it offered such a lousy view of the game. Expecting their starter to go at least four or five innings, they watched from the dugout during the early frames. So, both bullpens remained unoccupied for the second inning when Buhner nailed the Rangers' starter with a shot off his thigh.

As trainers rushed to the mound, Conor saw a flurry of activity in the Rangers dugout. A catcher, wearing full gear, began a long sprint toward the pen. Two pitchers followed him.

At first, all eyes fixed on the injured pitcher, so no one noticed the catcher's struggle at the bullpen gate. As the starter limped toward his dugout, the catcher's efforts became more frantic. Fans began to notice.

Initially, the laughter sounded polite and scattered.

When the Rangers manager and pitching coach rose to the top dugout steps, the catcher turned and held his arms wide as a signal of futility. The second base umpire jogged out to ascertain the problem. The manager raised his arms in a question mark. The umpire arrived and pointed at the top of the fence. One pitcher interlaced his fingers and made a cup of his hands.

Conor checked the camera wells. Every television camera in the stadium pointed at the bullpen gate. Announcers at their stations high behind home plate shook with laughter.

The catcher tossed his mask and glove and shoes over the fence. Then, with a helpful boost from the pitcher, grabbed the top of the fence and swung one leg up and over before disappearing on the other side. One of the pitchers followed suit.

The home plate umpire barked. The Ranger's manager yelled,

and a pitcher ran from the dugout to begin *his* warm-up on the field mound.

Between the third and fourth innings, the grounds crew tried drills and chisels to no avail.

At the beginning of the fifth inning, they dashed to the bullpen, carrying two stepladders. They leaned one against the outfield wall and tossed the other over the fence.

The remaining Rangers relievers trotted across the outfield. Before they scaled the fence, though, they paused, faced the Mariners bench, and performed a deep bow. Then they turned and repeated the gesture, displaying their butts.

"If the game wasn't being televised," Rangers pitcher Jeff Reardon advised Conor the next day, "we would have shown you the full moon."

"Everybody be alert, because they'll try something," Conor advised his mates the afternoon of the opener of the Rangers series in Seattle.

"I talked with security. They'll keep guys posted to make sure they don't do anything late at night. Keep your eyes open, anyway."

The Rangers couldn't retaliate in kind, Conor knew, because Kingdome bullpens were situated for all to see along each foul line. No locks, no gates, just a metal bench, a double mound toward the outfield fence and a pair of home plates back toward the dugouts. A big Igloo water jug sat at one end of the bench, and a canvass bag of bullpen baseballs rested on the Kingdome artificial turf at the opposite end.

Bullpen catchers who warmed relievers as the game continued had their backs to the batters, leaving them susceptible to sharply hit foul balls. Bullpen pitchers always performed protection duty, standing behind the catcher to deflect anything hit their way.

Conor drew sentry duty as the M's first reliever was told to get ready at the bottom of the sixth.

When Conor finally learned the details of the Rangers' reprisal, he recalled *The Shawshank Redemption's* climactic scene in which Andy Dufresne crawls through two hundred yards of sewer pipe, gagging and retching before he spills into a river to find a cleansing rain and freedom.

That's how Conor reconstructed Jeff Reardon's ordeal as he snuck through the bowels of the Kingdome and picked his way under the stands towards a metal wall beyond which lay the Mariners bullpen. At first, he walked over the detritus that had leaked down over the long course of a season. As he neared the wall, though, he ducked, squatted, then crawled as the stands lowered above him. Finally, he was reduced to slithering along among the petrified hotdog remains, popcorn kernels, sticky slather of spilled beer and pop to one of the small openings below the unsuspecting Mariners bullpen bench. He took first one, and then a second can of lighter fluid, aiming the narrow stream of liquid out the hole and patiently soaking the canvas bag of baseballs. Then waiting, waiting, waiting for the moment when the first reliever stood, and the catcher joined him. Running the last stream of lighter fluid along the ground and under the stands where he flicked the lighter, watched the line of flame flash toward the ball bag.

Standing at his sentry post behind the catcher, Conor heard a whoooomp and immediately felt a burst of heat as the ball bag ignited into a tower of flame. He turned and saw a column of fire almost five feet high, the bag totally involved. Panicked pitchers fled the bench.

The third base umpire called time out, and turning to confront a conflagration, began waving for the smattering of fans to flee.

Bullpen coach Bob Didier rallied the relievers, urging them to keep their wits and fight the fire. One brave soul used a spare shin guard and knocked the ball bag away from the crowd. The pitchers set up a Dixie Cup brigade, filling cups from their Igloo water jug, passing them pitcher to pitcher, the last man flinging three ounces of water at the blaze.

In that moment, Conor knew the Rangers had won. Television footage, beamed coast to coast on the next day's news broadcasts, showed Mariners pitchers passing pointy paper cones in a useless attempt to quench the inferno.

"Get out of the way," Conor screamed as he grabbed the Igloo jug and extinguished the fire.

The video ran everywhere. That wasn't the worst part, though. The worst occurred when Latham called two innings later for someone to start warming up and an enterprising reporter captured the additional sound bite. "We can't," yelled one of the pitchers. "We don't have any balls."

THE MEMORY I TREASURE MOST ABOUT 1990, THOUGH, HAD nothing to do with games or fights or fires.

Early that September we checked into our rooms for our final series against the Red Sox. A mix-up occurred when our traveling secretary distributed keys, because I stood alone in the penthouse of one of Boston's finest hotels.

The penthouse!

I opened curtains to a view of Fenway Park filling the foreground and the bustling blue expanse of Boston Harbor beyond. I recalled parting a set of curtains seventeen years earlier to find bars obstructing an alley view on the windows of the Bonneville Hotel in Idaho Falls. The Conman had come a long way from Idaho and Goodrum Martin. I only indulged my self-satisfaction for a moment, though, because I heard my father's voice.

"Don't get too full of yourself. Be mindful that just because you're here doesn't mean the work stops."

Always understand, getting to the penthouse is easier than staying there.

# thirty-seven

WHEN A.J. SHOWED ME THE BONUS SCHEDULE I pointed to the $20,000 payout at sixty-five appearances and told him Seattle would draw the line there. I saw that sort of thing a lot when I was a players' rep. And sure enough, I made exactly sixty-four appearances during the 1990 season. Still, I collected almost $100,000 worth of cha-chings. I posted a 2.89 earned run average.

Every bullpen pitcher had a great season that year. We became a cohesive group, everyone totally buying into team goals. Our thing was not allowing inherited runners to score. Scratch and bite and claw not to allow those runs. Today, I've got your back. Tomorrow, you've got mine.

Game appearances, though, aren't the only things putting miles on a pitcher's arm. A.J. knew that. He kept track every time I warmed up but didn't get into the game. He said I did that sixty times. See, relievers can be decoys. If an opposing manager is considering a pinch hitter for a given situation, his decision becomes *more complicated if both a righty and a lefty are getting ready. During a lot of the season, I was the only lefthander out there.*

And every pitch thrown in preparation took its toll.

For fourteen years, I'd indulged in cortisone. First, only a couple of injections a season. Then, creeping to five or six or more as the years passed. My back nagged me during Spring Training of 1990, so I took an injection. Six weeks later, another. By the second half, they shot me up every two weeks.

Don't get me wrong, Rita. Nobody ordered me to do it. This was a silent understanding. You know you need it. We know you need it. We know you can't refuse and still do your job. My trainer in West Haven, Walt Horn, had warned me years earlier. "You can't keep taking these injections. Cortisone doesn't dissipate from the body. You'll pay for it when you get older."

Back then, though, we were indestructible. That getting older thing drifted on the far, far horizon. More to the point, cortisone worked. My pain eased and 1990 became the pinnacle of my professional life.

Conor considered the champagne bottle, brought it halfway to his lips, then lowered it, feeling a tinge of disgust and regret.

And if I could, I'd freeze it all right there. Finish my champagne, get the fuck off this mountain, end Conman's story in October of 1990. Back when real life was mostly just a footnote to the main drama taking place on a pitching mound at center stage. When wife, family and friends existed within the narrow context of their relationship to the Conman's world of professional baseball. They all seemed happy as members of a supporting cast, each proud of the piece they owned of the Conman's success.

I can't do that, though, can I? Because only a few weeks later, the real world came pounding at our door.

Fall, 1987

"No, I can't go to Alaska. I've got work..."

"Hey, come on, Brad, nobody's that busy," Conor said. "I'll pay your way..."

"Connie, I can afford to go. It's just..." His voice trailed off.

"Just what?"

"Look, I've got a shot at being a judge, and I want that. I... I hate to put it this way, but Baze parties too hard. And you two together? I can't get caught in it."

"Yeah, Baze is a drinker," Conor said. "And some of his buddies smoke. I don't do any of that stuff, though. I enjoy spending time with him. Just because you're there, doesn't mean you have to be as wild as they are."

"Connie," Brad said, "you've got a significant career going. I'm not sure you see the whole picture. You should be careful, too."

Every other off-season or so, Conor flew to Alaska and spent a week with Basil.

Before the Japan gig, Basil paid Conor's way. Money never seemed to be an issue for him.

The first time Conor visited, Basil lived in an RV. Next time, Basil had bought himself a luxury trailer and an acre of land. Eventually, he owned a custom-built home situated on twenty acres. He also acquired a full array of toys. A Harley, snowmobiles, quad runners. And the parties were legendary. Conor didn't know how many women lived in Palmer, Alaska. The best-looking ones, though, showed up at Basil's house every weekend. Like the baseball culture of the seventies and eighties, weed and coke were plentiful on this frontier. Conor adopted the same approach when visiting Basil that he took with partying by some of his teammates during the coke and grass era of baseball. He enjoyed the spectacle. He didn't indulge.

Palmer, Alaska

"I TRIED," CONOR TOLD BASIL. "BRAD WON'T COME. HE'S nervous about something."

"It's the coke," Basil said.

Baze soaked in his hot tub, trying to sweat off the previous night's hangover. Conor sat against a wall with debris of the previous evening's binge scattered all around them. From some recess of the house came a woman's voice. "Baze! Why is my bra in the microwave?"

"It's not my fault!"

"Yeah, you might suggest to some of your friends..." Conor said.

"Brad's not nervous because my friends use it," Basil said. "He's nervous because I sell it."

"You... what? I... thought you didn't do drugs."

"I don't. I just sell 'em. Hey, don't look so shocked. This is the wild west. Almost everybody uses. How do you think they get through the winter? And someone's gonna sell it. Might as well be me."

"You could go to prison..."

"No, I can't. I sell to local cops. They won't arrest me. And there's no one else around. Besides, the money's too good. When I started, I made $60,000 a year. I can make $60,000 a month selling coke."

"You still work every day."

"Yeah. I like work."

Basil called Conor in San Carlos only a week later.

"I think," he said with a shaking voice, "that I may be going to prison."

We all had our wakeup calls. Mine was the prison girls' thing that made me realize how much I wanted and needed Kate in my life. A.J. struggled with gambling and alcohol, leading to a failed marriage which cost him millions before he found his way.

Basil's was the scariest.

Some guy got pissed at him for fooling around with his girlfriend and snitched about the drugs. If the locals weren't going to do something, the source said, he'd go to Anchorage and tell the state police. Nobody wanted state troopers poking around the wide-open slope.

Officers explained the situation when they arrested Basil. They had no choice. I made a panicked phone call to Brad. Help us find the right attorney.

"How good can an attorney be if he's practicing in Palmer, Alaska?" Brad said.

Because he hadn't been admitted to the Alaska bar, Brad couldn't officially represent Baze. But he could assist whoever we hired and make sure Baze was represented competently.

Brad flew to Palmer. He advised Baze that the feds offered him protection in exchange for names. Baze said no. Brad spent a couple of long days negotiating with local police and prosecutors. Baze didn't go to prison. He received two years' probation and community service with the tacit understanding he would maintain his silence. A second negotiation satisfied the Internal Revenue Service. The third negotiation was most worrisome.

The guys who fronted the drugs wanted their money.

"THE BIKERS SENT A GUY TO TELL BASIL HE HAS TO PAY UP or else," Brad told Conor.

"Or else what?"

"They left that to his imagination."

"How about the Palmer attorney?" Conor asked. "Can't he reason with them?"

"No, he lives there. He wants to have as little to do with bikers as possible. I can't say I blame him."

"Well, I don't have $80,000 to spare," Conor said. "A.J. does but Basil would never accept it."

"Yeah," Brad said. "I think the only option is for me to go talk to them."

"I'll go, too," Conor said. "I can't let you sit down with a bunch of bikers by yourself."

"No, Connie. You've got a career. You can't be consorting with known criminals. I'm sure that's against some major league rule. Maybe A.J. could—"

"Yeah, he probably could and I'm sure he would. But you and I both know the risk. Do you really want A.J. to get into a fight with a dozen outlaw bikers?"

"So, it'll have to be me," Brad said.

"Yeah, well, I'm going, too."

THE GYPSY BANDITS OPERATED OUT OF A DOUBLE-WIDE located at the end of a long gravel road, way out by the pipeline. Situated in the middle of a flat prairie, they could see anyone coming from a long way off.

Angry that he couldn't accompany Brad and Conor, Basil grudgingly gave them directions.

"You can't go," Brad insisted. "That would be stupid from both legal and health standpoints. I'm hoping you've resolved to put stupid things behind you. Give me a name and phone number so I can make an appointment."

Basil wrote a number on a piece of paper. "Ask for Shovelhead. He's kind of the appointments secretary."

A guy holding a shotgun greeted them as they pulled through a gate in the chain link fence surrounding the trailer. A row of a half-dozen motorcycles decorated the yard. The guy made a motion to roll down the driver's side window.

"You cops?"

"Um, we're here to see Shovelhead," Conor said through a dry throat. "We called earlier."

"You didn't answer my question," the biker said.

"No," Brad said from the passenger side. "We aren't law enforcement officials of any kind."

"You wired?"

"I beg your pardon?" Conor didn't understand.

"Are you wearing a wire? Do you have hidden recording devices?"

"God, no," Conor said.

The biker escorted them into the trailer where they saw a man with at least a foot-long beard sitting behind a desk. A second man, whom Conor estimated at eight feet tall and about six hundred pounds, stood off to one side. The man behind the desk didn't seem to take any notice of their entry. The giant's eyes bored into them.

"Sit down," said the desk guy, indicating a pair of folding chairs with an absent wave of his hand.

They sat. Desk guy studied a document. The giant growled. The man with the shotgun farted. "Beg pardon," he said.

"Um ... Mr. Shovelhead ..." Conor said, hoping to break the silence.

"Shovelhead's holding the shotgun," said desk guy. He

nodded his head slightly to his right. "This is Grinder."

"I see. And you are . . . ?"

"Percy."

"Percy?"

"Yeah, Percy." Now the man glanced up. "You wanna make something of it?"

Conor most certainly didn't.

Grinder growled.

Brad cleared his throat. "Percy, I'm Brad Grady, an attorney acting on behalf of Basil Doan."

"Who's this other guy?"

"I'm Conor Nash. I'm a friend of Basil's."

Percy stared at Conor. "Conor Nash? The baseball player?"

"Yeah." Conor felt a glimmer of hope that they might escape alive.

"We get Mariners games on TV," Percy said, nodding again toward the giant. "Grinder's a big fan. He loves Ken Griffey Junior."

Grinder growled acknowledgement.

Brad brought the conversation back into focus. "We want to discuss some resolution concerning the money Basil owes you."

"Eighty thousand dollars," Percy said.

"Yes. Well, as you undoubtedly know, the IRS took most of his assets so he's short of cash right now."

"Not my problem."

"Well, do you have a suggestion as to—"

"Yeah, pay us the eighty thousand."

"We can't," Brad said. "I would think you'd give Basil some credit for his silence. He turned down deals offered him to name names."

"Yeah," Percy said, "Basil is a standup guy. Very responsible. Was a pleasure doing business, for once, with someone who isn't a criminal. But business is business. We won't eat eighty thousand. Word will get around. Some of our other franchisees might get ideas."

"There must be some wiggle-room in that figure," Brad said. "I'm sure a significant portion of the eighty thousand is profit. Can we just find a way to make you whole on out-of-pocket expenses?"

"For instance?"

"Basil has a Harley and two snowmobiles the IRS missed. He owns them free and clear."

Percy tugged at his beard. "That Harley's a sweet ride. What condition are the sleds in?"

"If you know Basil, you know the snowmobiles are pristine, top-of-the-line. I can bring you titles this afternoon."

Percy looked at Grinder. Grinder growled.

"Two other conditions," Percy said. "First, Grinder wants an autograph."

Conor quickly agreed.

"And the second?" Brad asked.

Percy told him.

Grinder produced a new major league ball. Conor signed it, *Grinder, thanks for everything, The Conman.*

"Anything else?" Conor asked.

"Yeah," Grinder said, his voice rumbling through a bed of gravel. "Why the fuck can't you get Dave Parker out?"

"THAT'S IT?" BASIL ASKED. "THE HARLEY AND THE SLEDS, AND I'm off the hook?"

"One other thing." Brad told Basil, "Percy says you have to stay away from Grinder's sister."

"I can't believe," Conor said, "you were dating a biker gang girl."

"Not so much dating," Basil said.

"Well, in any case, Grinder's pretty pissed off."

"Hey," Basil said, "that wasn't my fault."

Basil still likes women and scotch, but he never again antagonized either bikers or the law.

Yes, in one way or another, without hesitation and asking nothing in return, Fat Brad rescued each of us. I'll never understand why he didn't allow us to do the same for him.

Conor relented and drank from the champagne bottle.

Here's to you Brad, you inconsiderate SOB.

thirty-eight

Phoenix
October 1990

"CONNIE, HAVE YOU TALKED WITH BRAD RECENTLY?" A.J. phoned Connor from San Francisco to relay his concern.

"No, A.J. Maybe a month or so, which is a little odd. He usually calls once a week."

"Same here," A.J. said. "But he hasn't called me, either. I've tried to reach him a couple of times this week. Something's going on."

"I figured he was just busy with the judge thing, and now the possibility of working on whatshisname's campaign."

"That's not it," A.J. said. "I'm no expert, but both times we talked, I heard a seriously depressed man. I mean go-see-a-therapist-depressed. Something dark is happening."

"Have you asked Millie about it?"

"She's weird, too. Like, angry weird. I think he needs our help."

We intended the week as Brad's reward for a lifetime of

unselfish, unwavering support, as well as a celebration of his professional achievement. He'd taken a couple of important steps toward his ultimate goal of a federal judgeship. He'd been named night court judge for the city of Fresno. A promising California gubernatorial candidate had invited Brad to become an advisor to his campaign.

We flew Brad and Millie to Phoenix and Basil down from Alaska. We got Brad a suite at the Biltmore and decreed that he could pay for nothing. He clearly did his best to pretend everything was okay. He laughed. He joked. As we recalled various outrageous moments of our lives, he extracted his teeth and agreed that, "Yeth, thir, that wath a good one."

He had an edge, though. Completely foreign to his nature. He displayed a lack of patience with cabbies and bellhops and waiters. We were accustomed to a Fat Brad who kept a careful rein on himself in social situations, who cringed at acts of inconsideration and guided us away from toxic situations.

CONOR TUGGED AT BRAD'S ELBOW, STEERING HIM PAST THE restroom, through a door by the kitchen, out to the parking lot.

"Hey, man, what's going on? This isn't you. Are you telling me, after all these years, A.J., Baze and I have finally rubbed off on you?"

Brad closed his eyes, wobbling a little as Conor steadied him.

"Connie, I'm sorry. It's been . . . A lot's happening. I . . . I apologize. I've had too much to drink . . ."

While Brad and I talked, his wife, Millie, stormed away from the dinner table, took a cab to Sky Harbor and flew home. Kate followed Millie out, but got no explanation as they waited for the cab.

Spouses weren't invited the next night as Conor, Basil and A.J. sought to get Brad to open up. He steered conversation away each time they approached an uncomfortable shoal. With each drink he became a little louder, a little more obnoxious. When two men at a nearby table took exception and asked Brad to tone it down, he stood and took a menacing step forward.

"Yeah? You want to take it outside?"

Confronted by this paunchy belligerent, the men might have been more than willing to accept Brad's offer. Brad was quickly flanked by A.J., Basil and Conor, though. The men shrank away.

Conor watched Fat Brad disappear into the boarding tunnel at Sky Harbor's Terminal Four the next afternoon.

"Something's really wrong," Conor said. "I've never seen him like this."

"Yeah," A.J. agreed. "I'd better go after him. I'll book an early flight."

Fresno, California

SGT. JORGE LEAL CONSIDERED HIS ASSIGNMENT THE WORST a police officer could draw.

He respected Judge Grady, even liked him. Their paths had crossed on several courtroom occasions, before the judge was a judge. He represented petty criminals, affording them their constitutional rights. Grady fought for his clients but wasn't the kind of attorney who constantly sought to scapegoat police.

And now that Grady worked night court, they saw each other more frequently. The judge seemed fair in his approach to both sides.

And these charges... shit, anyone could claim anything.

This kind of allegation, though, true or not, killed a career. Still, the charge had been filed. Leal had no choice.

He leaned back and closed his eyes. When he opened them again, the cab was already pulling away. He jumped from his cruiser and crossed the street at a quick walk. The judge stood in a wash of light spilling through an open front door.

"... I've got a restraining order."

The woman inside—Leal recognized her as the judge's wife—said, "You can't come in. You can't even stand in the front yard."

"Judge! Judge Grady!" called Leal. "Step away from the door, sir. Come to the sidewalk."

The judge's head snapped around. His expression startled Leal to the extent that his right hand dropped reflexively to a leather thong securing his sidearm.

Seeing the uniform, the judge's shoulders slumped. He dropped his suitcase where he stood. Eyes downcast, he shuffled trance-like across his lawn.

As he stopped a few feet from Leal and slowly raised his eyes, the police officer saw a defeated man.

"Judge, I'm sorry, I have to place you under arrest."

The judge said nothing, just stood, his eyes empty.

"Sir, the charge is rape of a minor. You have the right to remain—"

The judge waved a palm. "I know my rights. You don't need—"

"Yes, Judge, I do."

Leal completed his recitation.

The judge raised his eyes again and nodded.

"Judge, I need a verbal response."

"I understand my rights. I ... I don't need an attorney."

"Are... are you sure? I'll be glad to make a call..."

"Do you have to handcuff me?" The judge's voice bore a hollow ring, as if he was vacant inside.

"Um... no, Judge. No, I don't. You will need to ride in the back, though."

The judge raised his head again. Now a light snapped on behind his eyes. The assertiveness with which Leal was familiar returned. "I need to ask one thing."

Leal held open the passenger side rear door of his cruiser and raised his eyebrows, inviting the judge to continue.

"I need to get into my office."

"No, sir, we can't go to the courthouse. We have to—"

"No, my private office here at home. I have papers. If the wrong people see them, confidentiality of several former clients would be severely compromised. I have to be sure—"

"Judge, I can't let you do it. Think about it. Suppose those papers are germane to this case? Plus, the restraining order..."

"They are completely unrelated," the judge said. "These people relied on me to keep them... Look, I'll let you inspect the papers so you can ascertain they don't pertain to anything I might or might not have done. We'll put them in an envelope. I'll call my bailiff. Please. I can't let these people down. I have to get into that safe. At least ask my wife if I can get into the office for just a moment."

Under any other circumstances, Leal would ignore a suspect's plea and simply drive to the jail. But... the judge. He liked this man. He believed this man.

He asked the judge to remain at the curb while he knocked. The wife answered, accompanied by a man she identified as her brother. Officer Leal explained the judge's concern. When she balked, he heard the judge call, "Please, Millie. It's not enough you're helping to destroy me? You want to damage these other people, too? They aren't related to any part of this."

The woman, glared, nodded, then said, "I want him gone as soon as possible."

Leal beckoned.

The house sat among a neighborhood of ranchers and sprawled over its lot. The office was a converted bedroom. The judge hurried through his office door, as if achieving entry provided some sort of victory. He flipped the switch on a green-shaded banker's lamp, casting a square of light across a polished, wooden desk. He took a deep breath.

"The papers are in the safe," he said, waving to a wall painting.

The judge's wife and her brother followed Leal into the darkened room, waiting just inside.

"I think we should turn on the overhead light," the judge's brother-in-law said. "We just want to be sure he doesn't take something that belongs to Millie."

Millie bowed her head. She would not meet her husband's eyes.

"Good idea," the judge said, his voice cold, on the edge of menacing. "Turn on the light. I wouldn't want you to miss anything."

As light flooded the room, Leal said, "I'll have to open the safe, judge."

"No," the judge said as if he still held a position to issue an order. "The mechanism is tricky. If you try to do it, we could be here all night. I'll dial the combination and step back."

Without waiting for Leal's permission, the judge swung a painting away on unseen hinges to reveal a heavy knob fixed to a flat, steel-faced surface with a small handle. The judge deftly spun the combination. Nothing tricky about it.

Leal took a quick step forward. The judge jerked the safe open. His hand darted inside. Not an instant of hesitation.

"No judge, that's not what—" Leal didn't even register his own movement as he felt the heft of his sidearm. A glint of silver in the judge's hand! A gun? A gun! His wife stood in the doorway. No! No! The judge wouldn't... Leal hurried to bring his own weapon to bear, pressure on the trigger. The judge, though, spared him by turning away.

Leal watched helplessly as the top of the judge's head erupted in a flume of blood, bone, and tissue. The body thudded to the floor.

"Shit!" Leal said. "Shit!"

Still training his unfired sidearm Leal stepped to the body, kicking the judge's pistol away. He turned to quickly check on the others. Millie Grady wore an expression of abject horror. Her brother threw up on the hallway carpet.

thirty-nine

Tempe, Arizona

"Hey, Guillermo, there's a guy standing on the mound."

"What? What the fuck, man? I thought we were all locked up."

"Yeah, me, too. Want me to call someone? I think a police cruiser just drove through the parking lot. I could . . ."

Having overheard this exchange while hoisting a trash bag into a dumpster on the concourse running through the bowels of Tempe Diablo Stadium, Malcom Sleepsander let the home clubhouse door swing closed behind him. He skipped down the steps leading into shadows of the third base dugout.

"Hey, guys," he said. "Something going on?"

Guillermo pointed at the infield. "There's a guy out there. No one's supposed to be there."

Sleepsander followed the eyes of the two men as they faced the dark, empty expanse of stadium where the Mariners would soon begin preparation for their 1991 season.

A black silhouette towed the pitching rubber. This figure stared high into the night above the grandstand behind home plate where the hint of a crescent moon dodged gathering clouds.

"Give me a minute, guys," Sleepsander said. "No need to call anyone."

Sleepsander walked across the infield. He felt a smack of moisture on his bare head. As he strode across the grass, he saw plump dimples of unseen raindrops bloom across the hard-red clay of the mound.

"Hey, Conman."

"Hey, Sleepy."

"It's starting to rain," Sleepsander observed.

"Is it? I guess I didn't notice."

"Yeah. The grounds crew guys need to tarp the mound."

"I suppose."

The Conman didn't move. He continued to stare at the shadows where home plate lay. Rain began to fall in earnest. Sleepsander placed a hand on Conor's shoulder. "What's wrong?"

A new voice floated through the darkness. "Connie? We called Kate. She said you were getting some stuff at the clubhouse."

Two men Sleepsander did not know joined them.

"Hi, A.J., Baze," the Conman said. "I . . . I just didn't know where else to go."

Sleepsander sensed drama unfolding here. He stepped away, allowing these newcomers to embrace the Conman. Nobody spoke until, finally, Connor wiped rainwater from his eyes.

"You guys know I had a sister, right?"

"Yes," A.J. said. Basil nodded.

"She was only eight months old. Why would God do that? Take a child that way? Why would He let something like this happen to Brad? What kind of sense does this make?"

Neither A.J. nor Basil attempted an answer.

"Ever since I was seven years old," Conor said, his voice quivering, "this is where I ran to. This damned pile of clay. I could always hide here. Nothing else mattered. The world excuses all my sins when I stand on a pitching mound. I can stutter. I can fail chemistry. I can steal a bus. I can be a jerk and fight Wilbur Spalding... but out here, everything else goes away. The rest of all creation is... someplace else, you know?"

"Yeah," Basil said with a choked whisper, "we know."

"It's not going away this time, is it?"

"No," A.J. said. "No. It's not."

CONOR SLEEPWALKED THROUGH THE FUNERAL. BRAD GRADY had friends everywhere. He'd always been generous with his time, his support, his advice. Conor, A.J. and Basil weren't the only ones he looked out for. They, and a handful of others, attended Brad's service.

A.J. made arrangements. He tried pointlessly to talk with Millie, who'd been rendered helpless by the tragedy. The local Fresno newspaper coverage of Brad's death bordered on lurid. Most everyone within Brad's legal and political circles distanced themselves. Mercifully, A.J. supposed, his parents were both deceased. He had no siblings. The funeral home people worried who would pay.

Finally, A.J. called Conor. "We're taking him home. That's where he belongs."

Fat Brad's three closest friends shared the expenses. The graveside service proved awkward. Usually the case with suicides, Conor supposed.

They drove from the cemetery to a local bar, one from

which Conor's brothers had been banned years earlier, and chose the darkest corner.

"Are they sure?" Conor asked. "I mean, the whole thing wasn't an accident?"

A.J. sighed. "No, Connie. I asked everyone. The cop screwed up. No question about it . . ."

"A gun in the safe?" Conor asked. "Doesn't that seem a little . . . I don't know . . . coincidental?"

"It's Fresno. Everybody has a gun in their safe. No, Brad did it. At that moment, he just couldn't imagine any way to face us, to face up to—"

"Did he even do what they said? That kid's mom could claim anything. Maybe she saw a chance to shake Brad down . . ."

Basil waved a dismissive hand. "Can you imagine Brad not being willing to fight to save himself if he *hadn't* done it?"

The disaster had its roots in Brad's generosity. He helped a seventeen-year-old boy's mother avoid charges on a drug-related accusation. He found funds for her to enter a drug rehab facility. Her son had nowhere to go other than the streets. Brad allowed him into his home.

Released from rehab, the mother called police. Brad molested her son, she said. Police interviewed the kid and were convinced the charge was genuine. The woman called Brad's wife during their Phoenix trip. Asked for money to drop charges. Millie's anger at the woman wilted beneath her suspicion the allegation was true. She flew home, gave a statement, sought a restraining order.

"A couple of cops I talked to said it could have been a set-up," A.J. said. "There's no evidence or suggestion that Brad was a pedophile. Just this one time, I think the kid—who'd been previously arrested for soliciting, by the way—offered, and Brad succumbed to the temptation."

"But Brad wasn't gay."

"Oh, come on Connie," A.J. said.

"He was married," Conor protested.

"He hardly ever had a date in high school," A.J. said. "I don't know about college. because we weren't there . . . remember the hooker?"

The second year A.J. and Conor played baseball at Cañada, Basil came home from Alaska and they purchased an hour with a call girl at a fancy San Francisco hotel.

"Remember, we were worried he might still be a virgin?" Basil said.

San Carlos, California
1975

CONOR, BASIL AND A.J. WAITED AT THE HOTEL COFFEE SHOP as the hour passed.

"Well, how was it?" A.J. grinned when Brad joined them.

"I had a nice time," Brad said.

"Details," Conor demanded.

"Well, I'm not sure how appropriate it is to—"

"Oh, come on," Basil said. "It's us, and she's a hooker. You're not protecting anyone's reputation, here."

"Well, Audry is a very interesting girl. She's taking classes at—"

"Audry? Who's Audry? The escort place said her name was Tawny."

Brad rolled his eyes. "Tawny is her hooker name. You think anyone really names their daughter Tawny, unless they want her to grow up and be . . . well, a hooker?"

"Oh, no. No. Don't tell me," A.J. demanded. "You didn't do it, did you?"

Brad offered no response.

"See there, he didn't do it. We got him the hottest date in half of San Francisco and—"

"Hey," Brad said, "she's got a lot happening right now. Her heart wouldn't have been in it."

"She's a hooker. Her heart's never in it."

"She's a little confused. I told her I'd help her if I could."

THE POSSIBILITY BURDENED CONOR'S CONSCIENCE LIKE AN indictment.

"If… if he was gay, can you imagine what it was like for him? San Carlos? Being around… us?"

Nobody answered as they each retreated to memories.

During the Sixties and Seventies, San Francisco became the first American city to *out* itself, allowing its homosexual culture to be part of a gaudy display that was a piece of the sex, drugs and rock-and-roll generation. The patriarchs of many conservative and traditional families—like Hugh Nash—fled the city so their children wouldn't fall prey to the drug culture, a burgeoning minority population, and homosexuality.

Demeaning homosexuals was almost second nature to Conor's childhood—not with any real malice, he supposed, just in a belittling and ridiculing sort of way. Particularly so amid the locker room culture in which Conor, A.J., Basil and, yes, Brad, immersed themselves. How many times had words like *queer* or *homo* or *fag* rolled glibly off their tongues? Had this curious condition ever been personified before them, how cruel might they have really been?

And what would the effect be on a boy so anxious to share their friendship? How much of himself did he have to deny?

And how much denial could a person tolerate? How did he and A.J. and Basil feel about the possibility even now? As adults, the rhetoric had certainly been toned down. That was mostly a growing societal pressure towards political correctness, though. At their core, did they really view homosexuality any differently than their parents had?

"If Brad was sitting here right now," Conor asked his friends, "and confessed to being gay—not just in a curious way—but a full-blown homosexual, would it make a difference?"

A.J. turned the question back on Conor, who fell silent for a long moment.

"No," Conor finally said. "I mean, it's easy for me to say I'm not comfortable around some swishy guy who I know nothing about. But this is Brad, one of the best friends I've ever had. I hope I could accept it."

"I don't care what his secrets were," Basil said. "I loved the guy. All he ever wanted was to help people around him. He sure helped me."

"Yeah," A.J. said. "Me, too."

ALONE ON HIS MOUNTAIN CONOR TRIED FOR ABOUT THE millionth time to sort through his feelings toward Brad Grady. Conor had a low tolerance for grief. If he allowed, grief would paralyze him, consume him. He buried his father's death under single-minded purpose. With Brad, he substituted anger, understanding, though, he wasn't angry at Brad for who he might have been or for his crime.

I'm angry because you quit. *Quitting is fatal. Suicide is the ultimate quit. And the rest of the world has to find a way to get out of bed in the morning.*

forty

Phoenix
Off-Season
1990-91

CONOR SAVORED EVERY MOMENT OF THE 1990 SEASON, but he felt relief when it ended. He'd begun to suffer back pain early in August. With each injection, the cortisone seemed to be less effective.

"My recommendation," the doctor told him, "is back surgery."

"No," Conor said. "I'm thirty-six. Rehab from surgery would rob me of time I can't afford to give."

In lieu of an operation the doctor recommended a workout regimen, warning Conor not to throw until back muscles were stronger. As a result, Conor came to Spring Training of 1991 in great overall condition, but behind in his throwing schedule. He pushed his arm. His arm ached. Cortisone made the ache go away.

He wasn't as sharp as he'd been the spring before. He pitched okay, though. He'd put up two solid seasons. He enjoyed credibility among his coaches. He asked for patience. *I'll be ready. Let me get my work in. You know what I can do.*

A.J. negotiated a contract high on guaranteed salary—$450,000—and low on incentive payments.

Despite his slow start, Conor believed hard work, credibility established by his previous performance, and the guaranteed money would be enough.

They weren't.

"Here's the thing," Mariners manager Jerry Latham told him as the team prepared to break camp, "you've got options. Cassidy doesn't. He'd have to clear waivers—"

"Whoa, whoa, whoa. What's Cassidy ever done for this team?" Conor demanded, in no mood to be conciliatory. His defensive instincts had been sharpened by the constant presence of Brad's betrayal. "I told you I'd be ready, and I am."

"We're not keeping two lefties." Latham insisted.

The discussion deteriorated from there.

Conor had paid his dues. He'd posted great numbers during both 1989 and 1990. He'd done everything the Mariners asked. He'd compromised his body to assure his availability each time the bullpen phone rang. Cassidy had proven nothing. Conor had earned the right not to be the guy whose career was manipulated as a matter of bureaucratic convenience.

Soon, both men were shouting.

"I'm tired of hearing this shit," Latham finally said. "You've got no complaint. We're paying you $450,000 to pitch Triple-A ball. So, quit your whining."

Conor felt heat flush into his face. He found himself in sixth grade again under his father's orders, standing at Gary Shaw's front door, waiting to challenge the bully who'd beaten him time after time. Conor Nash would not be intimidated. Conor Nash would always—always—stand up for himself.

"I wouldn't suck your dick for $450,000," he said. "What makes you think I'd let you fuck me in the ass for $450,000?"

"Suck your dick?" A.J. said with a chuckle when Conor recounted the argument. "Probably not the smartest response, given the circumstances."

"Yeah."

"Connie, it's $450,000."

"Yeah."

"So, report to Calgary.

Conor sighed. "Yeah."

Calgary Cannons
1991

KATE FOUND HIS PASSPORT, PACKED HIS BAGS, AND CONOR Nash again became a Calgary Cannon. Manager Keith Bodie installed Conor as his closer. Like most of his minor league managers, Bodie loved the Conman.

Conor took the ball every time he could get it. He injected cortisone, both back and shoulder, every time he needed it. One afternoon, a doctor injected him four times. He got the save that night. The next morning his left arm and shoulder swelled like he'd been assaulted by a bicycle pump.

"You can't keep doing this," trainers told him.

But he had to. And not only for the sake of his career. The Conman knew that to earn his money—and honor the work ethic ingrained by his father—he had two job requirements at Calgary. One, to pitch. The other, teach young teammates about approach to the game, obligation, and the grind. Calgary's roster included kids who would become famous: Tino Martinez, Mike Blowers, Rich Amaral, Dennis Powell, Dave Burba, Jeff

Nelson, Scott Bankhead. All of whom would soon play critical roles in reversing the fortunes of a moribund Mariners franchise.

They needed an example. Conor pitched three nights after his allergic reaction and many nights thereafter. During his time at Calgary, he managed a 3.25 ERA over thirty-six innings, striking out thirty-eight.

As innings, outs, saves and injections continued to mount, Conor suspected the whole *suck your dick* thing still resonated in Seattle. His baseball angel, though, had a couple of surprises left.

"YOU KNOW WHAT?"

"What?"

"You should wear the Starman! costume and take lineup to the home plate meeting."

"No way," Conor said. "I can't..."

A host of minor league teammates, though, most of them at least a decade his junior—too young yet to be cynical and poised on the brink of the major leagues—started that chant.

Starman! Starman! Starman!

August. Las Vegas. The Cannons initiated a three-game series against the Stars.

The kids were playing great, but August can be a killer of both momentum and enthusiasm. The Conman knew the importance of little things that infused energy and passion during the dog days.

Somehow, somewhere, the kids had heard the story.

Conor's dismissive *no way*, evolved into, "I don't even know if they've still got the suit." The locker room erupted in cheers.

"Just don't tell Bodie. I don't think he'd let me do it."

"Yesssss! Yesss, yessss," said Don Logan, still Stars GM. "I'll get the suit."

Conor changed in Logan's office. The bullpen crew acted as scouts while he snuck through the concourse beneath the stadium and hid behind a door, one stiff star point and gloved hand exposed.

As he waited, he heard footsteps almost at a run. The steps slowed, then stopped.

"Um ... who's there?" asked a voice barely louder than a whisper.

Conor peeked from behind the door. There stood the same grounds crew kid from the Starman!'s last performance.

"Oh, my God," the kid said. "No. No. This can't be happening."

Conor slid into full view, waddled to the kid's side, and said, "Still got the keys to the go-kart?"

"Aaaaagggghhhhh!" the kid screamed. He turned and ran.

Calgary first-base coach John Majors typically presented the Cannons' lineup card to umpires at home plate. Bodie made out a lineup and put it on the top shelf of Majors' locker.

Knowing his routine, the players waited until a few moments before the plate meeting, when Majors disappeared into the bathroom for his pre-game dump. They grabbed the lineup card and smuggled it to Conor, still waiting in the darkened walkway.

"Shit," Majors said. "Shit, shit, shit!"

"What's wrong, Johnny?"

"I can't find the fuckin' lineup card. Bodie's gonna kill me."

"No sweat, Johnny. I got you covered." Resplendent and glowing as a five-pointed star, Conor waved the lineup card from across the clubhouse, briefly beheld Bodie's shock, and dashed onto the field.

The umpires initially flinched at Starman!'s charge. Being

minor league umps, though, they were inured to all manner of pre-game weirdness.

Most of Calgary's roster hung on the dugout rail and began to chant. Instantly, a bored mid-week crowd joined them, and the stadium rocked once again with *Starman!, Starman!, Starman!*

Conor handed over the card, flapped his hands in acknowledgment, and performed a jogging, waddling tour of the bases. He touched home plate, then veered into the Cannon's dugout, carefully avoiding eye contact with his manager.

Midway through the game, the bullpen phone rang.

"Conman!" barked the bullpen coach.

Uh, oh. This was too early for the closer to get up. Conor leaned forward and pointed to himself.

"He wants you!"

Oh, crap.

Conor shuffled along the dugout steps and began an apology he'd composed during his walk from the bullpen.

"Listen, Skip, I'm sorry. I thought the guys needed a little—"

"Hey, don't sweat it. I laughed pretty hard. Cassidy didn't cut it. Pack your stuff. They need you in Seattle tomorrow."

forty-one

Seattle Mariners
1991

THE MARINERS FINALLY WERE PLAYING FOR something. For fifteen years, Seattle had wallowed in mediocrity while its expansion twin, the Toronto Blue Jays, became a legitimate contender.

The 1991 Mariners, though, finally had a chance to finish above .500—an ignoble goal that might seem superfluous compared to ambitions of playoffs and World Series crowns. The players had completely invested themselves in this pursuit of respectability, though, and they would achieve their goal, laying a foundation for genuine success.

Conor loved the atmosphere he'd stepped into.

The third night of the home stand, the call came to protect a four-run sixth-inning lead.

He felt his back pinch as he quickly warmed. His shoulder ached. Nothing unusual. He'd see about an injection after the game. The happy home crowd, appreciative of last year's performance by the Conman, cheered his walk from the bullpen.

He ignored both back and shoulder through his warmup tosses.

The first hitter he faced dumped an awkward, opposite field bleeder over Vizquel's head at shortstop. He walked the next hitter on a full count, his shoulder complaining a little more with each delivery. The runners advanced on a double steal.

Conor knew just by feel his next fastball had nothing on it. The ball withered at the plate, then leapt from the bat like a bullet. Vizquel speared the ball, spoiling its deep-gap destiny, leaving runners at second and third.

Conor shook his left arm and cursed his shoulder.

"Fuck. Not now!"

As he began his windup, Conor somehow knew everything turned on this pitch. The struggle, the disappointment, the labor, the fleeting moments of success—indeed, his very identity—were all at stake. So many times, with no options left, a single game, a single performance, a single pitch, had dictated his fate. Time after time he'd risen to that challenge. As this fastball limped from his hand, though, he understood this night would not produce another miracle. He knew the truth the instant the ball rolled off his fingers—before a searing strip of pain stabbed his shoulder, before the tingling of his hand, before a wave of limp utter uselessness yanked at his left arm.

The ball reversed its course, streaking toward right centerfield, sinking too quickly for even Griffey to save him. Both runs scored. When Vizquel flipped him the return throw from the outfield, Conor left it nestling deep in his glove.

He waited for Latham's arrival.

Conor offered the baseball. Latham received it without comment.

To a smattering of polite applause, the journey ended.

Conor tilted the bottle high and allowed a few last drops to trickle down his throat. Flowing yellow and red snakes of headlights and taillights below him had been dissected into individual dots. Stars peppered the sky, their strength boosted by absence of a moon.

Who is Conor Nash if he can't pitch?

I really didn't expect to find the answer on a mountain. The only way that will happen is if this bottle has a genie at the bottom, so I can wish myself young and whole. He laughed. *Then again, why not? After all, this whole thing started with a wish in a tunnel.*

Boys, though, can believe in things that men can't. Conor's confessor wasn't real. Rita the baseball angel was only his personification of blind happenstance, wafting him here and there across the baseball landscape like the swirling winds at Candlestick.

If I was *the captain of my fate, how would the story end? Pitching into my forties? The left-hand relief specialist who hangs on and hangs on, being passed from team-to-team like an aging harlot, while Kate continued to wait* her *turn?*

Conor wanted to believe he was a better man.

But, to thine own self be true. Sure. I'd have settled for that. And what then? Would the end taste any less bitter because the champagne was a few years older?

They paid me to play baseball for sixteen years. Some players were fated to be the game's knights or kings. Others were pawns, sacrificed time and again for some nebulous greater good. I could compete with any of them, though. That's what gnawed at me. I proved it during a glorious season and a half when I was a decade too old.

Nine months out of sixteen years isn't enough, especially when excellence afforded me neither security nor justice.

This was the source of anger which turned me sullen and humorless for months. I could pick out men who'd manipulated me over the years and blame them, but they were too vague, too distant. Where was the satisfaction in being pissed off at people to whom my anger made no difference?

Conor needed to give voice to this visceral rage welling from his gut. What about Kate and her assertion she'd looked forward to this day as much as he dreaded it? His resentment slunk away as Conor searched his soul to find he couldn't be angry at Kate. Not that way.

But . . . Fat Brad. The fucking voice of reason?

Conor stood, wobbling a little with the effort, and screamed to the stars, "So you couldn't wait to put a gun in your mouth until I'd at least dealt with this shit! Fuck you, you coward! What was the hurry? Why couldn't you wait one more minute? And a minute after that. And then the minute after that? All you had to do was get past that moment when you felt you had to pull the trigger. No matter how bad it was, you had friends who loved you. You don't think we would have taken care of you? You think we'd have walked away? Life's not over because you can't be a fucking judge. A.J. would have made you a partner in a sports agency. You guys would have owned the world. Basil would've done anything for you."

Now tears streaked Conor's cheeks. "I would've . . . I would've . . . Fuck. You only had to get past that moment—"

"Are you talking about me, Connie, or are you talking about yourself?"

The voice came from behind him.

Conor turned with a start and there was Fat Brad, looking

only a little wavy and ethereal. "My God!" Conor gasped. "I had no idea I was this drunk."

"You're pretty drunk," Brad agreed. "So, you're gonna quit, too, huh?"

"I don't have any choice. Unlike you. I'm not deciding to—"

"Were you screaming incoherently, or did you hear what you said? No matter how bad it seems? People who love you? Life's not over just because you can't be a judge—or a pitcher? Getting past that moment?"

"Fuck you. I wouldn't even consider killing myself."

"You're too literal for your own good," the ghost said. "Your precious standards. All that failure and quit crap. Don't you understand your life philosophy should apply to a broader context than a pitching mound? There's all kinds of quit. Emotional suicide is every bit as devastating as any other kind. This is *your* moment, Connie. Sometimes, only the worst things can make the best things possible. Don't repeat my mistake. A bit clichéd, I grant you, but count your fucking blessings. Look at my wife, look at A.J.'s divorce. Look at all of Basil's women." The ghost paused briefly. "Kate is a gem, and you're pushing her away."

Conor sagged to the bench. The ghost sat beside him.

"Do you know," Conor asked, his voice a hard whisper, "how pissed off we are at you?"

"Yeah." The ghost sighed. "One day, though, you'll get over it. One day, my memory will be a comfort, not a torment. At least, that's what they tell me."

"They?"

"It's complicated. Don't draw any conclusions. And by the way, go easy on Val, would you? She does the best she can."

"Val? Who the fuck is Val?"

"Oh . . . right. You don't know. She's your baseball angel."

"My baseball angel is named Val? I thought her name was Rita."

"I don't know any Rita."

"So, there's a Saint Val?"

"Saint . . . No, you've been misinformed. Valarie certainly doesn't run with that crowd."

Conor turned with the shock of realization. "Valarie?"

"Yeah. Like your Dad always said, the Nashes look out for their own."

"Okay," Conor said, "we both know this is some sort of weird drunken dream. The baseball angel is something I made up. And I've assigned it a high degree of incompetence. If my sister is my baseball angel, why wouldn't she have done a little better job?"

"It's not like she had a lot of training," the ghost said. "It's sort of a learn-as-you-go thing. Like an angel internship."

"All the frustration?" Conor said. "All the releases? Wilbur Fucking Spalding? A shredded shoulder?"

"Your dad told you it wouldn't be easy. He didn't *want* it to be easy. He knew you better than anyone. You had to walk a crooked path to become the man you are. You'd be someone else entirely had it been easier. And I'm not sure you'd like that guy very much."

Conor shook his head. "The man I am? I don't even know who that is. I don't understand where that crooked path leads . . ."

"Yes, you do," the ghost answered. "It leads home. It leads to tomorrow, and the day after that. It leads to the privilege of embracing people who love and need you. And honestly, was it so bad? It's been quite a ride. Even knowing it all—A.J., me, Baze—we'd still give our left nut if Val had chosen us. So, suck it up, you little snotweasel. Quit feeling sorry for yourself. And give Al Rosen a call. Val might not be done yet."

The weight of chin on chest startled Conor awake. Standing, he turned a slow, complete circle. He was alone.

"See. I told you. A dream. Like in the movies..."

Lights sparkled below. Vague shadows of clouds above him began to mask what light was cast by the stars. He could barely make out his own cowboy boots.

"... but, God, that was weird, and... and... it's darker than fuck. How the hell am I supposed to get down from here?"

KATE PACED THE LIVING ROOM, TRYING TO FOCUS ON television rather than her concern over Conor's whereabouts. He sometimes saw a movie or went out with Basil—which always worried her a little. Not that she worried about the women who flocked to Basil. She trusted Conor to hold that phenomenon at a bemused arms' length.

No, the problem was that Basil still liked his scotch.

She thought of the last time she and Conor had met Basil at Swannie's—a downtown Seattle bar popular among Mariners players—after a game.

One Month Earlier

"UM... HI, KATE," BASIL SAID AS HE GAVE CONOR A SIDEWAYS look.

"What's wrong?" she asked.

"Why would anything be wrong?"

"You don't seem particularly thrilled to see me," Kate said.

"No... no... it's just..." He turned to Conor and

mouthed a couple of words Kate didn't understand.

"Tonight?" Conor asked him.

"I think so, and..."

"What?" Kate demanded.

"Circus Girl," Conor said. "Baze is worried that Circus Girl might be working tonight."

"Circus Girl?" Kate said. "Can the two of you be any more demeaning?"

"It's not like that," Basil said. "I don't know her name..."

Conor told Kate a waitress had developed a fixation concerning Basil. He wasn't interested in a continuing relationship.

"Is he ever?" Kate asked. "So... why Circus Girl?"

Basil started to answer. Conor cut him off. "He says she's clingy and... acrobatic. I've never met her. Sometimes Baze exaggerates..."

"Baaaaazzzzeee!" Her scream came from across the bar, the woman a blur as she charged at a full run.

Kate ducked as, a good ten feet from Basil, Circus Girl took flight.

Basil had only an instant to brace himself before they collided. He looked over the shoulder of this person, who clung like Velcro—arms wrapped around his neck, legs around his waist, her feet crossed and locked behind his ass—and shrugged.

Conor, Kate and Basil sat as Circus Girl resumed her waitress duties, her leering glances finding Basil time and again.

"Just tell her," Kate said. "Tell her you're not interested and..."

"I can't. I might hurt her feelings."

"So, what do you do? Eventually, I mean."

"I go to Alaska."

Kate shook her head. "I can't believe..."

"Kate, please. It's not my fault—"

"Basil," she said with exasperation, "has it *ever* been your fault?"

Basil adopted a look of genuine concern. He said nothing for several long minutes, finally breaking the silence with, "Well... maybe one time in... in... no. No, that wasn't my fault either."

EVEN BASIL, FOR ALL HIS ECCENTRICITIES, WOULDN'T ALLOW Conor out this late without at least calling.

The funk Conor had experienced over the past few months added to Kate's concern. She'd never underestimated how difficult retirement would be for Conor. She'd steeled herself for repercussions. She hadn't expected, though, his depression to run so long and so deep. Still, she clung to her faith that a day would come when something characteristically bizarre happened and Conor found humor in his life again.

She knew he wouldn't do something... something... well, anything irreconcilable.

Still, her heart pounded as she grabbed the phone before it rang a second time.

"Yes?"

"Mrs. Nash?"

The voice sounded grave and official. Kate felt her knees tremble. "Yes."

"This is Officer Gerard of the Phoenix Police Department. I'm calling about your husband—"

"Oh, my God," Kate gasped. "Please, please tell me he's okay."

"Well, yeah. For the most part. He's drunk, and he's pretty

scratched up. He's sitting in a pickup truck. And he's naked. Mostly. He's wearing boxer shorts and cowboy boots, and... normally, ma'am, we'd charge him with DUI and book him. But... um... if you'll come and get him..."

Kate closed her eyes and breathed a prayer of thanks. She knew now that Conor would be all right.

forty-two

He more or less fell down the mountain. When he managed to find a path, he couldn't see the switchbacks in the dark. After a couple of tentative, shaky steps, he'd walk off into some sort of prickly oblivion and go sliding and tumbling over cacti, rock and sand.

He'd meant to keep the empty Champagne bottle for his trophy case. Now it belonged to the mountain.

His final tumble brought him to rest on the parking lot's asphalt surface where his truck waited. Under the spill of the dome light, he assessed his damage. He had a cut across his forehead and a row of scratches along the left side of his face. One knee throbbed. Cacti spines and thorns posed the most immediate issue. His shirt and slacks were pincushions, nearly every inch of him pricked and needled.

He pulled his shirt painfully over his head, then slid gingerly out of his pants. His underwear had been spared the brunt of the assault, so he kept his boxers on, but his boots and socks were full of pebbles and goat heads.

He threw his shirt, pants and socks into the truck bed, then pulled his boots over bare feet. He slid carefully into the cab, gasping to catch his breath, and with everything tilting first one way, then the other, watched as a police car, its red and blue strobes flashing, pulled slowly to a stop.

A flashlight beam stabbed at his eyes.

"Sir, I want you to place your hands on the steering wheel."

"Sir, why are you naked?"

"I'm not naked. I'm wearing boxers and cowboy boots."

"Sir, have you been drinking?"

"Yes. Quite a lot."

"Do you have a drivers' license?"

"Yes."

"Where is it?"

"In my pants."

"Where are your pants?"

"Back there."

One officer held Conor in the glare of his flashlight while his partner inspected the truck.

"Yeah, here they are."

Holding them with a two-fingered grip by a belt loop, the officer gave Conor his pants. "Please remove your drivers' license from your wallet and hand it to me."

Conor took the pants. "Ow, shit, ow . . . ow . . . here!"

"Do you want to put on your pants?" the second officer asked.

"No." He pointed at the mountain. "I fell on a cactus and my clothes are all prickly."

"Well, have you got anything else to wear? Given your condition, we're going to—"

"Um . . . wait a minute, Jerry," the officer holding Conor's drivers' license said. He raised the license next to Conor's face.

"You're Conor Nash, the baseball player?"

"Well . . . yeah. I mean, I used to be . . ."

"The one who pitched for the Mariners?" the second officer asked. "I saw you at Spring Training."

"Yeah."

"Oh," the cop holding Conor's driver's license said, "he's a lot more than just a guy who pitched for the Mariners. I used to live in Las Vegas. You're looking at Starman!"

Kate brought Conor a pair of pants and t-shirt. They drove home along nearly deserted freeways. She didn't want to push him, so she waited. As they pulled into their driveway, Conor took her hand.

"I had to go up there and remember who I am," he said. "Not who I was. Who I am. Who my dad shaped me to be."

Kate leaned across the seat and kissed him.

"I'm sorry," he said.

"I know."

"I think everything will be okay."

"I know that, too."

"And my baseball angel's name is Val."

"What?"

CONOR WOKE THE NEXT DAY WITH A HEADACHE AND A mouth so foul and dry, he wondered if he'd fallen on his tongue the night before. He didn't know the time. Kate and the kids were gone, though, so he guessed mid-morning.

He rose to a sitting position, the movement accompanied by a chorus of protests from various parts of his body. He hunted for motivation to take a shower. Sooner or later, he knew, he'd have to pee, and then he'd have no choice but to actually stand up. Why rush it?

He glimpsed the telephone on the nightstand.

So, just a dream?

He wasn't sure he wanted to know. The phone sat right there, though, taunting him.

I dare you...

He dialed.

"My name is Conor Nash. I wonder if Al Rosen might be available..."

He held for a few minutes.

"Conman!" said Rosen. "What an amazing coincidence. We need a pitching coach in Everett, and we thought of you. Would you be interested?"

epilogue

Surprise, Arizona
Texas Rangers Spring Training Complex
February 2007

C ONOR ACCEPTED THE GIANTS' JOB, INITIATING A minor league coaching odyssey not unlike the journey he'd taken as a younger man. Other teams and other jobs waited. He'd just joined the Texas Rangers, ensconced in their brand-new Spring Training digs at a far-west suburb of Phoenix.

He arrived early for his first day and sat at the rear of the auditorium as other members of the Rangers coaching and scouting staffs entered in groups of threes and fours, taking their seats around him.

Director of Player Development Scott Servais called the meeting as part of preparations for Spring Training. They discussed both major and minor league personnel, who might be assigned where, who needed what specific attention, who might be salvaged, who might be released.

Finally, Servais said, "I want to be sure everyone agrees before we finalize Darren Whitehead's release. I'll remind you how good he was at A ball a couple of years ago—not to mention we've got three million dollars invested in this kid."

A wave of murmurs swept the room, one voice rising above the swell. "Kid can't throw a strike." And then another. "He's got the yips. You get the yips, you're done."

Servais listened to the chorus for a few moments before calling for silence. "Is there *anyone* who believes the kid is worth one more try?"

Shit. First day on the job. Conor's father, though, hadn't raised a coward. He lifted his hand. "I'd like to work with him."

June 2010

THE SHRILL RING OF THEIR BEDSIDE PHONE SENT A WAVE OF dread through Conor as he struggled awake. The clock said twelve twenty-five. A spectre of disaster hovered over midnight calls. The kids were old enough to worry about. Parents were elderly. Accidents happened.

"Conor?" Kate's voice quivered.

"I don't know," Conor said as he lifted the phone.

"Conman. It's Scotty. Sorry to call so late. I'm in Chicago with the team. We've got a rain delay. Anyway, I probably should have waited until tomorrow. But I thought you'd want to know."

"Um . . . know what?"

"Darren Whitehead."

"Darren? What happened?"

"He made his major league debut tonight. Threw in relief and retired both hitters he faced. Good job, Connie."

"What is it?" Kate asked.

"Scott Servais. A report on one of the kids I worked with."

"You're smiling. Good news?"

"Yeah."

"You're still smiling."

"Yeah. I'm thankful I got past my moment."

"Well," she said, punching him lightly on the arm, "I'm sure there are other moments waiting out there. We'll just keep working at it."

ACKNOWLEDGEMENTS

As always, I must first thank Nancy for allowing me to wander away from a perfectly good career and begin the adventure that took us on our path through baseball and now, writing. Thanks to Keith and Kathleen Comstock, Alan Schneider and Pat Doan for trusting me with their story. As always, I owe much to editors Laura Taylor, Shanna McNair and Scott Wolven. Randy Adamack of the Seattle Mariners and Ken Pries of the Oakland Athletics opened the door for Dave Henderson Baseball Adventures to host twenty years of Seattle Mariners and Oakland Athletics Fantasy Camps, where Keith and I met. Thanks to Nancy Henderson for her help and dedication to honoring Hendu's legacy. Thanks to our partners in DHBA, Brian Holman, Terry Lockhart and Jon Westmoreland. Thanks to Tom Giffen for opening broader baseball horizons. And finally, most heartfelt appreciation to Fielding Snow the man who shared this journey like a brother. It's been twenty- two years since we played that first game of catch in the Kingdome parking lot, buddy. What a long strange trip it's been.

Made in the USA
Columbia, SC
17 November 2019